KEY CONCEPTS IN INTERNATIO

Palgrave Key Concepts

Palgrave Key Concepts provide an accessible and comprehensive range of subject glossaries at undergraduate level. They are the ideal companion to a standard textbook, making them invaluable reading for students throughout their course of study and especially useful as a revision aid.

The key concepts are arranged alphabetically so you can quickly find the term or entry of immediate interest. All major theories, concepts, terms and theorists are incorporated and cross-referenced. Additional reading or website research opportunities are included. With hundreds of key terms defined, **Palgrave Key Concepts** represent a comprehensive must-have reference for undergraduates.

Published

Key Concepts in Accounting and Finance
Key Concepts in Business Practice
Key Concepts in Human Resource Management
Key Concepts in International Business
Key Concepts in Management
Key Concepts in Marketing
Key Concepts in Operations Management
Key Concepts in Politics
Key Concepts in Strategic Management
Linguistic Terms and Concepts
Literary Terms and Criticism (*third edition*)

Further titles are in preparation

www.palgravekeyconcepts.com

Palgrave Key Concepts
Series Standing Order ISBN 1–4039–3210–7
(*outside North America only*)

You can receive future titles in this series as they are published by placing a standing order. Please contact your bookseller or, in case of difficulty, write to us at the address below with your name and address, the title of the series, and the ISBN quoted above.

Customer Services Department, Macmillan Distribution Ltd,
Houndmills, Basingstoke, Hampshire RG21 6XS, England

Key Concepts in International Business

Jonathan Sutherland and Diane Canwell

First published 2004 by
PALGRAVE MACMILLAN
Houndmills, Basingstoke, Hampshire RG21 6XS and
175 Fifth Avenue, New York, N.Y. 10010
Companies and representatives throughout the world

PALGRAVE MACMILLAN is the global academic imprint of the Palgrave
Macmillan division of St. Martin's Press, LLC and of Palgrave Macmillan Ltd.
Macmillan® is a registered trademark in the United States, United Kingdom
and other countries. Palgrave is a registered trademark in the European
Union and other countries.

ISBN 1–4039–1534–2 paperback

This book is printed on paper suitable for recycling and made from fully
managed and sustained forest sources.

A catalogue record for this book is available from the British Library.

Library of Congress Cataloging-in-Publication Data
Sutherland, Jonathan.
   Key concepts in international business / Jonathan Sutherland and
Diane Canwell.
      p. cm. – (Palgrave key concepts)
   Includes bibliographical references and index.
   ISBN 1–4039–1534–2 (pbk.)
      1. International business enterprises—Dictionaries. 2. International
trade—Dictionaries. 3. International finance—Dictionaries. I. Title:
International business. II. Canwell, Diane. III. Title. IV. Series.

HD2755.5.S88 2004
338.8'8'03–dc22   2003070293

10 9 8 7 6 5 4 3 2 1
13 12 11 10 09 08 07 06 05 04

Printed and bound in Great Britain by
Creative Print and Design (Wales), Ebbw Vale

Contents

Introduction

The term 'international business' reflects the fact that international trade and, indeed, the establishment of businesses, are no longer restricted by national boundaries. There have been revolutionary changes in information technology, communication and transport which have brought businesses into a radically new and challenging environment. Increasingly, international business is ruled by interdependencies and strategies, and decision making must be taken with regard to a more global perspective.

Multinational, trans-national, multi-domestic or international business organizations are as concerned with the international environment in which they operate as they are with their home country's local environment. Tens of thousands of businesses routinely carry out international operations. These international operations, through diversification, access to cheaper supplies and access to new markets, have radically increased their opportunities. At the same time businesses face increasing and radically different risks, ranging from the economic and the political, to exchange rate and financial risks. All of these new opportunities and challenges require a radical rethink of how the business operates, where it operates, what it produces and who it employs. International businesses, although primarily interested in the exporting of their products and services to overseas markets, are also interested in securing products, services and raw materials from overseas nations.

The growth of international business has brought new terms and understandings, or in many cases misunderstandings, in the relationships between multinational organizations, their activities and the new nations with whom they deal. The term 'globalization' is one such misunderstood concept. Certainly the vast sum of foreign investments pouring into growing, or less developed, nations has been a significant factor over the last 50 years.

Whilst international businesses seek to find markets across the world, countries themselves have begun the slow process of forging new agreements and understandings between one another. Countries seek to cement their trade relationships, not only with traditional or close neighbours, but with countries literally located on the other side of the world. International business and international trade has undoubtedly affected and been affected by the growing number of economic and political unions around the world, ranging from the European Union,

NAFTA, and various African, Asian and Latin American intergovernmental treaties and unions.

The globalization of business requires a precise understanding of the culture, consumers, rules, regulations and policies of an increasing number of overseas nations.

The structure of the glossary

Every attempt has been made to include all of the key concepts in this discipline, taking into account currently used terminology, and jargon common throughout international business and trade around the world. There are notable differences in legislation and procedure when we compare different trading policies and standards in the United Kingdom, Europe, the United States, Japan, and the rest of the world. Increasingly in Europe, for example, there is a harmonization process in train which is gradually seeking to standardize regulations and procedures. Equally, organizations such as the World Trade Organization and the International Monetary Fund are seeking to harmonize and equalize regulations and procedures.

Each of the key concepts has been placed alphabetically in order to ensure that the reader can quickly find the term or entry of immediate interest. It is normally the case that a brief description of the term is presented, followed by a more expansive explanation.

The majority of the key concepts have the following in common:

- They may have a reference within the text to another key concept identified by a word or phrase that is in **bold type** – this should enable readers to investigate a directly implicated key concept should they require clarification of the definition at that point.
- They may have a series of related key concepts, which are featured at the end of the definition – this allows readers to continue their research and investigate subsidiary or allied key concepts.
- They may feature book or journal references – a vital feature for the reader to undertake follow-up research for more expansive explanations, often written by the originator or by a leading writer in that particular field of study.
- They may include website references – it is notoriously difficult to ensure that websites are still running at the time of going to print, let alone several months beyond that time, but in the majority of cases long-established websites or governmental websites, that are unlikely to be closed or to have a major address change, have been selected.

Glossary terms – a guide

Whilst the majority of the key concepts have an international flavour, readers are cautioned to ensure that they have accessed the legislation, in particular, which refers to their native country or to the country in which they are working.

It is also often the case that there are terms which have no currency in a particular country as they may be allied to specific legislation of another country; therefore readers are cautioned to check whether the description does include a specific reference to such law, and not to assume in all cases that the key concept is a generic one that can be applied universally to international business and trade.

In all cases, references to other books, journals and websites are based on the latest available information. It was not always possible to ensure that the key text or printed reference is in print, but the majority of well-stocked college or university libraries should have access to the original materials. In the majority of cases, when generic business books have been referenced, these are, in the view of the writers, the best and most available additional reading texts.

Absolute advantage

Absolute advantage is considered to be one of the simplest measures of economic performance. The assumption is that a country, or a business, can produce more of a particular product, using the same effort and resources, than other producers, giving that country or business an absolute advantage over the competitors.

In terms of international trade and business, 'absolute advantage' often refers to business or country specialization and is used to describe the maximization of benefits. True cases of absolute advantage are rare, but the more commonly used term to describe the advantage a business or a country has, in production terms, over its competitors is **comparative advantage**. Both absolute and comparative advantage fluctuate over periods of time.

Absorption

'Absorption' is a term used to describe the total investment and consumption of all households, businesses and government bodies, in terms of both domestic and imported products and services. Absorption can be compared with the actual production levels in a given country; when absorption is greater than production, the excess shows up on the country's **current account** as a deficit.

Acceptance

In international business terms, 'acceptance' has three different, but related meanings. Acceptance can apply to a **bill of exchange** that a **drawee** has accepted and is now unconditionally obliged to pay when it reaches maturity. The draft is presented for acceptance; the drawee becomes the acceptor and the date and place of payment are written on the draft.

'Acceptance' also refers to the drawee receiving a draft, thus entering into the obligation; or, more generally, an agreement to purchase goods or services under specific terms at a stated price.

Accession

'Accession' refers to the process of a country becoming a member of an international grouping or accepting an international agreement. The term has most commonly been used in relation to the **General Agreement on Tariffs and Trade (GATT)** or in relation to a country joining the European Community. In both cases the accession process involves a series of negotiations which aim to identify the obligations of the non-member country and what it must undertake or accept before it becomes a member of the international agreement. It is only when the accession process has been completed that the country will enjoy the full membership benefits.

> Marcou, Gerard, *Regionalisation for Development and Accession to the European Union.* Budapest: Central European University Press, 2003.

Accounting

Accounting, in its more general sense, involves the communication of a business's financial position to its providers of capital and, for tax purposes, to governments. It is also used to evaluate performance, control expenditure and make forecasts and plans.

In the field of international business, however, accounting is a far more complex discipline as businesses will need to adapt their accounting procedures to fall in line with the local demands in each environment in which they operate. There are a number of national differences in both accounting and auditing standards. While markets have become increasingly globalized over the past few decades, there may be a distinct lack of comparability between the accounting demands in each area in which a business operates. It can therefore be difficult for businesses to show why financial information appears to be different when based on the accounting practices of the various countries in which it has an interest.

A

Attempts have begun in order to institute a form of accounting standard harmonization, notably from the International Accounting Standards Committee (IASC). To date, their attempts have been rather limited. A multinational business, with subsidiaries in foreign countries, would be required to keep its accounting records and prepare financial statements in the currency of the country in which it is located. It is only when consolidated accounts of the multinational are compiled that the subsidiaries' financial statements have to be translated into the home country's currency. This, in itself, is a difficult task as exchange rates fluctuate and assets which are valued in a foreign currency also have to be translated into the home currency, but usually at the exchange rate in operation when assets were purchased. This leads to difficulties in making a multinational's balance sheet balance.

Inevitably there are distortions in both budgets and performance data when the results are translated into another currency. Increasingly, multinational businesses are seeking ways in which they can streamline this process and make the assumptions required more transparent.

Madura, Jeff, *International Financial Management*. Mason, OH: South Western College Publishing, 2002.

Acquisition

The most common use of the term 'acquisition' is in describing the process of one business purchasing another business, or indeed individuals purchasing an existing business.

'Acquisition' can also refer to the process of obtaining a loan or another form of finance, or to the purchase of a property by a business.

In international business terms, all acquisitions are subject to local, regional (EU) and national laws and regulations in respect of how other businesses are acquired or shares are purchased. In many cases businesses which are acquired by another company continue to operate as independent organizations, maintaining their original name, personnel and **organizational structure.**

Weston, J. Fred and Weaver, Samuel C., *Mergers and Acquisitions*. New York: McGraw-Hill, 2001.

Ad valorem tariff

An ad valorem tariff is a tax, charge or duty which is applied to products or services as a percentage of their value. *Ad valorem*, literally, means 'according to value'.

Administrative protection order

An administrative protection order is most commonly connected with **anti-dumping** and **countervailing duty** investigations, when it is used to prevent proprietary data being released. It is also used to control the disclosure of information related to national security in cases where businesses are being investigated for violations.

Gray, Rob and Bebbington, Jan, *Accounting for the Environment*. London: Paul Chapman, 2001.

A

Administrative (judicial) trade policy

Administrative or judicial trade policy instruments are used to deal with contentious issues on a case-by-case basis. They are often used to make market access investigations, deal with international trade disputes and investigate **anti-dumping**. These administrative trade policies have been widely criticized as further fragmenting domestic trade policy in various countries, notably the United States and within the European Union.

> De Bièvre, Dirk, *The WTO and Domestic Coalitions: Negotiated and Judicial Trade Policy in the European Union* (4th Annual Conference of the European Trade Study Group). Kiel: Institut für Weltwirtschaft (www.mpp-rdg.mpg.de/pdf_dat/etsg.pdf).

Advanced technology products

In the United States around 500 of the 22,000 commodity classification codes are deemed to be advanced technology. Many of these products are produced by businesses operating in the high technology field, such as bio-technology. The products are considered to be at the leading edge of technology in any given field. Businesses wishing to export these products must report to the US government in order to receive clearance.

> Paashuis, V., *The Organisation of Integrated Product Development (Advanced Manufacturing)*. Berlin and Heidelberg: Springer Verlag, 1998.

Advising bank

An advising bank handles letters of credit for a foreign bank and notifies the exporter that credit has been opened. The bank operates in the exporter's own country and informs the exporter of the conditions of the letter of credit, but without taking responsibility for the payment.

Advisory Committee on Export Policy (ACEP)

The ACEP is a US inter-agency dispute resolution body. The committee is chaired by a representative from the field of commerce and includes representatives for defence, energy, the state, arms control and disarmament, and intelligence.

Advisory Committee on Trade Policy and Negotiations (ACTPN)

The ACTPN is a US committee that consists of 45 individuals appointed by the President. They advise both the President and the government on trade policy and trade agreements. The members broadly represent the key economic sectors of the United States. The ACTPN is aided in the work by the Services Policy Advisory Committee (SPAC), the Investment Policy Advisory Committee (INPAC), the Inter-Governmental Policy Advisory Committee (AGPAC), the Industry Policy Advisory Committee (IPAC), the Agriculture Policy Advisory Committee (APAC), the Labor Policy Advisory Committee (LPAC) and the Defense Policy Advisory Committee (DPAC).

Affiliate

An affiliate, in international business terms, is a business which is wholly or partly owned by a business or an individual from another country. Officially an affiliate must be owned to the extent of at least 10 per cent by an overseas owner.

Agency for International Development (AID)

The AID was formed in 1961 and is used to deliver economic-assistance packages to developing countries on behalf of the US government. The AID has missions and representatives in many developing countries throughout the world.

www.usaid.gov

Air way bill (AWB)

Air way bills are a form of **bill of lading** applied to both domestic and international flights which are transporting products to a specific destination. These are non-negotiable instruments which serve as a receipt for the shipper. They indicate that the carriers have accepted the products and have obligated themselves to carry that consignment to a specified airport, under specified conditions.

See also **inland bill of lading, ocean bill of lading, through bill of lading.**

A

Alliance for Mutual Growth (AMG)

The AMG was established in 1993 and is an alliance between the United States and **ASEAN**. The alliance seeks to connect commercial initiatives with US policy in the South-East Asian region of the world. It also seeks to promote long-term relationships with businesses and countries in that region.

www.aseansec.org

Alongside

Alongside is a form of delivery method in which products are literally delivered alongside a transport ship, or within reach of the transport ship, enabling them to be loaded onto that vessel. In practice this means that the products must be delivered either to the dock at which the vessel is at rest, or to a smaller transport vessel, which can come alongside the larger vessel for reloading.

Andean group

See **Andean Pact.**

Andean Pact

The Andean Pact was established in Cartegena in 1969 and is a group of Latin American countries which seek to promote economic integration and political cooperation amongst their membership. The Andean group is also referred to as the *Pacto Andino* or the *Corporación Andino de Fomento*. In other cases it is also called the *Acuerdo de Cartegana*.

The members of the group are encouraged to specialize and provide financial and technical assistance to one another. Current members include Bolivia, Colombia, Ecuador, Peru and Venezuela.

www.comunidadandina.org

Anticipatory counter-trade

Anticipatory counter-trade is advanced purchases of products and services from the country of a customer which is undertaken by a supplier. These purchases are made in expectation of future sales which are linked to **counter-trade** requirements. In essence these are proactive purchases which may, or may not, be eligible for counter-trade credit unless approved by the country's authorities.

Mirus, Rolf and Yeung, Bernard, *The Economics of Barter and Countertrade*. Cheltenham: Edward Elgar, 2001.

A

Anti-dumping

If a business exports products at a price lower than the price it normally charges in its home market, it is deemed to have been **dumping** those products into a foreign country. The **World Trade Organization (WTO)**, under the terms of Article VI of the **General Agreement on**

Tariffs and Trade (GATT), provides for the contracting parties to apply anti-dumping measures. Negotiations during the **Uruguay Round** (1986–94) revised the anti-dumping agreement and provided more detailed rules in relation to determining whether a product had been dumped. In essence, the anti-dumping agreement seeks to protect the domestic industry by preventing the dumping of products, and setting up dispute settlement panels that deal with anti-dumping actions taken by domestic authorities.

The panels seek to establish a clear relationship between the dumped imports and any injury to the domestic industry, taking into account any relevant economic factors. Increasingly, procedures are being established across the world to ensure that all interested parties are given the opportunity to present their own evidence.

Gupta, R. K., *Anti-dumping and Countervailing Measures: The Complete Reference.* New York: Sage Publications, 1996.

Anti-trust law

Anti-trust laws seek to encourage competition by attempting to curb a business which has a monopoly, and to limit unfair business practices. Anti-trust laws aim to prevent abuses of market power by large businesses, and in some cases the government will step in to prevent a merger or an **acquisition** which would create a monopoly.

Different countries have different views on what constitutes a monopoly and, indeed, what kind of business behaviour is considered to be an abuse of power. In the United States, for example, the monopoly policy is firmly built on the Sherman Anti-Trust Act (1890). It prohibits contracts or conspiracies which restrain trade. During the 1970s, the Act was used against IBM but it failed. In 1982 the Act was successfully used to break up the monopoly which AT&T had established in the telecoms industry.

One of the highest-profile cases was launched against Microsoft in 1998, and it was found guilty of anti-competitive behaviour. It was proposed that Microsoft be broken up; negotiations continue as to how this case will be resolved.

In the UK, successive governments seem to have followed the US trend in basing their anti-trust policies on situations which could ultimately harm consumers. Throughout the rest of Europe, however, particularly within the European Union, national governments have allowed selected businesses to become virtual monopolies in an attempt to create national companies capable of competing throughout the world. However, from the 1990s the European Commission, keen to promote competition within the European Union, has become increasingly active in anti-trust policy. It is possible that as the markets become more globalized, an anti-trust watchdog operating throughout the world will need to be established. Currently it seems that the **World Trade Organization** may ultimately take up this challenge.

Hylton, Keith N., *Anti-trust Law: Economic Theory and Common Law Evolution.* Cambridge: Cambridge University Press, 2002.

APEC

See **Asian Pacific Economic Cooperation (APEC).**

Arab Cooperation Council (AAC)/Arab Maghreb Union (AMU)

These two organizations were created in 1989. The Arab Cooperation Council (ACC), with members including Egypt, Iraq, Jordan and North Yemen, seeks to promote economic cooperation and integration. Originally the ACC was intended to be a counterpart to the **Gulf Cooperation Council**.

The Arab Maghreb Union (AMU) has a similar purpose and its members include Algeria, Libya, Mauritania, Morocco and Tunisia. The union and the Gulf Cooperation Council seek ultimately to establish a common market.

Arab Maghreb Union (AMU)

See **Arab Cooperation Council (AAC)/Arab Maghreb Union (AMU).**

Arab Monetary Fund (AMF)

The AMF was created in 1976 and began its operations the following year, with its headquarters in Abu Dhabi. It seeks to correct the deficits in the balance of payments in most of the member states and promote monetary and economic integration. The fund is active in trying to address payment imbalances, stabilizing exchange rates, eliminating trade restrictions and creating capital markets. Its members include Algeria, Bahrain, Egypt, Iraq, Jordan, Kuwait, Lebanon, Libya, Mauritania, Morocco, Oman, Qatar, Saudi Arabia, Somalia, Sudan, Syria, Tunisia, the United Arab Emirates and the Yemen.

See also **Arab Trade Financing Program (ATFP).**
www.amf.org.ae/vEnglish

Arab Trade Financing Program (ATFP)

The ATFP was created in 1989 by the **Arab Monetary Fund** and is based in Abu Dhabi. The programme seeks to promote trade between Arab countries.

www.atfp.org.ae

Arbitrage

Arbitrage is the process of buying foreign currency, securities or commodities in one market and immediately selling them in another market. Profits are made as a result of the different rates of exchange or the different prices of securities or commodities in different markets. In other words, an asset will be purchased in one market and then the identical asset will be sold in another market at a higher price. An example would include the purchasing of Euros in London at a cheaper $ rate than is available elsewhere and then selling an identical amount of Euros in New York at a higher price.

Increasingly, however, arbitrage is becoming more difficult as a result of the **globalization** of the financial markets.

Graham, Mike (ed.), *The Arbitrage Handbook*. London: Fleet Street Publications, 2001.

ASEAN

ASEAN, or the Association of South East Asian Nations, was created in 1992, effectively establishing a free trade area known as the ASEAN Free Trade Area (AFTA). Member states agreed to cut their **tariff** rates within 15 years of the start date of January 1994. Manufactured goods in some 15 different sectors are subject to a tariff reduction of 5 per cent within 10 years.

Other fast-track sectors include pharmaceuticals, plastics, rubber, leather, copper and fertilizer.

See also **Association of South East Asian Nations (ASEAN)**.

www.aseansec.org

A

Asia-Pacific Economic Cooperation (APEC)

APEC was established in 1989 and is an informal group which allows the discussion, at ministerial level, of economic issues that affect the members. APEC consists of six **ASEAN** countries (Brunei, Indonesia, Malaysia, the Philippines, Singapore and Thailand) in addition to

Australia, Canada, China, Japan, New Zealand, South Korea, Taiwan and the United States.

www.apecsec.org.sg

Association of South East Asian Nations (ASEAN)

ASEAN has grown rapidly in the past decade, largely on the basis of the establishment of the ASEAN free trade agreement, along with high growth rates, increased purchasing power and huge infrastructure projects. It has been estimated that, in the ASEAN region, by 2010 the countries will enjoy a **gross domestic product** of $1.1 trillion and that over $1 trillion will have been spent in new infrastructure projects. The ASEAN region will, by that time, have nearly 690 million consumers.

www.aseansec.org

Automated Broker Interface (ABI)

The ABI is part of the US government's **Automated Commercial System**. It permits the transmission of data related to products being imported into the United States. Information is passed between brokers, carriers, importers, port authorities and data processing businesses which operate as service centres.

www.customs.ustreas.gov

Automated Commercial System (ACS)

The ACS is a US part-public, part-private computerized data processing and telecommunication system. It links members of the import trade to customs houses and government agencies, allowing them to transfer data electronically, deal with customs queries and obtain information on duties, taxes and fees. The ACS is an integral part of the information system used to compile US foreign trade statistics. It began operations in 1984.

www.customs.ustreas.gov

A

Backward vertical FDI

Backward vertical foreign direct investment occurs when an overseas business makes a direct investment or input into the domestic operations of another country. A prime example of this would be an international oil company investing in overseas drilling operations for oil which would be used for domestic refining.

Herrmann, Heinz and Lipsey, Robert E. (eds), *Foreign Direct Investment in the Real and Financial Sector of Industrial Countries*. Berlin: Springer Verlag, 2003.

Balance of payments

The balance of payments is a statistical summary of international transactions, 'transactions' being defined as the transfer of ownership of something which has economic value measurable in monetary terms, from one country to another. These may, of course, include the transfer of tangible or visible products, services (which are considered intangible), income on investments, and financial claims or liabilities. A transaction is an exchange of one asset for another, and as far as international transactions are concerned they are recorded on the balance of payments accounts using double entry. Each transaction gives rise to two offsetting entries of equal value, resulting in the credit and debit entries always balancing. Transactions are valued at market prices and are recorded when the ownership changes.

The **International Monetary Fund** defines the balance of payments as a statistical statement which shows the transactions in goods and services and income between one economy and the rest of the world. It also goes on to include changes in ownership of an economy's monetary gold, claims on and liabilities to the rest of the world, and transactions which are not mutually offsetting. The US, for example, produces seven quarterly balances, as can be seen in Table 1.

In the US, merchandise is deemed to be visible trade, which is the export and import of physical goods. Invisible trade is the receipts and payments for various services and other intangible goods (including copyrights, dividends and interest payments).

Table 1 US balance of payments

Balance	Description
Balance on merchandised trade	The net transfer of merchandised exports and imports.
Balance on services	The net transfer of services, including travel, business and professional services. From 1990 this excludes investment income.
Balance on goods and services	The sum of the balance on merchandised trade and the balance on services.
Balance on investment income	Net transfer of income from both direct and portfolio investments.
Balance on goods, services and income	The net transfer of merchandise plus services and income on direct and portfolio investment (comparable to net exports of goods and services, which are included in **gross national product**).
Balance on unilateral transfers	The net value of gifts, government grants and other contributions
Balance on current account	This includes transactions in products, services, income and unilateral transfers.

Clearly, as any outstanding money needs to be paid, theoretically a country's accounts must balance; but in reality the balances are often fudged because balancing is never quite as neat as in the accounts of individual companies and there will inevitably be inconsistencies. In situations where a country cannot pay interest on foreign debts, the country will find it impossible to borrow more money in the international finance market. An example is the Russian government in 1988, which was not able to increase taxes because its economy was collapsing and there were few sources within Russia itself to lend the government money. Situations such as these are known as 'balance of payment crises'.

Miller, Norman C., *Balance of Payments and Exchange Rate Theories*. Cheltenham: Edward Elgar, 2002.

Balance of payments accounts

Balance of payments accounts are the records of international transfers undertaken during a particular time period. Normally the accounts are divided into several sub-accounts, the most important being the **current account** and the **capital account**.

The current account is a record of all international transfers, products and services and combines the transactions of the trade account and of the services account. The merchandise (product) trade account records the international transactions for goods only, such as cars, food and steel. The services account covers the international transactions for services such as transport, insurance and brokering. The capital account is a record of all international transactions related to assets, including bonds, treasury bills, stocks, currency, real estate and bank deposits.

Balance of trade

The balance of trade is simply the difference between a particular country's imports and exports over a given period of time. If imports exceed exports then the balance of trade is said to be in deficit. If the imports are less than the exports then the balance of trade is said to be in surplus. Ideally a country would wish to literally 'balance' its balance of trade. In other words, broadly its imports should be equal to its exports. Obviously it is also desirable to generate a surplus rather than a long-term deficit.

Caves, Richard E., Frankel, Jeffrey A. and Jones, Ronald W., *World Trade and Payments: An Introduction*. London: Addison Wesley, 2001.

Bank Advisory Committee

The Bank Advisory Committee is an informal, unstructured organization which consists of the leading bankers who represent the interests of a debtor country's banking industry. They aim to develop restructuring plans to propose to the government. The debtor country's government then proposes the plans to the foreign lending governments. In many respects the Bank Advisory Committee has replaced the **London Club**.

B

Bank for International Settlements (BIS)

The Bank for International Settlements (BIS) was formed in 1930 and has its headquarters in Basel, Switzerland. The organization seeks to promote cooperation between the **central banks**, specifically related to international financial settlements. Members include Australia, Austria, Belgium, Bulgaria, Canada, Denmark, Finland, France, Germany, Greece, Hungary, Iceland, Ireland, Italy, Japan, the Netherlands, Norway, Poland, Portugal, Romania, South Africa, Spain, Sweden, Switzerland, Turkey, the United Kingdom and the United States.

www.bis.org

Banker's draft

A banker's draft is regarded as cash and is payable on demand and drawn by, or on behalf of, a bank itself. A banker's draft cannot be returned unpaid.

Barriers to entry

'Barriers to entry' is a term used to describe the way in which a business, or group of businesses, seek to keep competition out of markets in which they are currently operating. There are four main ways in which this is achieved:

- A business may have control over a specific resource, such as oil, or may have an exclusive licence to operate, such as a broadcast agreement.
- A large business which has significant **economies of scale** will have a competitive advantage because it can produce products and services at lower costs than those of its smaller rivals.
- A business may protect its market by investing considerable sums in advertising and marketing, making it very difficult for competitors to make any impression in the marketplace.
- Large and powerful businesses can make a competitor's venture into their market far more risky by raising the exit costs. In this respect they may have established a specific way of hiring employees, perhaps on long-term contracts, which has become the industry norm. It is therefore expensive for a newcomer to the market to try and then fail, as dispensing with staff would become prohibitively expensive.

Barter

B

Barter is one of the oldest forms of trade, where there is no financial transfer involved in the transaction. At its simplest, barter is the exchange of a package of either products or services for products and services of an equivalent value. Barters are still much used in international trade and may involve the exchange of products and services over a period of time, with both parties undertaking to make the transfer within a year.

Mirus, Rolf and Yeung, Bernard (eds), *The Economics of Barter and Countertrade*. Cheltenham: Edward Elgar, 2001.

Basel convention

The Basel convention came about in the late 1980s as a result of the dramatic rises in the costs of dealing with hazardous waste. There had been a trend for the developed nations to ship hazardous waste into developing countries and eastern Europe. The convention began to set up a framework for controlling the movements of hazardous waste. In 1999 the convention set up guidelines for minimizing hazardous waste generation:

- It actively promotes the use of cleaner technologies and production methods.
- It urges a reduction in the movement of hazardous waste.
- It seeks to prevent and monitor illegal hazardous waste movement.
- It funds the setting up of regional centres for training.

At its core the Basel convention seeks to establish environmentally sound management (ESM), which aims to protect health and the environment by minimizing waste production wherever possible. It is therefore concerned with the whole of a product's life cycle and its storage, transportation, reuse, recycling and final disposal, if necessary.

Countries which adhere to the Basel convention undertake to institute appropriate measures to implement and enforce the provisions of the convention. Each country is required to provide annual information on the generation and movement of hazardous wastes.

www.basel.int

Benelux Economic Union

'Benelux' is an acronym for 'Belgium, Netherlands and Luxembourg'. The Benelux Economic Union was established in the 1940s and fully established in the late 1950s. It was designed to promote the free movement of capital, products, services and workers throughout the Benelux region. The three countries were founding members of what is now the **European Union**, which has adopted many of the Benelux reforms. The Benelux Economic Union's ultimate goal of merging both the fiscal and monetary systems of the three countries was fulfilled in 2002 when the **Euro** replaced their own currencies.

B

Best information available (BIA)

Under the terms of the **General Agreement on Tariffs and Trade (GATT)**, when a business is cited as a respondent in an **anti-dumping** or a **countervailing duties** case and it either declines to provide information, or does not provide adequate information, the investigators may resort to the 'best information available' principle. This uses a collection of information, which may be provided by the petitioner or other sources, and determinations of the best information available are made on a case-by-case basis.

Big emerging markets (BEM)

The concept of big emerging markets represents a fundamental shift in both business and economic development. It has been brought about by the following:

- a shift from government-regulated markets to free markets based on private ownership and competition;
- the large-scale collapse of Communism in eastern Europe and the post-Communist transformation of up to 40 per cent of the world's population;
- the success of the East Asian nations.

This has brought about significant worldwide trends towards privatization and openness in many countries which at one time were bureaucratic and closed economies. It has also triggered regional and global integration based on competitive markets. The most significant BEMs can be found in central and eastern Europe, including Russia and the Caucasus, and in central and eastern Asia, notably China, Vietnam, India and Indonesia, as well as Latin America, including Mexico, Chile, Argentina and Brazil.

The United States Department of Commerce defines many of these countries as BEMs and specifically cites China, Taiwan, South Korea, India, Malaysia, the Philippines, Singapore, Thailand, Indonesia, Vietnam, Brazil, Argentina, Mexico, South Africa, Turkey and Poland.

US exports by 2000 to BEMs had reached $161 billion, virtually equal to the exports to the European Union and Japan combined. BEMs' **gross domestic product** is broadly equivalent to 25% of that of the industrialized world. This is expected to have reached 50% by 2010. BEMs are also expected to account for some 27% of the world's imports by 2010. The potential for growth is enormous; there are little more than 60,000 private cars in China and with the government expending huge sums on the road network infrastructure, this market is expected to explode in the coming years.

The BEMs do not necessarily have many of the characteristics of traditional trading partners. Many of the following are considered to be causes of concern for businesses wishing to trade with them:

- Generally their political stability is less predictable as changes occur faster, leading to increased risk. Some indeed still have authoritarian regimes.
- There is little or no regional or local government. At the very least it is under-developed.
- Economic stability is lower, exacerbated by incoherent economic policy.
- The physical infrastructure is under-developed.
- Education is also under-developed.
- With the occurrence of corruption, the enforcement of contracts is often more complex.

Despite the apparent drawbacks in dealing with the BEMs, many businesses cannot fail to be attracted by the potential profits and have adopted the corporate strategies outlined in Table 2.

Table 2 Strategies for dealing with BEMs

Strategy	Description
Quick buck	Essentially these are hit-and-run approaches to business, identifying a business opportunity on a one-off basis, avoiding the opportunity for longer-term cooperation, whilst simultaneously avoiding the risk of longer-term exposure.
Enclave	These are longer-term strategies in which the business builds an operation consisting of independent local supply networks.
Learning for earning	This involves the sacrificing of short-term profits in order to develop a better understanding of the market. The primary purpose is to build business confidence and stable relationships with partners in the emerging markets in order to produce higher profits in the longer term.
Integrative national treatment	This strategy approaches the market as if it were as sophisticated and developed as markets in which the business already operates. In other words, the business tries to treat the market in a similar way to the way in which it deals with its own domestic market. This is a long-term strategy which has not worked to any great degree to date.

B

Garten, Jeffrey E., *The Big Ten: The Big Emerging Markets and How They Will Change Our Lives*. New York: Basic Books, 1997.

Bilateral clearing agreement

Bilateral clearing agreements are reciprocal trade arrangements between governments. Both countries undertake to achieve a specified value of trade turnover over a given number of years. The value of this trade is expressed in terms of a major currency, such as the US Dollar or the Swiss Franc. Exporters in each of the countries are paid by specified local banks in the domestic currency.

Bilateral investment treaty

A bilateral investment treaty, specifically referring to the United States, ensures US investments abroad in **most favoured nation treatment** situations. It prohibits the imposition of performance requirements and allows the US investors to bring their own management into a foreign country without regard to nationality issues. The treaty ensures the right to make investment-related transfers and guarantees that any expropriation only takes place under international law. The treaty also guarantees access to impartial and binding international arbitration in cases of disputes.

Bill of exchange

A bill of exchange is a signed and written order by one business, which instructs a second business to pay a third business a specified amount of money.

See also **draft bill of exchange**.

Bill of lading (BOL)

B

A bill of lading is a contract issued to a transportation company (a shipper), listing the goods shipped, acknowledging their receipt and promising delivery to the person or business named. Bills of lading are also known as manifests or waybills.

In essence there are two different types of bill of lading: a non-negotiable, straight bill of lading, or a negotiable (shipper's order) bill of lading, which can be bought, sold or traded while the goods are actually in transit. In both cases, however, the customer will be required to produce an original or copy of the bill of lading to prove ownership before taking possession of the goods.

Bools, Michael, *The Bill of Lading – A Document of Title*. London: LLP Professional Publishing, 1997.

Bill of materials (BOM)

A bill of materials (BOM) aims to list all of the parts, components and individual items which were used to create or manufacture a specific product. In essence, a bill of materials is rather like a list of parts, but it goes one stage further than this as the components, parts and other items are listed as they were added to the product. In other words, a careful examination of a BOM indicates how a product was assembled. Some organizations refer to a BOM as a 'formula' or 'recipe'. Careful examination of the BOM should indicate to the organization the precise ordering of production units and processes within the premises. Assuming that most products are constructed or assembled in this manner, a BOM should help the organization to identify the most common route along which the product passes, on the shop floor.

Bi-national commission

'Bi-national commission' refers to the United States and Mexico Commission, which was set up to provide a forum and closer economic and commercial ties between the two countries.

Blocked currency

A blocked currency is a currency which cannot be freely transferred into convertible currencies and expatriated. The term is usually used to describe foreign-owned funds or other earnings in countries whose government exchange regulations prevent the money from being expatriated.

Bond

Bonds are debt instruments which can be bought and sold on the market. A bond pays a specific amount of interest on a regular basis and the issuer of the bond undertakes to repay the debt at a specific time, in full. Treasury bonds can be purchased via the Treasury Department in the US, but the majority of bonds are purchased through a brokerage company, who charge a fee for the transaction.

Bonded warehouse

A bonded warehouse is a building, or collection of buildings, which have been designated and authorized by a country's customs authorities in order to store goods which require a duty payment before they are released.

Boundaryless organization

'Boundaryless organization' is a term often applied to businesses which operate in several different countries throughout the world. Such organizations seek to eliminate any inefficient boundaries between their organizational levels and the operations of their workers. It has become increasingly important for businesses to be able to respond more meaningfully to the requirements of their customers, no matter where they are. This means that the business's functions and operations need to be fluid and efficient in order for information and connections to be made wherever required. This more flexible approach should mean that the business can enjoy greater growth.

Bretton Woods

The term 'Bretton Woods' refers to an international conference which was held at Bretton Woods, New Hampshire, in 1944. Arising out of this meeting the structure of the **international monetary system** was established and this led directly to the setting up of the **International Monetary Fund** and the **World Bank**. It was agreed at the meeting that exchange rates between members of the International Monetary Fund would be linked to the $US with a maximum variation of 1%. It was further agreed that the rates could only be adjusted in excess of this if a particular country's **balance of payments** had reached **disequilibrium**.

The arrangement hit a particularly difficult time in 1971 when US President Richard Nixon was forced to devalue the dollar as a result of economic difficulties at home and the escalating costs of prosecuting the war in Vietnam. By 1973 the fixed exchange rate system had been scrapped and all of the main currencies and their rates were set by market forces.

James, Harold, *International Monetary Cooperation since Bretton Woods*. New York: Oxford University Press, 1996.

British Overseas Trade Board

The British Overseas Trade Board is an integral part of the UK's Department of Trade and Industry (DTI). It advises the government on

B

international trade issues, specifically the promotion of exports, export policy and financing. The board itself is made up of government representatives and individuals from industry. The export departments of the board work in cooperation with the Foreign and Commonwealth Office in order to provide British businesses with assistance in international trade through various overseas offices.

www.tradepartners.gov.uk

Build/Operate Transfer (BOT)

BOT is a means by which debt and equity financing can be obtained for major overseas **turnkey** projects, such as the building of dams, electricity generating stations or even nuclear power plants. The normal understanding is that a foreign business will construct the facility and then operate it as a going concern, for profit, for a contracted number of years. At the end of this period the facility is transferred to local ownership. The revenues which are accrued from the running of the facility help to service the debt and generate the capital repayment for the original constructor.

Business Council for International Understanding (BCIU)

The BCIU was originally established by US President Eisenhower as an independent business association which sought to foster greater understanding between US businesses and visiting diplomats and heads of state. In more recent years the BCIU has broadened out from providing secondments to the association, for US ambassadors and senior diplomatic staff, and has now begun sponsoring discussions with foreign heads of government, ministers of finance and other foreign officials.

Business Information Service for the Newly Independent States (BISNIS)

The BISNIS was established in 1992 in the United States in order to provide a one-stop-shop facility for US businesses wishing to trade in the Independent States of the former Soviet Union. The BISNIS provides information on trade regulations and legislation, market data, commercial opportunities, financing, contacts and investments, in Armenia, Azerbaijan, Belarus, Georgia, Kazakhstan, Kyrgyzstan, Moldova, Russia, Tajikistan, Turkmenistan, Ukraine and Uzbekistan.

www.bisnis.doc.gov

B

Buy-American restrictions (BAR)

The Buy-American restrictions can be traced back to the Buy-American Act (March 1933) as amended by the Buy-American Act (1988) in the United States. In essence the restrictions can take a number of different forms, which include:

- the prohibition of public sector organizations from purchasing products or services from foreign suppliers;
- the establishment of local-content requirements for up to 100 per cent of the value of a product;
- the extending of preferential terms to domestic suppliers;
- the setting up of facilities for manufacturing (or assembly if appropriate) in the United States.

Under the terms of the Buy-American Act there are now four exceptions; these are:

- when the products or services are for use outside the United States;
- when the domestic market cannot supply given products or services;
- when the purchase of domestic products or services is inconsistent with public interest;
- when the cost of domestic products or services is deemed to be too high.

Under the terms of the Trade Act 1979 the restrictions under the Buy-American Act are waived for particular countries which grant reciprocal access to US businesses.

B

Cabotage

'Cabotage' is a term related to international shipping and transportation. It requires coastal and inter-coastal traffic to be carried by vessels which belong to the country which owns the coastline.

Calvo doctrine

The Calvo doctrine was named after an Argentine jurist and is now applied throughout Latin America and many other areas of the world. The Calvo doctrine, or Calvo principle, maintains that jurisdiction in the case of international investment disputes lies within the country in which the investment was originally located. In other words, the investor must use local courts in order to settle the dispute.

Capital account

The capital account, together with a **current account**, is a measurement of a country's **balance of payments**. Inherently these two accounts must balance. The capital account includes the net foreign lending, investment and changes in currency reserves.

See also **balance of payments.**

Capital controls

Capital controls are government-imposed restrictions on the movement of capital. Until relatively recently capital controls were fairly uncommon; there were major changes throughout the 1980s and 1990s and most developed countries scrapped their capital controls. Latin American countries imposed many capital controls during their debt crises of the 1980s. The majority of Asian countries scrapped theirs in the late 1980s and the 1990s. Capital controls tended to be lifted when free markets became more common and indeed they proved useless in preventing finance from leaving a country.

Most countries recognize that foreign capital plays an important part in the development of infrastructure and the overall health of a country's economy. Capital controls had unwanted side effects because they not only failed to keep money in the home country, but also deterred foreign investment. When there was an economic crisis in Asia in the late 1990s, capital controls came back to an extent, but the governments quickly realized that lifting controls meant that while money could leave the country, it could just as easily come in.

Ries, Christine P. and Sweeney, Richard J. (eds), *Capital Controls in Emerging Economies.* Boulder, CO: Westview Press, 1997.

Capital development initiative (CDI)

The capital development initiative, or CDI, is administered by the US Agency for International Development. Primarily it encourages infrastructure investment in countries in central and eastern Europe. Not only does the CDI provide both technical and financial services, but it also provides US businesses with up to 50 per cent of the development costs and feasibility study costs, primarily for projects in telecommunications, the environment and energy.

Capital flight

'Capital flight' is a term used to describe the rapid outflow of capital from a country. This usually occurs when a situation has developed, or may potentially develop, which scares investors sufficiently for them to lose their confidence in the economy. The process gathers momentum as there are sharp falls in the exchange rate of the country's currency, which simply speeds the capital flight. This becomes particularly difficult and dangerous to the economy when the capital flight extends to the country's own investors.

Walter, Ingo, *The Secret Money Market: Inside the Dark World of Tax Evasion, Financial Fraud, Insider Trading, Money Laundering and Capital Flight.* New York: HarperCollins, 1991.

Capital lease

A capital lease is a type of lease which is classified, and counted for, as a purchase by the leasee, and by the leasor as a sale. It must meet the following criteria:

- The leasor transfers the ownership of the asset to the leasee at the end of the lease term.

- The lease contains an option to purchase the asset.
- The lease term must be equal to at least 75 per cent of the estimated economic life of the asset.
- The present value of the minimum lease rental payments must be equal to at least 90 per cent of the market value of the leased asset in respect of related investment tax credits.

Caribbean Basin initiative (CBI)

The CBI is a US programme aimed to increase economic aid and trade preferences for some 28 states within the Caribbean area. Under the terms of the Caribbean Basin Economic Recovery Act (1983), 12 years of duty free treatment for most goods was instituted. This initiative was extended permanently under the terms of the 1990 US Customs and Trade Act. There are some 23 countries which are eligible for the benefits, these include Antigua, the Bahamas, Barbados, Belize, British Virgin Islands, Costa Rica, Dominica, the Dominican Republic, El Salvador, Grenada, Guatemala, Guyana, Honduras, Jamaica, Montserrat, the Dutch Antilles, Nicaragua, Panama, St Kitts-Nevis, St Lucia, St Vincent and the Grenadines, and Trinidad and Tobago.

www.mac.doc.gov/cbi/webmain/intro.htm

Caribbean Common Market

The Caribbean Common Market, or CARICOM, was established in 1973 and aims to provide mutual economic support and development between the 13 English-speaking Caribbean countries. The members are Antigua and Barbuda, the Bahamas, Barbados, Belize, Dominica, Grenada, Guyana, Jamaica, Montserrat, St Kitts-Nevis, St Lucia, St Vincent and the Grenadines, and Trinidad and Tobago.

www.caricom.org

CARICOM

See **Caribbean Common Market**.

Carnets

A carnet is a customs document which permits the holder to send sample merchandise temporarily to particular countries, without paying associated duties. Different countries have a variety of customs regulations and the problems which may arise from these different customs

procedures can be avoided by obtaining a carnet. In essence it is a standardized international customs document which allows the duty free,
temporary admission of particular goods into countries which are signatories to the ATA Convention (Admission Temporaire/Temporary
Admission Convention passed in Brussels on 6 December 1961 as a
customs convention for the temporary admission of goods). Under the
terms of the ATA Convention commercial samples can include advertising materials, and medical, scientific or other professional equipment.
Carnets tend to be valid for 12 months.

Carriage and insurance paid (CIP)

See **carriage paid to (CPT).**

Carriage paid to (CPT)

Both 'carriage paid to' (CPT) and 'carriage and insurance paid' (CIP) are
trade terms used to describe the exact terms of a transaction which
undertakes to pay carriage to a specific named destination. They are
used as an alternative to the term 'CIF', which is a commercial acronym
meaning 'cost, insurance and freight'.

Cartel

A cartel is an informal group of businesses that attempt to regulate
production, pricing and marketing practices in order to maximize their
power in the market and limit competition. In essence this means that
two or more businesses willingly cooperate to fix prices, allowing them
to restrict their output in order to continue to control the market. The
purpose of the cartel is to increase profits by reducing competition.
Increasingly, governments have sought to identify and combat cartels
with a variety of **anti-trust laws**, but businesses rarely refer to their
agreements with one another on paper, making it difficult to break up
cartels.

Berge, Wendell, *Cartels: Challenge to a Free World.* Beard Books.com, 2000.

Cash against documents

Cash against documents is a method of paying for products and services,
in which the documents which transfer the ownership of those products
and services are given to the buyers once they have paid cash to an intermediary (often a commission house) who is acting on behalf of the seller.

Cash in advance (CIA)

This is a form of payment for goods, in which payment is before the shipment is despatched. This form of payment oc products such as specialized machinery have been built to order in advance offers an exporter in international business the security knowing that the goods have been paid for and that there will not be any debt-collection issues. Payment is usually made either by direct bank transfer or, perhaps, by cheque. The latter may in fact be at variance with the desire to receive payment before shipment, as overseas cheques may take as long as six weeks to clear. The difficulty arises when buyers are concerned that the goods will not be sent if payment is made in advance, and with the internationalization of banking, cash in advance is becoming a less used means of doing business.

Central African Customs and Economic Union

The Central African Customs and Economic Union was created in 1966 in order to develop a Central African common market, with common external tariffs. The members include Cameroon, the Central African Republic, Chad, Congo, Equatorial Guinea and Gabon.

Central African States Development Bank

The Central African States Development Bank was established in 1975 and began operations in early 1977. It provides loans for its members' economic development and support for integration projects. Its members include Cameroon, the Central African Republic, Chad, Congo, Equatorial Guinea and Gabon.

Central American Bank for Economic Integration (CABEI)

The Central American Bank for Economic Integration, or the CABEI, was founded in 1960 and began operating in 1961 in order to promote development and economic integration amongst its members. The CABEI is an institution of the **Central American Common Market**. Its members include Costa Rica, El Salvador, Guatemala, Honduras and Nicaragua.

www.bcie.org

Central American Common Market

The Central American Common Market, or CACM, was originally begun

Cash in advance 27

y operational until 1973. Its members
ith the **Central American Bank for**
ACM aims to move towards regional
nt of a common external tariff.

used to describe institutions such as the
ited States, or the Bank of England in the
United King-   central bank was created in Sweden in the
middle of the seven... ith century. In Europe the powers of the
European central banks were effectively transferred to the **European
Central Bank** in Frankfurt with the adoption of the **Euro** in 1999. The
central bank's function was to set short-term interests and generally
oversee the health of the country's financial system. It would act as a
lender of last resort to commercial banks should they find themselves in
financial difficulties. During the 1990s, notably in the UK, central banks
have become increasingly independent from political intervention and
now, in the UK, the Bank of England sets the interest rates without
government interference.

Independent central banks theoretically concentrate on the long-term
needs of the economy, avoiding short-term fixes, which are often
adopted by governments. Above all, central banks are concerned
primarily with the reduction of inflation, whereas politicians tend to be
concerned with both inflation and its impact on employment.

Center for Trade and Investment Services

The Center for Trade and Investment Services (CTIS) was established in
the United States in 1992. In cooperation with the Agency for
International Development, the CTIS attempts to promote US business
involvement in generating economic development in **lesser developed
countries**.

Certificate of inspection/manufacture/origin

A certificate of inspection is a document which certifies that particular
merchandise, such as perishable goods, was in an acceptable condition
immediately before its shipment.

A certificate of manufacture is a document which certifies that the
manufacturing process has been completed and the products are now
available for the buyer.

A certificate of origin states precisely where goods have originated from, which is sometimes vital in the case of exports.

Certified trade mission

A certified trade mission, in US terms, is usually planned and organized by state development agencies, sometimes by trade associations or chambers of commerce, and in other cases by export groups. These trade missions must follow the international trade administration criteria in order to receive US government sponsorship. The missions are led by a representative of a sponsoring organization.

Collectivism

'Collectivism' means a set of commonly held beliefs and practices, usually based on ownership of capital. It is often used as an alternative word for 'corporatism'.

Colombo Plan

The Colombo Plan, or more formally, the Colombo Plan for Cooperative Economic Development in South and South East Asia, was established in 1951. Its scope covered a number of countries across Asia and the Pacific region, with the purpose of promoting economic and social development.

COMECON

COMECON, or the Council for Mutual Economic Assistance, was in operation between 1949 and 1991. Its establishment was prompted by the Marshall Plan. It linked the Soviet Union with Bulgaria, Czechoslovakia, Hungary, Poland, Romania, East Germany, Mongolia, Cuba and Vietnam. Associate members were Yugoslavia and Albania. In 1987, COMECON agreed that relations should be established with the **European Community** and it established a free-market approach to international trade in 1990. It was formally disbanded the following year.

Command economy

A command economy occurs in a situation where the government controls virtually all aspects of economic activity. Perhaps the most prominent example of a command economy was the Soviet Union.

There are very few examples of command economies in the world today.

Schutz, Eric, *Markets and Power: Understanding the West's Modern Command Economy.* Armonk, NY: M. E. Sharpe, 2001.

Commercial invoice

A commercial invoice is essentially a bill for goods, sent to the buyer by the seller. Commercial invoices are also essential for customs, in order to determine the value of the goods while calculating any relevant duties or taxes. There is no single standard for a commercial invoice, but they tend to have some or all of the following features:

- the seller's contact information;
- the buyer's contact information;
- the **consignee**'s contact information (assuming this is different from that of the buyer);
- the invoice date;
- a unique invoice number;
- sales terms (in **incoterms** format);
- payment terms;
- currency of sale;
- quantities and descriptions of the merchandise;
- a statement of certification that the invoice is correct.

Committee on Trade and Development (CTD)

The Committee on Trade and Development, or CTD, was originally established in 1965 in order to consider how the **General Agreement on Tariffs and Trade (GATT)** could assist in the economic development of the **lesser developed countries**. In the United States in 1975 the Committee on Foreign Investment in the United States (CFIUS) was established in order to assist the country in organizing major foreign governmental investments.

www.wto.org/english/tratop_e/devel_e/d3ctte_e.htm

Common Agricultural Policy (CAP)

The common agricultural policy, or CAP, is a set of regulations which aim to merge the agricultural policies and programmes of the member states of the **European Community**. It also seeks to promote regional agricultural development, protect the living standards of those who work in agriculture, stabilize the agricultural markets, increase productivity and address issues arising out of the delivery of food supplies. The CAP levies an import duty amounting to the difference between the European Community target farm prices and the lowest available market prices of imported goods. It provides subsidies and promotes the export of farm goods produced within the European Community that cannot be sold at the target prices.

Ingersent, K. A., Rayner, A. J. and Hine, R. C., *The Reform of the Common Agricultural Policy.* Basingstoke: Palgrave Macmillan, 1997.

Common market

A common market, notably the **European Community**, is a group of countries which have a common external **tariff** and may, or may not, allow labour mobility. Common markets tend to have common, or similar, economic policies in each of the member states.

Swann, Dennis, *The Economics of Europe: From Common Market to European Union.* London: Penguin Books, 2000.

Commonwealth

The British Commonwealth is the most notable example of this form of free association, and until the 1990s had some 50 members. A commonwealth lacks a charter, a treaty or a constitution and simply promotes mutual assistance, cooperation and consultation between its sovereign-independent members.

www.thecommonwealth.org

Commonwealth of Independent States (CIS)

The Commonwealth of Independent States, or CIS, was created in 1991, originally with 11 republics which had formed part of the Soviet Union. The original members were Russia, Ukraine, Belarus, Moldova, Armenia, Azerbaijan, Uzbekistan, Turkmenistan, Tajikistan, Kazakhstan and Kyrgyzstan. Georgia joined the CIS in 1993.

www.cis.minsk.by

Communautés Européennes (CE)

'Communautés Européennes', or 'CE', is a mark applied to products, or their packaging or paperwork, which serves as a declaration of conformity within the European Community. It came into force in January 1993 and is, in effect, a European Community national safety mark which represents third-party testing or certification, as well as quality assurance and approval. Products which do not have an authenticated CE mark are, in theory, prohibited, as are products that improperly show the CE mark without having gone through the correct procedures.

Comparative advantage

Comparative advantage is a means by which the relative efficiency of a particular business or country is measured. Certain businesses or countries are inherently, or have become, more efficient or productive with similar resources. Comparative advantage can be differentiated from **absolute advantage** in the sense that a comparative advantage is an advantage by degree, rather than in absolute terms.

Hall, Peter A. and Soskice, David (eds), *Varieties of Capitalism: The Institutional Foundations of Comparative Advantage*. Oxford: Oxford University Press, 2001.
Porter, Michael E., *Competitive Advantage of Nations*. New York: Free Press, 1998.

Compensatory and contingency financing facility (CCFF)

The compensatory and contingency financing facility was introduced by the **International Monetary Fund** in 1963 and provides aid to its members who are experiencing **balance of payments** problems. Originally it would fund shortfalls in export earnings or increases in serial import costs. It is now applied more broadly to fluctuations in commodity prices, shortfalls in tourism receipts and other situations. Changes in international interest rates or prices and the impact on primary imports and exports usually can trigger a CCFF payment.

www.imf.org

Competition policy

The term 'competition policy' refers to the steps that a national government or a world body adopts in relation to its attempts in controlling the way in which international businesses trade in a fair and reasonable manner. Many national governments have specific competition policies, but ever since the signing of the **General Agreement on Tariffs and Trade (GATT)**, ministers from the **World Trade Organization** have sought to harmonize competition policy. There is a close relationship between trade and investment, and competition policy, and with increased **globalization** there is concern that competition is not fully free, particularly with regard to trade within businesses (trade between subsidiaries and other subsidiaries, and with headquarters). Indeed over one-third of the $6.1 trillion in world trade for products and services (late 1990s figures) was within companies. In 1996 the World Trade Organization set up a working party to look into competition policy to examine the impact of foreign investment on competition in markets.

> Stopford, John M., Strange, Susan and Henley, John S., *Rival States, Rival Firms: Competition for World Market Shares*. Cambridge: Cambridge University Press, 1991.

Competitive advantage

The term 'competitive advantage' refers to a situation where a business has a commercial advantage over the competition by being able to offer consumers better value, quality or service. Normally, a competitive advantage would be measured in terms of lower prices but in the case of more benefits and greater quality, higher prices are possible as a result of the competitive advantage enjoyed.

> Porter, Michael E., *Competitive Advantage: Creating and Sustaining Superior Performance*. New York: Free Press, 1985.

COMPRO

COMPRO is an on-line trade data retrieval system. COMPRO is maintained by the International Trade Administration, which is part of the US Department of Commerce. It is used within the Federal Government trade community and other agencies.

Conférence Européenne des administrations des postes et des télécommunications (CEPT)

CEPT, or the European Conference on Postal and Telecommunication Administration, aims to establish standards, many of which have been taken up by the **European Telecommunications Standards Institute**. Its work revolves around the harmonization and simplification, as well as improvement, of the European postal and telecommunications services. CEPT is based in both Paris and Berne.

Confirming

Independent businesses provide this financial service, in which they confirm an export order in the seller's country and then make payment for the goods in the currency of that country. The process of confirming is common within Europe, but is at present under-developed in the United States.

Consignee

A consignee is a business, representative or individual to whom a shipper, or seller, sends merchandise. The consignees present the required documents, and are then recognized as the owners of the merchandise when they have paid customs' duties. More generally the term 'consignee' also applies to anyone to whom products are shipped.

Consignment

A consignment is the delivery of merchandise from the **consignor** to a business or representative (**consignee**).

Consignor

In international business terms, a consignor is an individual or a business that sells or ships merchandise to a **consignee**.

Consolidation

The term 'consolidation' has various meanings applied in business. 'Consolidation' can mean the merging of two or more organizations into a new organization which has a different structure. It is different from a merger in that it combines all of the assets and liabilities of the combining businesses.

'Consolidation' can also refer to loans and debts. It applies to loans in the sense that a large loan is taken out by a business to eliminate all of its smaller loans. A consolidated debt combines all monies owed as a more manageable and controllable single debt.

Businesses also use the term 'consolidation' to apply to invoices. A consolidated invoice covers all items which have been shipped to a particular customer over an agreed period of time. This eliminates the need to invoice individually for each purchase or set of purchases.

Consolidation is also used to describe the process by which a manufacturer or supplier will merge all of the products and raw materials bound for a particular geographical area. In international trade, for example, either consolidation occurs at the docks, where several individual orders are placed in a single container for shipment, or alternatively, transportation to a particular area may be delayed until such a time as it is economically viable to ship the various small orders as a single lot.

Constant returns to specialization

'Constant returns to specialization' assumes that the units of resources which are required to produce a particular product remain constant, regardless of where the country is on its production possibility frontier (PPF). In practice, however, many countries do not specialize but produce a range of different products. It may also be the case that any gains that can be made from specialization are actually exhausted before specialization is completed. It is essential to understand that different products use different resources in different proportions and that not all resources are of the same quality.

Containerization

'Containerization' is a shipping term and refers to cargo-carrying containers up to 48 feet in length. They are limited to this length so that they can be more easily loaded onto trucks, trains or ships without the requirement to unload the contents of each container.

Degerlund, Jane (ed.), *Containerization International Yearbook 2003*. Colchester, Essex: Informa Maritime and Transport, 2003.

Controlling interest

The term 'controlling interest' refers to the point where an individual or other business gains ownership of more than 50 per cent of another business's voting stocks or shares. Controlling interest can be achieved with significantly less than 50 per cent, assuming that the rest of the shares either are not actively voted or are owned by a number of smaller shareholders.

Convention on Contacts for the International Sale of Goods

The UN Convention on Contacts for the International Sale of Goods (CISG) came into force in 1980 and established uniform legal rules governing international sales contracts and rights. The CISG applies to all contracts between businesses from two different countries, as long as those countries have ratified the convention. The United States, for example, adopted the convention in 1988.

www.un.org/law

Cooperative contract

A cooperative contract is an agreement between two businesses to engage in joint economic activity. This is a form of international **strategic alliance**. Usually a simple written or oral contract is agreed, and determines the cooperation between the two businesses over a specified time. During this time, managers and employees from the two businesses have an opportunity to learn more about one another before a more formal alliance is created.

Co-production

Co-production is a licensing arrangement between businesses which enables foreign businesses to learn how to manufacture, assemble, maintain, repair or operate specific products or machinery. In the US, co-production is a government programme, either at government-to-government level or through specifically designated commercial businesses, and is usually limited to defence markets.

van Witteloostuijn, Arjen, *Market Evolution: Competition and Cooperation*. New York: Kluwer Academic Publishers, 1995.

Copyright

Copyright is an exclusive statutory right of an individual or business to exploit the benefits of a particular product over a given period of time. There is considerable variation in the national standards of copyright protection and enforcement across the world. Certain countries have little or no copyright control and openly exploit the advantages of replicating copyright material or products, without reference to their owners. This has become a considerable problem, particularly when these copycat products have been exported and purport to be the original product itself.

See also **intellectual property rights.**

Cornish, William R. and Llewelyn, David, *Intellectual Property: Patents, Copyrights, Trademarks and Allied Rights*. London: Sweet and Maxwell, 2003.

Core competence

Core competences have two specific definitions. The first is the identification of the key skills, knowledge and experience required of an individual to carry out a specific job role.

The other definition refers to the ability of employees or managers to be adaptable in the sense that they could work in an alternative remote location, specifically abroad. In these cases core competences examine the adaptability and resourcefulness of the managers in operating in what may be an unknown overseas environment.

Core competences, or capabilities, are also often related to the key skills or abilities of an organization, or its 'central expertise'.

Stone, Florence M. and Sachs, Randi T., *High-value Manager: Developing the Core Competences for your Organization*. New York: Amacom, 1996.

Core list

'Core list' is a term most closely associated with US national security controls that came into effect in 1991. It covers ten major areas, known as the core list:

- Materials
- Materials processing
- Electronics
- Computers
- Telecommunications and cryptography
- Sensors
- Avionics and navigation
- Marine technology
- Propulsion systems and transportation equipment
- Miscellaneous

Cost and freight (CFR)

Under the terms of cost and freight, the seller quotes a price to the buyer which includes the cost of goods and the cost of transportation to a particular point of debarkation. Insurance is left to the buyer. This is a typical form used for ocean shipments.

Cost, insurance and freight (CIF)

Cost, insurance and freight is a means by which a seller can quote for the cost of goods, including the insurance and transportation to a given debarkation point. It is typically used for ocean shipments. Otherwise **carriage and insurance paid** would be used.

Cost of capital

Cost of capital is a means by which an investor who supplies capital can expect a return that is commensurate with the risk to which that capital is exposed. It can also be used to describe the cost of raising money.

Typically, as far as a business raising capital is concerned, it would include the returns which the investor demands for lending or investing the money, the potential risks of the project and the returns that would be provided by alternative investments at a similar risk.

Council of Europe

The Council of Europe, based in Strasbourg, was established in 1949 in order to encourage both unity and social and economic growth within Europe. Its members include Austria, Belgium, Cyprus, Denmark, Finland, France, Germany, Greece, Hungary, Iceland, Ireland, Italy, Lichtenstein, Luxembourg, Malta, the Netherlands, Norway, Portugal, San Marino, Spain, Sweden, Switzerland, Turkey, and the United Kingdom.

www.coe.int

Counter-purchase

See **counter-trade.**

Counter-trade

'Counter-trade' describes a situation where a seller accepts goods or services in part-, or whole payment for its products. Counter-trade, therefore, includes **barter**, buy-back, **swaps**, switches, or triangular trade (in which the value of products is traded between three different businesses). **Offsets** are also part of counter-trade, but in some cases a distinction is made, as counter-trade is considered to be a reciprocal exchange of goods and services, which is often used to alleviate the problems importers may have in terms of foreign exchange shortages. Offsets, in this sense, are related to the advancement of industrial development and may often include equity investment.

Counter-purchase is one of the most common forms of counter-trade. The exporters will agree to purchase a quantity of goods from a country in exchange for the products that they have exported. The products may be completely unrelated, but are of equivalent value.

In buy-back situations exporters who deal with the technology of whole facilities and heavy equipment may agree to purchase a percentage of the eventual output of the facility. Switch trading can be likened to barter, but involves a chain of different buyers and sellers, often in different markets.

Counter-trade is particularly useful when a business exports goods to a country whose currency is not freely convertible. Equally that country may not have sufficient foreign exchange reserves to purchase these goods. In many cases counter-trade will be the only way in which an export deal can be completed and many businesses have recognized that by insisting on being paid in hard currency, they are at a competitive disadvantage.

As a counter to this, businesses may view counter-trade as simply encumbering them with poor quality or unusable goods, which cannot provide a decent profit.

See also **offsets**.

Mirus, Rolf and Yeung, Bernard (eds), *The Economics of Barter and Countertrade.* Cheltenham: Edward Elgar, 2001.

Countervailing duties

Countervailing duties are imposed by a country accepting imported goods in order to counteract any subsidies which the exporters were granted by their own governments. This duty is allowed under the terms of the Code on Subsidies and Countervailing Duties, assuming that the country which is importing the products can prove that the subsidy would otherwise cause damage to its domestic businesses. In the US, countervailing duties must be ratified by the **International Trade Commission**.

Mirus, Rolf and Yeung, Bernard (eds), *The Economics of Barter and Countertrade.* Cheltenham: Edward Elgar, 2001.

Court of International Trade

The Court of International Trade (CIT) was established in 1890 and deals with civil actions against the United States arising from import transactions. The CIT deals with situations involving **anti-dumping**, product classification and **countervailing duties**, in addition to unfair trade practices which have been referred to them by the **International Trade Commission**. The court can hear and determine cases arising from any location within the jurisdiction of the United States. The judges are appointed for life by the US President.

www.cit.uscourts.gov

Credit risk insurance

Credit risk insurance is simply insurance which is designed to cover the risk of non-payment for goods which have been delivered.

Schaeffer, Hal, *Credit Risk Management: A Guide to Sound Business Decisions.* New York: John Wiley, 2000.

Credit tranches

Credit tranches underpin the policies of the **International Monetary Fund**. Under this system, credit is made available to a country in four tranches, each of which is equivalent to 25 per cent of the members' quota. *Tranche* is the French for 'slice'. A member may be granted the use of the IMF in the first credit tranche if it appears to be making efforts to overcome its **balance of payments** problems.

www.imf.org

Cross-cultural literacy

Cross-cultural literacy has become an increasingly important concern for businesses engaged in international trade. The desire is to pay regard to the customs and business etiquette of other countries in which a business may trade. Increasingly, multinational businesses are trying to understand the cultural differences between nations and how this affects the way in which business is practised. Cross-cultural literacy involves a sensitivity to the customs and culture of other nations, without which, potentially important business opportunities would be lost.

Although English has become the dominant business language in the world, the speaking of foreign languages would not only be beneficial, but may often be expected in other cultures in order to cement positive business relationships.

Cross-licensing agreement

A cross-licensing agreement is a business understanding which allows two organizations, often in different parts of the world, the right to develop products and services using one another's technology, data and expertise. The agreement is mutually beneficial and may also involve the interchange of staff and management in order for them to work alongside, replace or shadow their counterparts in the other organization.

Culture

The term 'culture' can be applied not only to specific nations or parts of a country, but also to businesses, which may have their own particular form of culture. The term 'culture' itself is a complex collection of knowledge, beliefs, morals, laws and customs – notably however, values and norms, which are considered to be at the centre of culture. Values themselves are abstract ideals, possibly revolving around what is right, wrong or desirable. Norms are the social rules and guidelines that direct appropriate behaviour in certain situations. Values and norms are at the very heart of any form of social system or organization.

There have been many attempts to categorize different forms of culture and to explain why particular forms of culture are more, or less, prevalent in business organizations, particularly those that operate across the world.

In business organizations, however, one of the dominant features is a sense of **collectivism**, presenting a series of common, mutually binding standards to which all who work for the business are expected to conform. Increasingly, economic progress and **globalization** have driven cultural change. Businesses operating abroad seek to develop their **cross-cultural literacy** by employing the nationals of their host countries and attempting to deal with what could be considered **ethno-centric behaviour**. Clearly both the value systems and norms of a new country in which a business is operating can affect its chance of success. One of the main differences across frontiers concerns ethics; whilst ethical principles are universal, they differ. Any international business needs to firmly establish a coherent set of ethics of the highest order in terms of morals, in order to avoid falling foul of any particular country's ethical standards.

Currency board

A currency board is a monetary institution which issues domestic currency that is backed by foreign assets. The domestic currency is convertible to an overseas anchor currency at a fixed rate. The currency to which the domestic currency is pegged is usually chosen for its international acceptability, convertibility and, above all, stability. The currency board's reserves are equal to at least 100 per cent of all the notes and coins in circulation. The currency board generates profits arising from the difference between the interest earned on its reserved assets and the expense of keeping the notes and coins in circulation. Market forces determine the money supply, and the only true function of the currency board is to be able to exchange domestic notes and coins for the anchor currency at the given fixed rate. Currency boards do not act as lenders, either to the domestic banks or to the government. Currency boards tend to occur in countries where the national currency has had extreme difficulties, and may also occur in countries where the currency is internationally traded.

Balino, Tomas J. T. and Enoch, Charles, *Currency Board Arrangements: Issues and Experiences.* Washington, DC: International Monetary Fund, 1997.

Currency crisis

A currency crisis may occur in a country where there is a dramatic degree of volatility in the exchange rate. Between 1970 and 1996 alone there were over 160 currency crises or crashes. They have become a very frequent feature, which is fuelled by a sudden loss of confidence in the value of the currency, a widespread threat of bankruptcies, a severe recession, a financial panic or a speculative attack on the currency.

Dooley, Michael P. and Frankel, Jeffrey A. (eds), *Managing Currency Crisis in Emerging Markets.* Chicago, IL: University of Chicago Press, 2003.

Currency speculation

Under normal circumstances the exchange rate of a particular currency is based on its performance or value against other currencies. A country's exchange rate is essential as it determines how that country is involved in international trade and investment. Movements in exchange rates directly affect the nation's interest rate levels. The exchange rate management system requires stability and attempts to ensure that the exchange rate is at an optimum level. Currency speculation, however, occurs during periods of instability. Indeed, market forces can force governments to try to stabilize their exchange rates; most fail. In essence, currency speculation involves purchasing or selling a currency in the hope that the exchange rate will move favourably, allowing the dealer to make a profit by either selling or buying.

Many countries are powerless to stop this form of speculation. Indeed some 95 per cent of all currency movement is speculative, leaving just 5 per cent for genuine international trade and investment. Speculation, by buying or selling an asset to take advantage of a future price change, is inherently a risk. In other words, currency speculators make a subjective judgement of possible movements in the exchange rate in the future. Currency is bought and sold and a country's **central bank** will then try to defend the currency by matching the increased supply of the currency in accordance with demand. This is usually achieved by increasing interest rates, making the local currency more attractive.

Global financial speculation moves vast sums of money around the world and has successfully destabilized many developing countries, not to mention countries such as the United Kingdom, in recent years.

Henderson, Callum, *Currency Strategy – A Practitioner's Guide to Currency Trading, Hedging and Forecasting.* New York: John Wiley, 2002.

Currency swap

See swaps.

Currency translation

Currency translation is the process of converting assets and liabilities from a foreign currency into the home currency for inclusion on the business's financial statements. The process usually involves the following:

- Fixed assets are translated into the home country's currency at rates which were prevailing on the date of the **acquisition**, and adjusted for any profits or losses.
- Monetary assets and liabilities in foreign currencies are translated into the home currency at the foreign exchange rates pertaining to the balance sheet date.
- Revenue and expenses in foreign currencies are recorded in the home currency, again at the rate ruling for the month of the transactions.
- Any gains or losses arising out of the translation are reported as part of the profit or loss.

For other operations, assets and liabilities are again translated into the home currency at a rate related to the balance sheet date, and revenues and expenses are recorded in sterling, with gains or losses arising from the translation being dealt with by the business's reserves.

Guithues, Denise M., *Foreign Currency Translation: A More Useful Approach.* Ann Arbor, MI: University of Michigan Research Press, 1986.

Current account

See **balance of payments**.

Current account deficit/surplus

A current account deficit or surplus is shown on a country's **balance of payments**, detailing the relationship between the exports and imports of products and services. A current account deficit occurs when the value of the exports is lower than the value of the imports. A current account surplus occurs when the value of the exports is higher than the value of the imports.

Pitchford, John, *The Current Account and Foreign Debt.* London: Routledge, 1995.

Current cost accounting

Current cost accounting is a method of valuation. The methodology states that assets and goods which are used in production are valued at either their estimated or their actual current market prices at the point when production takes place. Current cost accounting is also known as 'replacement cost accounting' as it shows the true current value of assets and stock.

Groot, Tom and Lukka, Kari (eds), *Cases in Management Accounting: Current Practices in European Countries.* London: Financial Times, Prentice Hall, 2000.
Horngren, Charles T., Bhimani, Alnoor, Datar, Srikant, M. and Foster, George, *Management and Cost Accounting.* London: Financial Times, Prentice Hall, 2001.

Current rate method

The current rate method involves the translation of all overseas currency balance sheets and income-statement items at the current exchange rate.

Customs Cooperation Council (CCC)

The Customs Cooperation Council (CCC) was established in 1950 and is based in Brussels. The council is a technical organization which not only studies various countries' customs problems, but also attempts to harmonize customs systems in order to promote trade. The organization has a membership of around 150 countries.

www.wcoomd.org

Customs house broker

A customs house broker, as far as US customs service definitions are concerned, is an organization or individual that can transact customs business on behalf of other businesses. Customs house brokers deal with the entry and admissibility of merchandise, its classification and valuation, as well as the payment of duties and taxes or other charges. Customs house brokers are licensed under Part III of Title 19 of the US Code of Federal Regulations (Customs Regulations).

Customs union

The best known example of a customs union is the **European Community**; it is, in essence, an agreement between two or more countries to remove trade barriers between one another. They also seek to establish common tariff and non-tariff policies pertaining to imports from countries which are outside the customs union. The main purpose of customs unions is to create trade by encouraging the consumption of other members' products, as opposed to domestic products, and to divert trade from countries which are outside the union in favour of trade with other member countries.

C

D'Amato Act

'The D'Amato Act' is the common name for the Iran and Libya Sanctions Act (1996). The D'Amato Act can be seen as an instrument of US foreign policy in respect of imposing sanctions on individuals or businesses that would choose to invest in either the Iranian or Libyan oil or gas industries, or indeed sell particular goods, services or technology to Libya. It was introduced just 5 months after the **Helmes–Burton Act**. At that particular juncture the US classified both of these countries as sponsors of terrorism and owners of weapons of mass destruction. Underpinning this move was a fear by the United States and its allies that in continuing to trade with these two countries, national security and foreign policy interests would be compromised. Given that both countries are highly reliant upon their oil and gas industries, the D'Amato Act would block foreign investment and, in turn, have a drastic impact on their economies, thus reducing the two governments' funds which could be passed on to terrorists.

The D'Amato Act also sought to force Libya to comply with several United Nations Security Council resolutions. The D'Amato Act was just one feature in a continued campaign by the United States against both countries, which had been proceeding for several decades. The US had already prohibited domestic trade and investment in both Libya and Iran.

The Act is named after Senator Alfonse D'Amato, who introduced the legislation into the US Senate in September 1995. The most contentious part of the Act was that it authorized the US President to impose sanctions upon individuals, businesses or corporations who knowingly invested in Iran or Libya. The penalties would be the withdrawal of the assistance of the **Export–Import Bank of the US** (meaning that guarantees, insurance and credit were withdrawn), or the denial of their right to receive exports from the US, effectively removing their export licences.

Deed of assignment

A deed of assignment is a banking arrangement between a business which holds a letter of credit and, usually, the supplier of products or services, who may require a payment to be forthcoming and need to receive assurance that the payment will be made.

Deed of protest

A deed of protest is a document showing that a protest has been made. A bank may be required to provide one of these if a **bill of exchange** is not paid, accepted or honoured.

Deferral principle

The deferral principle states that the parent company of a foreign subsidiary is not taxed on the income of that subsidiary until it has received a dividend from the subsidiary. The United States does not recognize the deferral principle.

Deficit

A deficit, in the general sense, is a situation where the sum of the debts exceeds the sum of the credits. It is usually applied to the **balance of payments** or indeed any international transactions and is, clearly, the reverse of a surplus.

Delivered at frontier

'Delivered at frontier' literally means that the seller undertakes to ensure the safe delivery of merchandise to the frontier of a country, before the customs border. The term usually applies to road or rail deliveries, but can also be used for other forms of transportation. Once the merchandise has been delivered to the frontier, the seller's obligations have been fulfilled.

Delivered/duty paid

'Delivered/duty paid' represents a seller's maximum obligation in terms of delivery. It is in stark contrast to **ex-factory** or **ex-works**. Delivered/duty paid means that it is the seller's responsibility to clear the products for import, but the seller may not necessarily be responsible for **Value Added Tax** or other similar taxes, noting this as, for example, 'exclusive of VAT and/or other taxes'.

Demurrage

'Demurrage' refers to delays of scheduled departures of a vessel, usually

D

extra time which may be taken for loading and/or unloading the vessel. The term is applied to situations where the shipper or the charterer of the vessel is responsible for the delay, and not the vessel's operator.

Tiberg, Hugo, *The Law of Demurrage*. London: Sweet and Maxwell, 1995.

Depreciation

Depreciation is a systematic reduction of the acquisition costs of fixed assets, such as machinery, over the period during which those assets were of benefit to the organization. Depreciation is, in effect, a paper-based accountancy exercise which seeks to take account of the fact that the value of fixed assets gradually decreases over a period of time and that those attendant losses should be written off against the expense accounts of the organization.

In the US this process is known as 'amortization', which is the systematic reduction of the value of primarily intangible assets, such as goodwill or intellectual property. The value of these intangible assets, such as a breakthrough in manufacturing processes, reduces in value over a period of time as they are either replaced or copied by other competitors.

'Depreciation' can also be used to describe a fall in the value of a country's currency, when the currency falls on the exchange market, relative to other currencies or a weighted average of other currencies.

Depression

A depression is exemplified by a period of prolonged, negative economic growth. Depressions can be differentiated from recessions as depressions represent the lowest point of a country's trade cycle. Recessions effectively become depressions if they last a considerable period of time. Whilst there was undoubtedly a severe depression in the 1930s, the economic downturn during the late 1980s and early 1990s is probably more accurately described as a recession, rather than a depression. With the increasing globalization of markets, economic difficulties in major international trade countries tend to have a negative impact upon the economies of trading partners.

James, Harold, *The End of Globalization: Lessons from the Great Depression*. Boston, MA: Harvard University Press, 2002.

Deregulation

Deregulation is the process of removing either legal or quasi-legal restrictions on competition. It is an integral part of free market policies, during which liberalization of trade is pursued in order to improve the overall competition and economic activity. However, deregulation, which involves the cutting of 'red tape', still stifles many areas of international trade. In the US alone it has been estimated that regulations cost over $300 billion per year.

The process of deregulation is often coupled with a government moving industries out of state ownership and into private hands, allowing them to operate more freely in the marketplace, coupled with the deregulation of that market, in order to attract more competitors and, overall, generate a better and fairer market for consumers.

Derivatives

Derivatives are a form of leveraged instrument that may be linked either to items such as foreign currencies, government bonds, share prices or interest rates, or to specific commodities, such as coffee, gold or sugar. These items may be purchased or sold at a future date. Derivatives can also be linked to future exchange according to contractual obligations. The instrument, which is a contract, is tradable and has a market value. In essence, the derivative is purchased at a specific price and then, ideally, sold at the correct time when the value of that derivative has increased.

Hull, John C., *Options, Futures and Other Derivatives*. Englewood Cliffs, NJ: Prentice-Hall, 2002.

Devaluation

Devaluation has three different meanings. It may be used as an alternative description for **depreciation**. 'Devaluation' can also be used to denote the fall in the value of a currency, which had been pegged at a particular value. It can also be used to describe a fall in the value of currency in terms of gold or silver, or indeed the sudden fall in the value of one currency compared with other currencies.

D

Devaluation usually occurs when there is a sharp fall in a currency which is part of a fixed exchange rate system. In some cases, devaluation has been a part of government policy and on many occasions devaluation has taken place as the result of **currency speculation**.

Devaluation can have short-term competitive benefits, but in the longer term, higher prices erode these benefits.

See also **j curve**.

Edwards, Sebastian, *Real Exchange Rates, Devaluation and Adjustment: Exchange Rate Policy in Developing Countries*. Cambridge, MA: MIT Press, 1989.

Development bank

Development banks may be involved in activities worldwide, nationally or regionally and aim to encourage economic development by lending or investing money in businesses in a specific region.

Diminishing returns on specialization

The term 'diminishing returns on specialization' is the converse of **economies of scale** and is often referred to as 'diseconomies of scale'. The concept suggests that the larger the operation, the smaller the additional benefit received by the business as a result of producing more. This can be applied to many different business situations, for example if employees are already well paid, a slight increase in payment would have little impact on their productivity. It would be more effective to pay a small increase to workers in a developing country, who would respond far more positively to an increase in pay. To a business that operates in a developed economy, the term implies an approach that is widely different from what it suggests to those who operate in **lesser developed countries**. Capital does not suffer from diminished returns as greatly in developing countries as it does in developed countries.

Directly unproductive profit-seeking activities

Directly unproductive profit-seeking activities are those that have no directly productive purpose. They do not increase the utility of a product or service as far as a consumer is concerned and are wholly designed to increase profits. Typically, they would include attempts to distort the market in order to achieve a higher profit without adding value.

Dirty float system

A dirty float system involves a currency which floats in terms of its value compared with other currencies, and which is prone to government intervention. Governments adopting this system will attempt to manage the fluctuations in the currency's value in order to maintain desired exchange rates.

Discount rate

Discount rates are the rates at which future values are diminished each year to make them comparable to present values. Discount rates are also the rates at which **central banks** charge commercial banks for

D

short-term loans of reserves. They are an essential tool of monetary policy.

Disequilibrium

Disequilibrium is essentially an inequality between supply and demand. Ultimately it is an untenable state when applied to an economic system and an equilibrium, which balances both supply and demand, will be sought by businesses involved in the affected area of trade, or by countries which have identified this disequilibrium.

Kirzner, Israel, *How Markets Work: Disequilibrium, Entrepreneurship and Discovery*. London: Institute of Economic Affairs, 1997.

Dispute settlement/dispute settlement mechanism

Under the terms of the **General Agreement on Tariffs and Trade (GATT)**, the **World Trade Organization** appoints a three-person panel to hear and adjudicate in cases of trade disputes between parties, essentially made up of members of the World Trade Organization. The panel produces a report of the dispute settlement mechanism and its conclusions, which is then reviewed by an appellate body.

www.wto.org

Distributor

In international trade terms a distributor is a foreign business or agent which sells in a particular country on behalf of a supplier. It sells for the supplier directly and, in order to facilitate this, maintains a stock of the supplier's products.

Dollarization

Dollarization takes place when a country adopts a foreign currency to use alongside or instead of its own domestic currency. Panama is an example of a country which has used the US dollar as its primary currency, whereas Andorra had two currencies, the French franc and the Spanish peseta, prior to the arrival of the Euro.

When a country becomes officially dollarized, it becomes part of a unified currency zone with the country whose currency it has adopted (the issuing country). In effect an officially dollarized country relinquishes its independent monetary policy and adopts the monetary policy of the country of the currency it is using. Within the currency zone, **arbi-**

D

trage keeps the prices of similar products and services within a narrow band. Inflation rates tend to be similar, as are interest rates. The supply of money is determined by the **balance of payments**. The monetary base is determined by the issuing country. If the country spends less, it can acquire more currency.

Countries tend to adopt dollarization when they have had a history of poor monetary performance or when they have established a very close relationship with another country as a major trading partner.

Flowers, Edward B., *The Euro, Capital Markets and Dollarization*. Lanham, MD: Rowman and Littlefield, 2002.

Downstream dumping

Downstream dumping occurs when an overseas producer sells products, usually components or raw materials, to a producer in another country. The product is then further processed and shipped to a third country.

See also **dumping**.

Draft bill of exchange

A draft bill of exchange is a written and unconditional order for payment from the **drawer** to the **drawee**. The draft directs the drawee to pay a specified sum of money in a particular currency on a particular date to the drawer. There are two other variants: a sight draft requires immediate payment on sight of the bill and a time draft requires payments at an agreed date, or set of dates, in the future.

Drawee

A drawee is an individual or a business on which a **draft bill of exchange** is drawn and which then owes the amount stated on that bill of exchange.

Drawer

A drawer is an individual or a business which issues or signs a **draft bill of exchange** and is thus entitled to receive payment from the **drawee**.

Dumping

'Dumping' is a sales-related term which has considerably negative connotations. Dumping is the practice of selling obsolete products and services into an overseas market at a lower price (often) than had been charged in the home market. Normally products and services which have reached the decline stage of their product life cycle are identified as being ideal candidates for dumping procedures. Dumping is not entirely restricted to obsolete products as the practice can be seen as a means by which a business can achieve a significant influx of income by reducing the margins on a product or service overseas, whilst retaining the margins at home. Typical examples of products which have been dumped in this way are those in the consumer electronics industry, notably from Japan and South Korea. The US and the European Union have begun to set up protectionist measures to prevent this practice.

A rather more sinister form of dumping involves the selling of products which have not met with safety standards or other criteria in the home market. Overseas markets are chosen which have less protection for their consumers, notably in the pharmaceuticals market where potentially dangerous drugs which have been either banned or restricted in use in the home market, are sold openly overseas.

Under Article VI of the **General Agreement on Tariffs and Trade (GATT)**, **anti-dumping** duties can be imposed which are equal to the difference between the price sought in the importing country and the normal value of that product in the exporting country. Since dumping implies the sale of commodities in foreign markets at a less than fair value, it is considered to be unfair and will directly affect domestic producers of competing products. A business can only sustain sales at below cost, or close to cost, if it has some means of subsidizing these sales. Dumping is used by dominant businesses to undermine their rivals, and often falls foul of **anti-trust law** allowing the country to add duties to the cheap imports which they believe are being dumped into their markets.

Jackson, John H. and Vernulst, Edwin A. (eds), *Anti-dumping Law and Practice: A Comparative Study*. Ann Arbor, MI: University of Michigan Press, 1990.

D

Dutch disease

The term 'Dutch disease', unsurprisingly, is derived from the Netherlands, where the discovery of natural gas and the exports the industry generated had a massive impact on the country's other industries. A substantial increase in a particular industry in terms of its exports directly affects the country's currency and causes it to appreciate, thus making it more difficult for other industries in that country to compete worldwide.

Duty

Duties are taxes which are imposed by a country via its customs authorities. Duties can be based upon the value of the goods being imported (**ad valorem tariff**). Other duties can be based on weight or quantity (specific duties) whilst other duties are based on a combination of the value of the products and other factors (compound duties).

Duty free

'Duty free' means, literally, 'without tariffs'. 'Duty free' describes imports which would normally attract a tariff but where, for a particular reason, the imports are exempt from duty. The most common form of duty free is afforded to international travellers, who may import a certain amount of goods up to specified limits on a duty free basis.

Dynamic gains from trade

Dynamic gains from trade are the benefits which businesses may enjoy from international trade, in addition to the normal gains they would enjoy from increases in the number and value of transactions. Dynamic gains from trade allow, or infer, a greater gain or benefit to the business than purely monetary forms of measurement. Many countries have benefited far more from international trade than the gains that would normally be directly associated with the value of that trade. The inference continues that increases in international trade propel funds around the domestic environment, creating a form of multiplier effect. This means that income received from international trade generates both direct and indirect domestic employment and internal trade and makes a valuable contribution to the country's economy and infrastructure.

Baldwin, Richard, *Measurable Dynamic Gains from Trade*. Cambridge, MA: National Bureau of Economic Research, 1989.

D

E-business

The term 'e-business', or 'electronic business', was probably coined by IBM in 1997. It used the term as part of a major advertising campaign. E-business is the process of conducting business using elements of the Internet. E-business is a more generic term than **e-commerce** because it transcends the acts of buying and selling, to include collaboration with business partners and the servicing of customers. In effect, e-business is a fusion of business processes, applications and organizational structure. The vast majority of businesses are now incorporating e-business as part of their overall planning procedures. Typically, in manufacturing for example, the Internet can be used to buy parts, components and supplies. Providing the organization is satisfied with the quality of products (which would certainly entail the receiving of samples), the global implications for supply are enormous. It is perfectly feasible for a manufacturing organization to now access, interrogate and evaluate organizations remotely in ways that would have been impossible in the past. The convenience and availability of suppliers, notwithstanding the attendant delivery costs, may continue to revolutionize the supply and fulfilment functions of the manufacturing industry.

Eclectic paradigm

The eclectic paradigm is a theory put forward by John Dunning. It suggests that three advantages justify the establishment of a business, usually a multinational, in another country through direct investment. The three advantages are ownership, location and market internalization. The business will enjoy closer control, and reduced transaction costs due to its location in that market, and it will also enjoy the environmental advantages of the host country. Dunning suggested that if one of these three advantages is lost, then the multinational will undoubtedly divest itself of the business.

Dunning, John H., 'Toward an Eclectic Theory of International Production: Some Empirical Tests', *Journal of International Business Studies*, 11 (1980).
Dunning, John H., 'The Eclectic Paradigm of International Production: a Restatement

and some Possible Extensions', *Journal of International Business Studies*, 19(1) (1988), pp. 1–32.

Eco-label

An eco-label is a mark which is awarded by the **European Community** to businesses that can prove that their products have a significantly lower impact on the environment than similar products. The concept was introduced in 1992 and eco-labelling criteria now provide businesses with commercial benefits as a reward for producing products which are more environmentally friendly and designing production processes which produce less pollution.

Zarrilli, Simonetta, Jha, Venna and Vossenaar, Rene (eds), *Eco-labelling and International Trade*. Basingstoke: Palgrave Macmillan, 1997.

E-commerce

'E-commerce', or 'electronic commerce', is a term specifically used to describe the buying and selling of products and services via the Internet. In many respects the term has been superseded by **e-business**, as the latter description is taken to encompass more aspects of trade using the Internet. In effect, e-commerce is a paperless exchange of information via emails, bulletin boards, the electronic transfer of funds, and fax transmissions. These tools allow online buying and selling in a wide variety of consumer and industrial sectors.

Economic and Social Council (ECOSOC)

The Economic and Social Council, or ECOSOC, was created in 1945, primarily to coordinate both the social and the economic functions of the United Nations. The council is concerned with international development, world trade, the impacts and progress of industrialization, the use of natural resources, human rights issues, the status of women, population growth, drug trafficking, science and technology, and the prevention of crime. ECOSOC has five regional commissions and six functional commissions.

See also **United Nations Regional Commissions.**

www.un.org/esa/coordination/ecosoc

Economic exposure

In international trade terms, 'economic exposure' refers to the impact that changes in exchange rates may have on a business's value. This is usually measured by the impact the exchange rate changes have had, or may have, on its future cash flows.

Friberg, Richard, *Exchange Rates and the Firm: Strategies to Manage Exposure and the Impact of EMU*. Basingstoke: Palgrave Macmillan, 1999.

Economic risk

When a business involves itself in projects overseas, providing finance for that project, economic risk is assessed on the basis that the project's output may not generate sufficient revenue. The assessment of the revenue generation is usually based on the firm's ability to cover its own operating costs and to be in a position to deal with its debt obligations to the financing organization, or to other lenders.

Shiller, Robert J., *The New Financial Order: Risk in the 21st Century*. Princeton, NJ: Princeton University Press, 2003.

Economic sanction

Economic sanctions seek to punish, or isolate, particular countries by imposing economic penalties until such a time as their behaviour, or stance, on particular issues are resolved. Economic sanctions can range from the prohibition of trade, the ceasing of financial transactions, the removal of economic or military assistance, or other measures aimed to bring the country back into line, usually with international standards. Sanctions are often selective and may target particular forms of trade or financial transactions. In other cases all aid programmes may be ceased. Sanctions seek to uphold international norms and deter the country from taking actions which are objectionable to the international community. Sanctions are seen as a viable alternative to invasion or military occupation and are purely designed to force that nation's government to change its policies.

Sanctions can be multilateral, usually under the auspices of the United Nations. However, in many cases sanctions are unilateral or bilateral, when one or more countries without the support of the international community at large choose to impose economic sanctions. It has been estimated that over 60 per cent of economic sanctions fail and that these sanctions have drastic impacts upon countries which would normally have been engaged in economic relations with the target nation. Indeed it was calculated that in 1995 alone the US economy lost $15 billion in exports as a result of imposing economic sanctions on other countries.

Arguably the most successful use of economic sanctions was against the apartheid regime in South Africa, although it is hotly debated

E

whether economic sanctions really did play a crucial role. It was, perhaps, the fact that overseas companies feared the effect upon their share prices should they invest in South Africa that caused them not to invest or trade with the country.

Cortright, David and Lopez, George A., *Smart Sanctions: Targeting Economic Statecraft.* Lanham, MD: Rowman and Littlefield, 2002.

Economic Support Fund (ESF)

The Economic Support Fund, or ESF, is a US agency which provides economic assistance to countries as an adjunct to the furtherance of US economic and foreign policy. Often the economic support comes with strings attached, including US access-rights agreements or military-base rights. The countries are chosen by the US State Department and the funding can provide support for the country's **balance of payments** or for the importation of commodities.

www.usaid.gov

Economic union

Perhaps the clearest example of an economic union is the **European Union**. Economic union was achieved in January 1999 when 11 of the then 15 countries of the **European Community** took the step to merge their national currencies and adopt the **Euro**. An economic union aims to bring about currency stability and low inflation through the creation of an independent **central bank** (in this case the **European Central Bank**).

Businesses within the economic union have the advantage of only having to deal with one currency, making prices and wages across the economic union more transparent, while simultaneously increasing competition, as it is easier for businesses to sell throughout the union. Essential to an economic union is the setting of a central interest rate and exchange rate and although countries within the union lose this flexibility, it is ultimately hoped that the union will become an optimal currency area as a result of the common monetary policy.

Artis, Michael and Nixson, Frederick, *The Economics of the European Union: Policy and Analysis.* Oxford: Oxford University Press, 2001.

Economic zone

Economic zones are specifically designated areas of a particular country which have special investment incentives. The purpose of the economic zone is to attract inward investment through treating the area, to all intents and purposes, as a **duty free** zone in which both imports and exports are not taxed or are taxed at a much lower rate than the rest of the country. To some extent these economic zones replicate development areas, where businesses wishing to invest in these areas receive greater benefits for their investment, usually to bring that zone into line economically with the rest of the country. The economic zones tend to be areas of high unemployment which have had historically low investment. There are several economic zones in the People's Republic of China and the **newly independent states** of the former Soviet Union.

Hoyle, Brian S., *Cityports, Coastal Zones and Regional Change*. Chichester: John Wiley, 1996.

Economies of scale

Strictly speaking, 'economies of scale' is an economics-related issue. However, it has considerable implications for marketing options. The basic concept revolves around the fact that a business needs to build up a critical mass. In other words, it must be large enough or powerful enough relative to the market to be able to influence it and to enjoy any degree of success. It is notoriously expensive to establish a presence in any but the smallest markets. The concept suggests that small businesses are simply too small to register any impact on larger markets. Businesses need to be able to assign a certain percentage of their turnover towards product development and marketing activities. However, in the case of small businesses, this percentage, in real terms, will inevitably be miniscule.

Once a business has reached a point where it is a large trading entity, it can enjoy many of the benefits associated with larger-scale production or distribution. In other words, as the size and scope of the business increases, the generally held view is that the unit costs are driven down. The corollary is that having achieved economies of scale, the business will have more funds available to further improve its market position. One of the main reasons behind this is that fixed costs and other overheads can be spread over ever-increasing units of output. However, there are inherent difficulties and increased costs, which are known as diseconomies of scale, when increased average costs occur that are due to the difficulty of managing large operations.

E

Katrak, Homi and Strange, Roger (eds), *Small-Scale Enterprises in Developing and Transitional Economies*. Basingstoke: Palgrave Macmillan, 2001.

Eco-tourism

Eco-tourism has flourished over the past two decades and although there is no clear definition of the term, the International Eco-tourism Society defines it as 'responsible travel to natural areas that conserves the environment and sustains the well-being of local people'. In essence, eco-tourism is the growing trend towards travel to destinations where the flora, fauna and cultural heritage are the primary attractions. Unfortunately the effects of tourism on fragile environments, species and local ways of life have had negative impacts. This is partly due to many international tourism businesses 'greening' their products.

Eco-tourism presents a tremendous challenge to the governments of nations where it has become developed. Whilst the economic benefits of eco-tourism are clear, the balance between those benefits and the gradual degradation of the environment as a result is attracting greater attention. Eco-tourism is generally, but not exclusively, designed for small groups, and true eco-tourism seeks to minimize the negative impacts on both the natural and the socio-cultural environment. The revenue received from the tourism can provide the means by which the natural areas can be protected, and offers economic benefits for the local communities. Providing for eco-tourism continues to benefit the communities, and the environment, land and facilities which were otherwise regarded as non-productive by the host nation will not be converted into agricultural land. Clearly there are increased employment opportunities locally which will increase the possibility of other local businesses providing for the community. Assuming that improved knowledge and awareness of environmental issues continue hand-in-hand with the maintenance of the natural areas, successful eco-tourism should continue to provide much-needed economic support.

Honey, Martha (ed.), *EcoTourism and Certification: Setting Standards in Practice.* Washington, DC: Island Press, 2002.

E

Ecu

The Ecu, or European Currency Unit, unlike the **Euro** was not a currency. It was a weighted basket of currencies of **European Union** countries. On 1 January 1999, one Ecu became one Euro, and on that date all official Ecus were converted into Euros. Any reference to the Ecu would now refer to the Euro.

EFTA

See **European Free Trade Association (EFTA).**

Emerging markets

The **World Bank** classifies economies with a gross national income per capita of $9,266 or more as high-income countries. An emerging market is a country which is trying to change and improve its economy in order to reach that broad target. One of the emerging markets is China, which is considered an emerging market despite its vast resources and huge population.

The term 'emerging markets' was coined by Antoine W. van Agtmael, who worked for the World Bank's **International Finance Corporation**. Emerging markets attract various forms of international financial support in order to assist their economies, either through the World Bank itself or from the **International Monetary Fund** or the more wealthy nations. They also receive assistance in the form of reduced tariffs for their exports.

Emerging markets have become attractive propositions for those wishing to make high returns on their investments. However, there are greater risks in investing in emerging markets, since many suffer from both economic and political upheaval.

Mobius, Mark, *Mobius on Emerging Markets*. London: Financial Times, Prentice-Hall, 1996.

Enabling clause

Under the terms of Part I of the **General Agreement on Tariffs and Trade (GATT)**, a developed country is allowed to give more favourable treatment to developing countries and more special treatment to the least developed countries with whom it trades. This is notwithstanding the provisions for **most favoured nation treatment** which are part of GATT.

Escape clause

An escape clause is a provision allowed by the **World Trade Organization**. It allows countries to suspend tariffs or other trade agreement concessions on certain goods which they import from another country. The escape clause is triggered when the imports have reached a quantity which will cause serious difficulties for domestic producers who compete with those imported goods.

Escrow

Escrow is a payment service which, although it is strongly associated with Internet transactions, can also be used for conventional purchases

E

and other transactions. The Escrow system seeks to reduce the risk associated with Internet or overseas transactions by operating as a licensed third party which receives payment from the buyer on behalf of the seller. Once the buyers' funds have been verified and secured, the sellers are contacted and told that they can deliver the products to the buyers in the safe knowledge that payment has been made. Notably, the funds received on behalf of the buyers are not released to the sellers until the buyers confirm to the Escrow service that they are satisfied with the merchandise.

Ethnocentric behaviour

See **Ethnocentrism**.

Ethnocentric staffing

Ethnocentric staffing is an approach which many international businesses prefer when filling key management positions in overseas operations. The approach revolves around appointing nationals from the parent country to key roles in the new business or operation abroad. As more businesses have set up international operations they have begun to realize that staffing along these lines does not always necessarily work since the staff, although competent, trusted and aware of the way in which the international business operates, are unaware of the differences in **culture** in the country in which they are now operating. This tendency is known as cultural myopia.

See also **expatriate failure** and **expatriate managers**.

Bechet, Thomas P., *Strategic Staffing: A Practical Toolkit for Workforce Planning*. New York: Amacom, 2002.

Ethnocentrism

Ethnocentrism is the belief that a particular set of norms and values enshrined in a particular **culture** is inherently superior. Ethnocentrism has considerable implications for international business in as much as a foreign business's involvement in an overseas market may well be coloured by ethnocentric behaviour which may not allow that business to understand, appreciate or value the culture in which it now operates. Continued ethnocentric behaviour will ultimately prove to be counter-productive and many businesses actively seek to dispel ethnocentric attitudes, either through training and orientation, or by employing from the very beginning individuals from the cultures or nations involved.

Mehmet, Ozay, *Westernizing the Third World: The Eurocentricity of Economic Development Theories*. London: Routledge, 1999.

Euro

The Euro is the primary currency of the **European Union** and was officially launched in January 1999, effectively replacing the **Ecu**. On 1 January 2002 it became legal tender, replacing the currencies of 12 European countries. The adoption of the Euro was seen as an essential step towards full economic and monetary union within Europe.

Euro-12

On 1 January 2002 the **Euro** replaced the national currencies of 12 of the 15 **European Union** countries. The adoption of the Euro was the largest and most significant currency change in Europe and indeed the world. The term 'Euro-12' is used to describe the 12 countries which on 1 January 2002 adopted the Euro and jettisoned their old currencies. The Euro-12 are Austria, Belgium, Finland, France, Germany, Greece, Ireland, Italy, Luxembourg, the Netherlands, Portugal and Spain.

Eurobonds

A Eurobond is an international bond which is denominated in a currency that is not native to the country in which it was issued. In other words, a Eurobond could refer to a Japanese bond issued in US dollars or a US bond issued in Japanese yen.

Walmsley, Julian, *Global Investing: Eurobonds and Alternatives*. Basingstoke: Palgrave Macmillan, 1991.

Eurocreep

'Eurocreep' is a term used to describe the spread of the use of the **Euro** into countries which have not officially adopted that currency. Eurocreep has become a marked trend, particularly in countries which either intend to adopt the currency at a later date, or have intentions to join the **European Community** at a specified point in the future. For countries already in the European Community, but which have chosen not to adopt the Euro officially, the Euro is technically legal currency and for practical purposes the acceptance of the Euro as legal tender is advantageous.

E

Eurocurrency

Eurocurrency is currency which is deposited, either by businesses or governments, in banks outside their own country. The **Euro** prefix only describes the geographical origins of the first markets in securities. Many Euromarkets are located in Asia and the term 'Eurocurrency' can be transposed as either a **Eurodollar** or Euro sterling. Eurocurrency is a convenient way in which borrowing for international trade and investment can be facilitated. The Eurodollar is the most common form of Eurocurrency.

The Eurocurrency market communicates electronically, and deals take place between banks, institutions, businesses and governments. In effect, the Eurocurrency market was the first offshore market.

Gibson, Heather D., *The Eurocurrency Markets, Domestic Financial Policy and International Instability.* Basingstoke: Palgrave Macmillan, 1989.

Eurodollar

Eurodollars are deposits of US dollars in financial institutions or banks outside the United States. To all intents and purposes a Eurodollar is identical to a US dollar. They are often referred to as offshore dollars.

The prefix **Euro** simply reflects the beginning of the trend of holding deposits offshore. The deposits are often placed abroad to avoid currency exchange costs and taxation and they have become an important aspect in the creation of credit for international trade.

Burghardt, Galen, *The Eurodollar Futures and Options Handbook.* New York: McGraw-Hill Education, 2003.

European Bank for Reconstruction and Development (EBRD)

E

The bank was established in 1991 in order to support the private sector in the newly democratic central and eastern European countries. The EBRD is involved in some 27 countries in central Europe and central Asia. It is owned by some 60 countries and two intergovernmental institutions.

The bank finances industries and businesses, mainly privately owned, but it also supports some publicly owned companies. It has been involved in restructuring former state-owned enterprises. Its primary function is not only financial support and business assistance, but it is also concerned with moving countries closer to becoming market economies.

The EBRD also promotes co-financing and the direct investment of foreign funds, along with the mobilization of domestic capital.

www.ebrd.com

European Central Bank (ECB)

The first appointments of board members of the ECB took effect on 1 June 1998. This coincided with the period in which 11 European Union member states agreed to adopt a single currency (the **Euro**). The ECB and the national **central banks** of all of the European Union member states form the **European System of Central Banks (ESCB)**.
Primarily, they are charged with managing the Euro system by:

- defining and implementing monetary policy within the Euro area;
- conducting foreign exchange operations;
- holding and managing the official foreign reserves of the member states;
- promoting the smooth operation of payment systems.

The ECB is managed by an executive board and a general council comprised of the President and Vice-President of the ECB and the governors of the national central banks of each of the member states. The ECB's capital amounts to some 5 billion Euros and it has reserve assets of 40 billion Euros.

www.ecb.int

European Commission

The European Commission was created in 1957 under the terms of the **Treaty of Rome**. It currently has a staff of some 17,000 and is, perhaps, one of the most controversial of the **European Union**'s institutions.
Based in Brussels, it draws up treaties, laws and policies which ultimately have precedence over European Union member states' domestic laws. Some 20 commissioners have specific remits, such as environment or transport. Commissioners are nominated by member states and each commissioner has his or her own cabinet to support the work. The commission presents legislative proposals to the Council of Ministers and if these are approved, then it is the commission's responsibility to administer the new legislation.
In essence, the commission has the following responsibilities:

- The right to initiate draft legislation.
- The presentation of legislative proposals to the European Parliament and Council.

E

- The responsibility for implementing the European legislation, budget and programmes.
- Guardianship of treaties and European Community law.
- Representation of the European Union internationally, where it negotiates agreements.

The European Commission is, in effect, the European Union's executive body.

www.europa.eu.int/comm/index_en.htm

European Committee for Standardization (Comité Européen de Normalisation) (CEN)

The CEN, along with the European Committee for Electro-technical Standardization (CENELEC) and the **European Telecommunication Standards Institute (ETSI)**, are the three European standardization bodies, who prepare European standards in specific areas.

Standards are prepared either at the request of the **European Commission** or when asked for by industry. The basic function is to create harmonized standards, or conformity, within the European Union.

The CEN has clear procedures which aim to guarantee:

- openness and transparency;
- consensus;
- national commitment from European member states;
- technical coherence at European level;
- integration with other international work.

www.cenorm.be

European Community (EC)

The six original members of the European Community were Belgium, France, Italy, Luxembourg, the Netherlands and West Germany. The European Community was formally established under the terms of the **Treaty of Rome** in 1957. The term 'European Community' actually refers to three separate regional organizations which operated under separate treaties: the European Coal and Steel Community (1951), the European Economic Community (1957) and the European Atomic Energy Community (1957). The European Economic Community was renamed the European Community in 1992.

Since 1967, however, the European Community has had four common institutions, namely the **European Commission**, the European Council, the European Parliament and the European Court of Justice.

www.europa.eu.int

European Development Fund (EDF)

The European Development Fund finances development cooperation under the terms of the **Lomé Convention**. The first fund was set up in 1960 to provide aid to Africa, the Caribbean and the Pacific. New partnerships have been developed, including PHARE (central and eastern Europe) and TACIS (former Soviet Union states). Around 6 billion **Euros** are committed to development funds each year. Currently the fund is active in around 100 states across the world. Around 71 Asian/Caribbean/Pacific (ACP) states receive in excess of 2 billion euros each year.

www.europa.eu.int/comm/development/index_en.htm

European Economic Area (EEA)

The European economic area came into existence in 1994 and originally covered 17 countries, which were the 12 member nations of the **European Union**, plus Austria, Iceland, Finland, Norway and Sweden. The purpose of the EEA is to facilitate research and development, the promotion of tourism and the implementation of environmental, social and consumer policy. The six countries which remained part of the **European Free Trade Association (EFTA)** in December 1992 (Austria, Finland, Iceland, Lichtenstein, Norway and Sweden) signed a protocol in the following March to proceed into the EEA. Switzerland remained outside the EEA, but there are now provisions for the country to participate at a later stage. Lichtenstein also remains outside the EEA.

Border controls between the members of EEA and former members of EFTA have been relaxed. However, the EEA is not a **customs union** but a **free trade area**.

www.europa.eu.int/comm/external_relations/eea

E

European Free Trade Association (EFTA)

Iceland, Lichtenstein, Norway and Switzerland are the four EFTA countries. They have a European agreement with the Baltic States, Estonia, Latvia, Lithuania, Bulgaria, the Czech Republic, Hungary, Poland, Romania, Slovakia and Slovenia.

EFTA is an international organization which promotes **free trade** and economic integration. It manages the **free trade area**, participates in the **European economic area (EEA)** and has centres in Geneva, Brussels and Luxembourg. EFTA originally had seven members (Austria, Denmark, Norway, Portugal, Sweden, Switzerland and the United Kingdom) and was established in 1947 in order to implement the Marshall Plan. By 1995, EFTA was much reduced in size, with many of its former members opting for full or partial EU membership.

www.ecb.int

European Investment Bank (EIB)

The European Investment Bank was established in 1957 as an independent institution under the terms of the **Treaty of Rome**. It is designed to assist in the steady development of the **European Community**. The EIB provides loans and guarantees to both public institutions and businesses in order to facilitate regional and structural development, as well as achieving cross-border objectives.

www.eib.org

European Monetary and Cooperation Fund (EMCF)

The EMCF was created in 1973 and later revised in 1979 to link it more closely with the **European Monetary System**. It was originally intended to support the **Ecu** and act as a reserve system for the **central banks**. The fund is used to keep account of short-term borrowings and to support the currencies of member states through intervention in foreign-exchange markets.

European Monetary Institute (EMI)

E

The EMI was established in 1994 under the provisions of the **Maastricht Treaty**. It manages national currency reserves for the **European Community**'s **central banks** and was originally concerned with fostering worldwide acceptance for the **Ecu** (now the **Euro**). Its other primary functions were to strengthen the coordination between the monetary policies of the member states, as well as studying the policies, procedures and infrastructure required for more centralized monetary policies.

www.ecb.int

European Monetary System (EMS)

The European Monetary System was adopted by the **European Community** in 1979. Its function was to stabilize the exchange rates between member countries' currencies. The European Monetary System has four major components: the **Euro**, the **Exchange Rate Mechanism**, credit facilities and transfer arrangements. In the run up to the adoption of the Euro the major tool of the European Monetary System was the Exchange Rate Mechanism, which pegged the currencies of each of the member states to the Euro and only allowed them to fluctuate slightly (2.25% on either side of the Euro value).

Masson, Paul R., Krueger, Thomas H. and Turtelboom, Bart G., *EMU and the International Monetary System*. Washington, DC: International Monetary Fund, 1997.

European Norm (EN)

European Norm is a common European product certification mark which is primarily used to harmonize European safety standards. In electrical products, for example, ENEC is often printed on the product, standing for European Norms Electrical Certification. The key benefits of the EN symbol are that it is formally recognized in upwards of 20 European countries. It demonstrates that the products have been independently tested to any relevant European safety standard. Since it is also a requirement for the manufacturer's quality systems to comply with **ISO 9002**, buyers can be reassured that a factory inspection has been carried out at least twice a year and that product surveillance checks have taken place. The ENEC mark was launched in 1992 and this mark alone covers more than 30,000 different products.

European Organization for Testing and Certification (EOTC)

The European Organization for Testing and Certification was established in 1990 by the **European Commission**, the **European Free Trade Association (EFTA)** and other European standards bodies. The EOTC operates conformity assessment issues in Europe, but does not in itself test or certify products or services.

www.eotc.be

European Patent Office (EPO)

The European Patent Office, or EPO, was established in 1973 and is based in Munich. The organization aims to provide a cheaper, easier and more reliable patent protection by granting patents across Europe; in other words, providing a single, unified, European patent law.

www.european-patent-office.org

European Research Coordination Agency (Eureka)

The Eureka agency was created in 1985 and is based in Brussels. The organization aims to coordinate advanced technology projects which are being undertaken by European businesses. Eureka also encourages European collaboration in order to achieve international competitiveness.

www.eureka.be

European System of Central Banks (ESCB)

The primary objective of the European System of Central Banks (ESCB) is to maintain price stability by supporting the economic policies of the community, whilst upholding the concept of an open market, with free competition and an efficient use of resources. The ESCB attempts to control prices by maintaining inflation rates to as close to 2 per cent per year as possible. It achieves this by:

- undertaking economic analysis which looks at current economic developments and how they may affect price stability;
- undertaking monetary analysis of long-term inflation trends and the relationship between the availability of money, and prices over the longer term.

The ESCB offers standing facilities and requires credit institutions to hold minimum reserves with national **central banks**.

www.ecb.int

European Telecommunications Standards Institute (ETSI)

The ETSI was established in 1988, largely as a result of the inability of the European Conference of Postal and Telecommunication Administrations (CEPT) to deal with the workload associated with common European standards and specifications. ETSI continues to pursue standards development across the telecommunications industry. It is based in Sophia Antipolis, France.

www.etsi.org

European Trade Union Confederation (ETUC)

The ETUC was founded in 1973 and is a pan-European organization which represents European trade unions. It is based in Brussels and has a membership of 78 national trade union confederations from 34 European countries, in addition to 11 European industry federations. Altogether, it has 60 million members. The ETUC is recognized by the **European Union**, the council of Europe and **EFTA** as the single representative of cross-sectoral trade union organizations at a European level.

www.etuc.org

European Union (EU)

The term 'European Union' was introduced in 1993 when the **Maastricht Treaty** came into force. In effect, the term European Union is an umbrella explanation of the **European Community** and Europe's integration efforts. The European Community has transformed itself from what was essentially a trade area in 1957, under the terms of the **Treaty of Rome**, to a political and economic union which can be more accurately described as a European union.

www.europa.eu.int

Evidence account

An evidence account is an agreement between an overseas supplier and a government agency in a developing country. Evidence accounts are used to stimulate reciprocal trade. The agreement notes the trade conditions between the exporting foreign business and the jurisdiction of the developing countries, and the effect these will have upon that trade. Evidence accounts usually require cumulative payment turnovers for particular goods and not necessarily payments for each individual transaction. The payments need to be balanced in agreed proportions over a specified period of time, which may be up to three years. The trade flows are then monitored and financial settlements are made through banks which have been designated by both parties.

Ex

'Ex', in international trade terms, means literally 'from' and is used in trade or price terms as a prefix, such as in **ex-factory** or **ex-dock**. The 'ex' is used to signify that the price that has been quoted applies at the point of origin of the product. This forms the basis of a quotation, indicating that the seller agrees to make the goods available to the buyer at a specific place.

Exchange rate

An exchange rate is the price of a particular currency as expressed in terms of another currency. In other words, the number of units of one particular currency that will be needed to exchange it for a unit of another currency. Exchange rates are affected by investor expectations, interest rates, confidence in the currency, the state of a country's **balance of payments** and many other factors.

Sarno, Lucio and Taylor, Mark P., *The Economics of Exchange Rates*. Cambridge: Cambridge University Press, 2003.

Exchange Rate Mechanism (ERM)

The Exchange Rate Mechanism was brought into effect in 1979 and aimed to bring together the currencies of the member states of the **European Community**. The ERM achieved this by maintaining parity between the exchange rates of the member states' currencies, setting limits to how far the exchange rates could vary between any two currencies. If the exchange rates reached the maximum limit, then the **central banks** of the two countries involved were expected to intervene in the market to bring back parity, which had been previously agreed. Originally the ERM was applied to Belgium, France, West Germany, Luxembourg, the Netherlands and Denmark. Italy joined in 1990, Spain in 1989, the UK in 1990 and Portugal in 1992. However, disruptions in 1992 caused the UK to withdraw.

Minikin, Robert, *The ERM Explained: A Straightforward Guide to the Exchange Rate Mechanism and the European Currency Debate*. London: Kogan Page, 1993.

Exclusive economic zone

Under the terms of the 6th session of the 3rd United Nations Conference on the Law of the Sea (UNCLOS), nations agreed to control and take responsibility for both the living and non-living resources of the sea for 200 miles off their coastline. They also agreed to allow free navigation to other countries beyond a 12-mile limit. Clearly these exclusive economic zones require a comprehensive management system and the ability of the nation to monitor activity over this potentially vast area. In order to facilitate this, governments have taken steps to place patrol and enforcement assets to protect fisheries, seabed mining and oil exploration. The nations are also responsible for the prevention of smuggling, piracy, illegal immigration and money laundering activities.

Ex-dock

'Ex-dock' is a price or trade term literally meaning 'from dock'. Effectively the seller continues to own the goods until they are unloaded on a dock or at a port of discharge. Under the terms of ex-dock the selling price includes all the costs involved, including the cost of unloading the goods from the vessel.

Ex-factory

'Ex-factory' is a price or trade term which means that the seller continues to own the goods until they are picked up from the factory in which they were made. In this instance the selling price is literally the cost of the goods, with no other charges attached.

EXIMBANK

See **Export–Import Bank of the US.**

Expatriate cycle

Business organizations involved in either acquiring, running or cooperation with foreign businesses need to ensure that they have an effective system to manage their expatriates. Increasingly, businesses are taking a strategic approach to the use of **expatriate managers**, which is shown in Figure 1.

E

Figure 1   The expatriate cycle

By following this cycle, organizations can more clearly link foreign assignments to operational requirements and make an assessment of whether the use of expatriates is the most cost-effective way of running overseas operations.

Expatriate failure

The deployment of **expatriate managers** continues to be a trend despite the fact that many of the managers fail to cope with the additional pressures and potential clashes of **culture** in overseas environments. As can be seen in the **expatriate cycle**, careful selection procedures need to be put in place in order to choose the most appropriate candidates. Traditionally, successful expatriates have high self-esteem and self-confidence, added to which they are willing to communicate in foreign languages and understand other cultures. In this respect training is an important aspect in reducing expatriate failure and should include practical, language and cultural training. Many businesses have also realized that training needs to be extended beyond the expatriate managers themselves, to include their partners and, perhaps, offspring.

Expatriate managers

Businesses involved in international trade, and specifically those who set up operations abroad, tend to use expatriate managers for the following reasons:

- to control and coordinate operations;
- to transfer skills and knowledge;
- for general managerial development.

Employing managers from the originating country has been estimated to cost between three and four times as much as employing a local individual. Traditionally, expatriate managers who had taken overseas assignments could expect promotion on their return, but increasingly the larger financial packages are disappearing as organizations move towards equalizing the terms and conditions of locally employed staff and of expatriates. In the past, expatriates could expect to be either on domestic salaries or better, often in countries where the cost of living was considerably lower.

Experience curve

The term 'experience curve' has had a direct application for many businesses over a number of years, in as much as it describes improved performance of both the organization and individuals within that organization, over a period of time, as they repeat and become competent in tasks. Experience-curve analysis is the study of this phenomenon and indeed it has an additional dimension in terms of international trade, with the experience curve being steeper in the sense that there is more to learn and understand, and then practically demonstrate, when businesses deal with overseas markets.

It has been proved that there is a direct and consistent relationship between the growth in product volume and the reduction in unit product cost. Each time production doubles, costs decline by between 20 and 30 per cent. The experience curve itself relates the cost per unit output to the cumulative volume of output since a production process was first begun. Costs per unit of production decline as the cumulative volume of output increases. The production process, repeated time after time, allows the business and employees to learn from experience and adjust the production process in accordance with their acquired knowledge, thus reducing costs. Numerous studies suggest that these costs tend to decline at a relatively stable percentage each time the cumulative volume produced is doubled.

Clearly, the experience curve, or learning curve, of the organization and of its employees have different dimensions, particularly in the case of setting up production facilities abroad. None the less, the fundamental phenomenon of the experience curve and its cost-saving implications are still ultimately enjoyed.

Experience curve pricing

Experience curve pricing occurs as a business attempts to expand its overall **market share** by setting a low price which higher-cost competitors cannot possibly match. Taking the concept of the **experience curve**, established organizations that have gradually increased their overall output enjoy cost savings and are thus able to pass on a proportion of these saved costs to the final market price. Having achieved this position, the organization can then take advantage of the difficulties which competitors will have in matching its prices, inevitably leading to a larger market share, particularly in price-sensitive markets. Each time the market share increases, the organization can increase its output, thereby enjoying even greater cost savings as it proceeds along the experience curve.

E

Export Administration Review Board (EARB)

The Export Administration Review Board (EARB) is a US cabinet-level export licensing dispute resolution group. It was established in 1970 and is chaired by the Department of Commerce, with representatives from the Departments of State, Defense, Energy, and Arms Control and Disarmament. The board is the final review body which resolves differences between different agencies' views on the granting of export licences from the US. Cases which the EARB cannot resolve are passed to the President of the United States for resolution.

www.bxa.doc.gov

Export broker

An export broker is an individual or a business which takes a fee for bringing together buyers and sellers in the international market. In effect an export broker operates rather like an introduction agency and attempts to smooth and facilitate the interaction between the buyer and the seller, but does not actually take part in the sales transactions.

Export credit agency

An export credit agency is invariably a government body which provides subsidies to encourage exports. Loans may be appropriate to foreign buyers who wish to purchase domestic products. Alternatively, guarantees may be made on loans made by banks to domestic businesses in order for them to produce exports which will ultimately pay off the loan. The export credit agency, in effect, insures the producers against non-payment of the loan. For the most part, export credit is offered for political reasons rather than economic reasons, primarily to encourage the country's earnings, to help with the **balance of payments** and, more generally, for employment generation.

See also **Export Credit Guarantee Department (ECDG)**.

Gianturco, Delio E., *Export Credit Agencies: The Unsung Giants of International Trade and Finance*. Westport, CT: Greenwood Press, 2001.

Export Credit Guarantee Department (ECDG)

The British Export Credit Guarantee Department was established in 1919 and is now a part of the Department of Trade and Industry (DTI). It remains the primary source of British export credit. The ECGD aims to assist exporters by providing them with insurance against the risk of not being paid for their exports. It also guarantees to banks that have provided finance to British businesses, primarily exporters of capital goods, a facility at a low rate of interest. In effect, the ECDG provides short-term underwriting facilities.

www.ecdg.gov.uk

Export Enhancement Act 1992

The Export Enhancement Act of 1992 is US legislation which formally requires the **Trade Promotion Coordinating Committee (TPCC)** to issue an annual report detailing the strategic plan for overall trade promotion efforts and describe how these efforts have been implemented. The TPCC is required to establish a strategic plan, explain the rationale behind any of the identified priorities, and attempt to improve their coordination. The TPCC, under the terms of the Act, makes annual proposals to the President in the form of an annual unified budget for trade promotion. Overall, the Act seeks to identify priorities, improve coordination and eliminate duplication of effort.

Export–Import Bank of the US (EXIMBANK)

This independent agency came into existence in 1934 and is charged with the financing of exports from the US in the form of support programmes, guarantees, loans and insurance. The bank underwrites a proportion of the risk associated with the financing of production, and the sale, of US goods and helps finance overseas customers who wish to purchase US goods, particularly in cases where those customers cannot obtain finance from other lending organizations. Above all, the EXIM-BANK seeks to match other foreign governments' subsidies by helping US businesses obtain credit at lower rates from lenders and providing financial incentives to foreign buyers.

www.exim.gov

E

Export licence

An export licence is a document which may be required in some countries in order to authorize some, or all, exports. In many countries export licences are only required for specific products or under special circumstances. In the US an export licence is also used as an individual validated licence, which authorizes the export of particular goods in specific quantities to a named destination.

Export management company (EMC)

An export management company is a business which operates to all intents and purposes as the export department for several different manufacturers. The EMC seeks export opportunities and manages the transaction process on behalf of the businesses with whom it deals. The usual arrangement is based on a commission, a salary, or a standing charge plus commission. In some cases an EMC may actually purchase products from the manufacturers with whom it deals and then sell on the products at a profit. The exact relationship between each EMC and the manufacturers, and indeed the end purchasers of the products, depends upon the nature of the market in which they are operating and the types of overseas markets in which they are involved.

Albaum, Gerald, Duerr, Edwin and Strandskov, Jesper, *International Marketing and Export Management*. London: Financial Times, Prentice-Hall, 2001.

Export quota

An export quota may be either the target objectives or specific restrictions on the volume or value of exports, as set by the government. Normally restrictions may be set in order to protect the domestic market from shortages of materials, or they can be used in order to ensure that the prices of specific commodities are not driven down by over-exporting.

Export revolving line of credit

An export revolving line of credit (ERLC) is essentially financial assistance to businesses in the form of guaranteed loans which assist them in bridging the gap in their working capital while production and stock-holding are under way, until the point when they receive payment from an overseas buyer for what they have produced. In the US, for example, ERLC is available via the Small Business Administration (SBA). It will provide up to 85 per cent of the ERLC up to a limit of $750,000. In essence, the ERLC covers the exporter for defaults of their own making but not for defaults by the foreign buyer. The exporters would be expected to have their own export credit insurance or letters of credit. In the US, ERLC can be used to finance labour and materials required for manufacturing, or to purchase stock in order to provide the necessary stock for an export order. It can also be used to help develop overseas markets. ERLC cannot be used to purchase fixed assets, but it can be used for advice, business travel, or attendance at trade shows.

Gianturco, Delio E., *Export Credit Agencies: The Unsung Giants of International Trade and Finance*. Westport, CT: Greenwood Press, 2001.

Export subsidy

Under the terms of the **General Agreement on Tariffs and Trade (GATT)**, it is noted that export subsidies distort trade and have an impact on normal competition. They also hinder fair-trade objectives. An export subsidy is a payment to exporters from their home government, perhaps in the form of a low-interest loan or other economic inducement, to help them sell products into a foreign market. GATT does not define precisely what export subsidies are, or whether these practices will ultimately be deemed undesirable.

Bourgeois, J. H. J. (ed.), *Subsidies and International Trade*. New York: Kluwer Law International, 1991.

Extended Fund Facility (EFF)

The Extended Fund Facility (EFF) is an arrangement by the **International Monetary Fund** to provide assistance to countries in order for them to meet their **balance of payments** requirements. EFF payments are made in larger cash amounts than are available under normal **credit tranche** policy.

www.imf.org

Externalities

Externalities are either costs or benefits which arise out of an economic activity which affects individuals other than those actually engaged in the economic activity itself, but they are not reflected in prices. Pollution, for example, is considered an externality which would have an immediate and long-term impact upon a local population despite the fact that the polluting business is providing much-needed jobs and contributing to the country's **balance of payments**.

Externally convertible currency

'Externally convertible currency' applies to situations where non-residents can convert their holdings of domestic currencies into a foreign currency. Usually the ability of residents of the country to make a similar conversion is limited.

E

Ex-quay

'Ex-quay' is used to describe price or trade terms which specify that the seller makes the goods available to the purchaser at the quay or wharf at the destination which has been named in the sales contract. The seller bears the costs and risks up to that point. There are two forms of ex-quay contract. The first is 'duty paid' and the second is 'duties on buyer's account', the latter meaning that the liability to clear the goods for import is met by the buyer.

Ex-ship

'Ex-ship' can be differentiated from **ex-quay** in as much as the seller pays to transport the goods on board a ship to the destination named in the sales contract, and not for its unloading or forward transportation.

Ex-works

'Ex-works' is another term used to describe **ex-factory**, ex-warehouse or ex-mill. The price quoted on the sales contract applies at the point of origin of the goods and the seller agrees to make the goods available to the buyer at that specified place on a particular date. All transportation and other associated costs from that point are borne by the buyer.

E

Factor endowments

Factor endowments are the primary factors of production of a given country. In essence this means the different ratios of capital to labour and the fact that goods differ in their input requirements, notably in terms of ratios between rents and wages and the fact that some goods require more capital per man hour than others. Primarily the endowment factors include labour, capital, land and, in some cases, natural resources. The concept of factor endowments is very much based on the **Heckscher–Ohlin Theory**. A similar model, known as the Stolper–Samuelson Theorem, states that as the price of goods goes up, the return on factors used intensively in their production goes up by a larger percentage, while the return on other factors of production falls.

Lal, Deepak, *Unintended Consequences: The Impact of Factor Endowments, Culture and Politics on Long-Run Economic Performance.* Cambridge, MA: MIT Press, 2001.

Factoring

Factoring occurs when an exporter transfers the title of its foreign accounts receivable to an independent factoring house. Factoring houses specialize in financial accounts receivable, purchasing them at a discount off the face value of the account. Factoring in international trade is less common than the factoring of domestic receivable accounts.

Salinger, Freddy, *Factoring: The Law and Practice of Invoice Finance.* London: Sweet and Maxwell, 1999.

Factors of production

In international trade, factors of production are significant as they describe the inherent nature of the economic activity of a given country. Typically, factors of production include the available assets in terms of land, labour, capital and enterprise. Each country has its own distinct blend of factors of production, often described as **factor endowments**.

FASB

FASB, or the Financial Accounting Standards Board, in cooperation with the International Accounting Standards Board (IASB), attempts to set standards in international trade activities which are broadly comparable in terms of quality standards with those used in the US and other more developed countries. The FASB attempts to ensure that the quality of information is comparable across national boundaries, and continues to progress the concept of international standards.

www.fasb.org

Fast track

The concept of fast tracking was first introduced into the United States in 1974; it was improved in 1979 and was an integral element of the Trade Act (1988). Fast tracking attempts to streamline the negotiation of US trade agreements by ensuring that votes on legislation related to the trade agreements are undertaken within a fixed period and that few amendments are made to that legislation.

Federal Reserve System (FRS)

The Federal Reserve System is better known as the FED and was established in 1913 as the United States' **central bank**. The system has 12 Federal Reserve districts, each with its own regional Federal Reserve Bank. Seven governors, based in Washington, form the Federal Reserve Board, which oversees the operations of the FRS. The Federal Open Market Committee determines the monetary policy of the system.

www.federalreserve.gov

F

Final determination

The term 'final determination' refers to the US **International Trade Administration**. The ITA investigates sales which are at less than fair value and must make a final determination within 75 days of the date of a preliminary determination. Assuming the primary determination has proved that the sales were made at less than a fair price, the exporter may request a postponement. Conversely, if it was not found true, then the petitioner can request a postponement. In both cases, however, postponement cannot be for more than 135 days. Essentially these final determinations are made in accordance with **anti-dumping** investigations and the ITA ultimately renders a decision, with its final determination, as to whether anti-dumping took place.

www.ita.doc.gov

Financial structure and management

The financial structure and management of foreign projects require a considerably different approach from that to investments at home. Normally a business would use capital budgeting techniques, but must make a distinction between the cash flows to the project and cash flows to the parent company. In many cases the host government may choose to adopt a policy which effectively blocks the repatriation of cash from foreign investment. In order to use capital budgeting techniques, a business will need to assess risks which may arise from its location in an overseas country. These risks may include both political and economic situations. Also, capital may be cheaper on the global market than in the domestic market and a business may choose to secure finance from the global capital market. Again this borrowing may be restricted by regulations imposed by the host government. The business may choose to consider local debt financing in countries where the local currency is unstable, particularly if it may depreciate.

Whatever the objectives of the business, it will attempt to utilize resources in the most efficient manner and may use a variety of different means to transfer funds from one country to another. Dividend remittances are one of the most common methods. The manipulation of transfer prices can also be used, particularly to minimize tax liabilities and to protect against foreign exchange risks. The business may also be able to work around government restrictions, as well as reducing tariff payments. Other businesses choose to use fronting loans, channelling cash from the parent company, via a third party, to a foreign subsidiary. Above all, the financial structure and management of foreign subsidiaries aims to reduce a business's **economic exposure** and has become a considerable business in itself in moving a business's assets and distributing them.

F

Grou, Pierre, *The Financial Structure of Multinational Capitalism*. New York: St Martin's Press, 1986.

First-mover advantage

The concept of a first mover, or first-mover advantage, suggests that considerable benefits accrue to a business that is the first to enter a market. This is not just on account of the fact that the first-mover business can begin to erect **barriers to entry**. It may also be that potential competitors recognize that the business already has that first-mover advantage, and are reluctant to throw funds and effort into trying to wrestle control of the market from them. None the less, in the majority of cases, competition will follow, often learning from the mistakes made by the first mover, enabling the newcomers to avoid these and learn how best to deal with this new market.

Fisher effect

The Fisher effect was proposed in the 1930s by Irving Fisher. He suggested that changes in the expected rate of inflation would lead to an equal change in the nominal interest rate, which would, in effect, keep the real interest rate unchanged.

Fisher, Irving, *The Theory of Interest*. New York: Macmillan, 1930.

Fixed exchange rate

A fixed exchange rate is usually synonymous with a **pegged exchange rate**. The use of the word 'fixed' is somewhat misleading, since it implies that there is a lower chance of change. In reality, however, countries fail ever to have a truly fixed rate of exchange.

Fixed rate bond

A fixed rate bond is a form of saving which provides a guaranteed interest rate over a specified period of time.

Floating exchange rate

A floating exchange rate occurs where a country allows its currency to fluctuate freely with the rate being determined purely by market forces. The country does not seek to intervene in the exchange market, either by government action or through the intervention of its **central bank**.

Larraain, Felipe and Velasco, Andres, *Exchange-rate Policy in the Emerging-Market Economies: The Case for Floating*. Princeton, NJ: Princeton University Press, 2001.

Flow of foreign direct investment

The flow of **foreign direct investment (FDI)** into developing countries has risen considerably over the last decade. In 1989 this figure stood at

$59.6 billion, but by 2000 it had reached $241 billion. During the same time the stock of foreign direct investment into these developing countries had risen from $257 billion in 1990 to $2,032 billion in 2000. The net flow of the foreign direct investment component into these developing countries stood at $24.3 billion in 1990 and $178 billion in 2000 – in other words, 60% of the total long-term resource flows, or 78% of the private long-term resources, to all developing countries.

The flow of FDI is concentrated into Asia, Latin America and the Caribbean, which on average between 1989 and 1994 accounted for 92.5%, rising to 95.2% by 2000. Areas such as Africa and the **lesser developed countries** in the Pacific area saw a proportional drop over the same period from 7.5% to 4.8% of FDI inflows. The top ten recipients of FDI inflow during the period from 1992 to 1998 were China, Brazil, Mexico, Argentina, Poland, Chile, Malaysia, Venezuela, the Russian Federation and Thailand, collectively receiving 70% of all FDI inflows. The main reasons for this are fundamentally the market size and increasingly strong economic stability.

Akinkugbe, Oluyele, *Flow of Foreign Direct Investment to Hitherto Neglected Developing Countries*. Discussion Paper 2003/02, United Nations University. World Institute for Development Economics Research, Helsinki, 2003.

FOB (free on board)

'FOB' is a pricing term which means that the quoted price for particular goods includes the delivery costs of those goods to a vessel provided by or for the purchaser. The term 'FOB' has to be qualified by a named location, such as the shipping port or destination. The seller is liable for all risks to the goods up to the point where the title passes to the buyer; from then on the buyer is liable for charges and risks.

See also **free onboard (FOB)**.

Foreign access zone (FAZ)

FAZ describes the Japanese form of a **free trade zone**, which was created in an effort to improve Japan's trade balance and stimulate the economic growth of the immediate region. FAZs tend to be established near airports and seaports which have facilities for distribution, warehousing and wholesaling, and other facilities. FAZ emphasizes imports rather than job creation. It is part of the Japanese Law on Extraordinary Measures for the Promotion of Imports and the Facilitation of Foreign Direct Investment in Japan (1992).

F

Foreign availability

The US Bureau of Export Administration conducts periodic reviews in order to determine the foreign availability of selected commodities or technologies which are subject to export control. The reviews have four criteria in order to determine foreign availability:

- comparable quality;
- actual availability;
- source;
- available quantities.

The foreign availability issue is very much tied to US export control, normally of commodities or technologies which would require an **export licence.** If specific commodities or technologies are deemed to be available under the criteria of the review, it may be deemed prudent to reconsider the US stance on the exporting of such items.

Foreign Corrupt Practices Act

The US Foreign Corrupt Practices Act (1997), as subsequently amended in 1998, expressly forbids US individuals, businesses or foreign subsidiaries of US businesses from offering foreign government officials incentives in order to obtain business, or to retain existing business.

www.usdoj.gov/criminal/fraud/fcpa.html

Foreign debt crisis

'Foreign debt crisis' refers to situations where countries that have borrowed considerable sums from abroad find it increasingly difficult, if not impossible, to pay even the interest on their debt, let alone addressing the original loan. A prime example of this is Latin America, where in 1985 the combined debt was $300 billion. It now stands at over $750 billion. This is despite the fact that between 1992 and 1999 the region paid some $913 billion in debt servicing charges. In this example the overseas debt consumes some 56% of the region's income from exports.

The foreign debt crisis has marked impacts upon the poverty levels in affected countries. Again in Latin America, some 44% of the population is considered to be poor, a figure which accounts for some 224 million individuals, of whom 90 million are destitute. The foreign debt crisis also affects infant mortality rates, which, again in Latin America, are 35 for every 1,000 live births.

There have been attempts to assist in the reduction, or the writing off, of these foreign debts, yet there has been little headway and the net outflow of cash from these poorer countries to richer countries continues at an even greater pace. Mexico, for example, has a current foreign debt of over $163 billion, twice what it owed less than 20 years before. The net impact upon Mexico has seen an increase, over the same period of time, of the price of basic goods at a rate of 560%, whilst real income has only increased by 135%.

Ray, Edward John, *US Protectionism and the World Debt Crisis*. Westport, CT: Greenwood Press, 1989.

Foreign direct investment (FDI)

Foreign direct investment means investing directly in production in an overseas market, usually by purchasing an existing business, establishing a new one or buying a part-share in an existing business. In the period between 1990 and 1997 the value of international trade grew by around 60 per cent. At the same time FDI doubled. The key recipients were countries which were members of the **Organization for Economic Cooperation and Development (OECD)**, although Asia was a considerable recipient.

FDI can be considered to some extent as a substitute for trade, but in fact FDI and trade are complementary in as much as international businesses recognize that even if a product originated in a foreign country, its production or processing in a host country is of more benefit to this country. The United States is one of the largest investors in FDI. The majority of their activities take the form of mergers, as opposed to setting up new subsidiaries.

There are various versions of FDI, principal among which are the following:

- *Horizontal FDI* – which is when a business invests in a similar form of industry to what it is involved in at home.
- *Vertical FDI* – which is when the investment in an overseas industry either provides inputs into or sells outputs to the business's domestic operations.

There are several factors which have characterized FDI over the past two decades or more:

- a rapid increase in the total volume of FDI;
- a decline in the importance of the US as a source of FDI;
- an increase in FDI into developing nations in eastern Europe and Asia;
- the US becoming a recipient of FDI;

F

- an increase in FDI in developing nations in order to reduce transport costs and the cost of tariffs.

Akinkugbe, Oluyele, *Flow of Foreign Direct Investment to Hitherto Neglected Developing Countries*. Discussion Paper 2003/02, United Nations University. World Institute for Development Economics Research, Helsinki, 2003.

Foreign exchange exposure

Foreign exchange exposure is a measure of the sensitivity of a business's cash flow to changes in **exchange rates**. It is notoriously difficult to estimate the exposure of a business since the exposure is related to net foreign currency revenues and profit margins and many businesses shield themselves, by hedging, from the larger-scale effects of exchange rate changes. Changes in the exchange rate can affect a business for a number of different reasons:

- It may produce products for both export and domestic sales.
- It may use both imported and domestic components.
- It may produce the same products or different products at similar plants abroad.

All of these issues may well expose the business to potential foreign exchange considerations and difficulties.

Bodnar, Gordon M. and Gentry, William M., 'Exchange Rate Exposure and Industry Characteristics: Evidence from Canada, Japan, and the USA', *Journal of International Money and Finance*, February 1993, pp. 29–45.

Jorion, Phillippe. 'The Exchange-Rate Exposure of US Multinationals', *Journal of Business*, July 1990, pp. 331–45.

Foreign exchange market

The primary function of the foreign exchange market is the conversion of currency. Many international businesses are active in the foreign exchange market in order both to facilitate their international trade and to make investments. They may well invest any available cash in short-term money market accounts, or indeed engage in **currency speculation**. Foreign exchange markets also provide insurance against **foreign exchange risks**. Foreign exchange risks can be reduced by using **forward exchange rates**, or by engaging in currency **swaps** (the simultaneous purchase and sale of an amount of foreign exchange for two different value rates).

Shamah, S. B., *A Foreign Exchange Primer*. New York: John Wiley, 2003.

Foreign exchange option

A foreign exchange option is an arrangement by which a buyer and a seller of foreign currencies agree a specific rate of exchange at some future date. The purchaser of the foreign currency may either choose to exercise the right to purchase the currency at that date, or pass up the option. The seller receives a fee for tendering the option. Purchasers may choose to exercise the option at any time. In Europe the currency exchange is actually made on the original date but in the US the exchange can be made within two days of the purchaser exercising the option.

Walker, Joseph, *How the Option Market Works*. New York: NYIF, 1991.

Foreign exchange risk

See foreign exchange exposure.

Foreign Portfolio Investment (FPI)

Foreign portfolio investment (FPI) is an investment instrument that can be easily traded and in some cases may be less permanent and tend not to represent the controlling stake in a particular business. FPIs include equity instruments (stocks and shares) or debt (bonds) of foreign businesses which do not represent a long-term interest. FPI can be differentiated from **foreign direct investment** as the funding comes from more diverse sources, such as pension or mutual funds. FPI investments usually look for interest payments or dividends from non-voting shares. FPI investments tend to be short-term compared with foreign direct investments, and account for around a third of investment. Collectively, FPI and FDI account for around 90 per cent of capital flows into developing countries and are growing at a time when lending from commercial banks, or the **World Bank** or the **International Monetary Fund**, are diminishing. FPI and FDI are the most important phenomena of **globalization**.

Hopkins, Peter and Hayes Miller, C., *Country, Sector, and Company Factors in Global Equity Portfolios*. London: Blackwell, 2002.

F

Foreign trade zone

Foreign trade zones (FTZs) are the US equivalent of **free trade zones**. These are restricted-access sites near ports of entry, and aim to encourage operations and activities on US soil, which might otherwise have been carried out abroad. Goods are brought into the zone and are exempt from both state and local taxes. The zones are licensed by the US Commerce Department's Foreign Trade Zones Board and are supervised by the Customs Service. Normal quota restrictions do not apply; however, the Foreign Trade Zones Board can limit or deny zones in specific cases.

Once exported goods have moved into the foreign trade zone they are considered to have been exported and are eligible for tax rebates.

Forfaiting

Effectively, forfaiting is a form of supplier credit. It requires the exporter to surrender possession of the receivable cash from exports by selling them at a discount to a forfaiter. The transaction is guaranteed by a bank in the importer's country. In some cases there may also be a guarantee by the importer's government and the exporter would approach the forfaiter while formulating the structure of the transaction. Once the forfaiter has committed to the deal, a discount rate is set. Forfaiters usually use **bills of exchange** or promissory notes (both of which are unconditional and easily transferable).

There is a difference between forfaiting and export **factoring**; forfaiters usually work on a medium- to long-term basis in terms of receivable cash (180 days to 7 years). Factors tend to work in the short term (up to 180 days). The other major difference is that forfaiters tend to work on a one-off basis, whilst factors prefer to have a longer-term relationship with the exporting business. Equally, forfaiters tend to work on larger projects or deals, mainly with capital goods or commodities, whilst factors tend to operate within the area of consumer goods. Ultimately, forfaiters are rather more flexible and are willing to work in the developing areas of the world, whilst factors need reliable, legal, and financial and credit frameworks and information.

Ripley, Andy, *Forfait Finance for Exporters*. London: International Thomson Business Press, 1996.

F

Forward exchange rate

A forward exchange rate is a price which is set between a buyer and a seller for the delivery of a foreign currency on an agreed date. Technically, if the transaction will take place more than a week into the future it is called a 'forward exchange transaction'. If the transaction is to take place within a week it is known as a 'spot transaction'.

Anderson, Torben Juul, *Currency and Interest-rate Hedging: A User's Guide to Options, Futures, Swaps and Forward Contracts.* New York: NYIF, 1994.

Forward vertical foreign direct investment

Forward vertical FDI occurs when overseas businesses make an investment in an industry which directly utilizes the output of their domestic production. For example, a manufacturer of steel may well consider the purchase of steel fabrication industries as a viable form of forward vertical FDI. Not only does the purchase guarantee a demand for the domestic industry's products, but it also establishes **barriers to entry** in the overseas market for competing businesses that produce the same products as the domestic production units. The major considerations when contemplating forward vertical FDI are the knowledge and understanding of how products are used further up the channels of distribution. This may involve establishing new sales and service centres in areas of industry in which the investing business has little knowledge.

Akinkugbe, Oluyele, *Flow of Foreign Direct Investment to Hitherto Neglected Developing Countries.* Discussion Paper 2003/02, United Nations University. World Institute for Development Economics Research, Helsinki, 2003.

Framework agreement

During the Tokyo Round of the **General Agreement on Tariffs and Trade (GATT)**, thoughts turned to improvement in the international framework for the conduct of world trade. The result of the negotiations brought about four agreements which are collectively known as the framework agreement. These are:

- Differential and more favourable treatment for, and reciprocity and fuller participation by, developing countries in the international framework for trade.
- Trade measures taken for **balance of payments** purposes.
- Safeguard actions for development purposes.
- An understanding on notification, consultation, dispute settlement and surveillance in the GATT.

F

The term 'framework agreement' can also be applied to the Enterprise for the Americas Initiative, during which bilateral framework agreements were established in order to eliminate counterproductive barriers to trade and investment. This bilateral framework agreement sought to open trade and investment, protect intellectual property rights, observe workers' rights and resolve trade and investment problems as quickly as possible. The initiative also established a Council on Trade and

Investment in order to monitor trade and investment relations. The framework agreement did not bind the signatories to implement specific trade liberalization measures.

Franchise

A franchise is a form of business in which a franchisor enters into a business relationship with a franchisee. The franchisor grants the franchisee a licence to use their common trade name, or trademark, in return for a fee, and during the association the franchisor will render assistance to the franchisee. It is essentially a licensing system which affords the franchisor the opportunity to expand, with the capital required to enable that expansion being provided by external sources.

In the US alone franchising generates some $800 billion per year and employs around 9 million people. Franchisees enjoy considerable benefits, which include:

- The ability to open a franchise business which is already a proven success.
- Receipt of full training and continued support from the franchisor.
- The ability to enjoy the benefits of national advertising.
- A guarantee that the franchisor will not sell a similar business to a competitor in the immediate area.

Free alongside ship (FAS)

'Free alongside ship' is a contractual arrangement for trade in which the seller undertakes to deliver goods to the buyer at the port of embarkation. From that point on, the buyer assumes responsibility. It is a common way of valuing internationally traded goods, which does not include the cost of the goods' shipment from the exporting country to the importing country.

F

Free onboard (FOB)

'Free onboard' is an international trade term which states that the price paid for goods includes the delivery costs to, and the loading onto, a particular carrier at a specified point. There are four other variants of free onboard, which are:

- *FOB freight allowed* – which is essentially the same as FOB except that the buyer pays the transportation charges and the seller reduces the price by that amount.

- *FOB freight pre-paid* – again similar to FOB except that the seller pays the freight charges for the inland carriage of the goods.
- *FOB named point of exportation* – in this variant the seller is responsible for getting the goods to a named port of exportation.
- *FOB vessel* – the seller is responsible for the goods and the export documentation until the goods are onboard a vessel.

Free trade

'Free trade' is a general term which is used to describe the ability of individuals or businesses to take part in economic transactions with other countries, free from restraint or regulation. The scope of free trade is measured as a sum of all imports and exports. The most significant change which has brought about the growth of free trade in the world was the **General Agreement on Tariffs and Trade (GATT)** and its successor, the **World Trade Organization**. Indeed, in the 50 years from 1950 to 2000 world trade increased by 1,600%, three times the rate of growth of the world's total output. Exports grew over the same period, in comparison with **gross domestic product**, from 7 to 15%. Free trade has not had a huge impact on traditional trading partners; Canada, for example, is still the largest trading partner with the United States, and the majority of European countries still trade primarily with other European countries. Those countries that have particular natural resources, such as oil or agricultural products, trade more freely across the world, whereas many of the **lesser developed countries** rely on simple manufactured products such as clothing, for which they find markets across the world.

Gilpin, Robert, *Global Political Economy: Understanding the International Economic Order.* Princeton, NJ: Princeton University Press, 2001.

Free trade agreement

F

A free trade agreement is an arrangement between two or more countries in which they undertake to allow the exchange and flow of products and services across their borders, with little or no impediment. A free trade agreement can be differentiated from a **common market** as it does not include labour mobility, the adoption of common currencies, the framing of uniform standards or the establishment of common tax policies. Usually members of **free trade areas** under this agreement apply their own individual tariff rates to countries which are outside the agreement.

Kreinin, Mordechai E., *Building a Partnership: The Canada–United States Free Trade Agreement.* East Lansing, MI: Michigan State University Press, 2000.

Free trade area

Many free trade areas were set up as a result of the **General Agreement on Tariffs and Trade (GATT)**. The free trade areas are cooperative arrangements between two or more countries where, effectively, all trade barriers are removed between those in the free trade area. Usually, but not exclusively, the free trade area is a **customs union** with a common external tariff. In some cases, however, the countries which are part of the free trade area do set their own different tariffs for countries outside the free trade area.

Free trade zone

A free trade zone (FTZ) is often known as a **duty free** zone or a customs free zone. The term itself is generic and simply refers to an area set aside by a country in which commercial and industrial activities can take place which allow the importing of foreign raw materials, components and finished goods which do not have to have duty paid. Should the merchandise be exported then the duty free treatment is given to re-exports. Typically the zones are near ports of entry and are used to either store, assemble, process or manufacture prior to re-export into the country proper. Usually manufacturing uses both foreign and domestic components.

Freely convertible currency

A freely convertible currency is a currency which has no limits on the amount which can be transferred from a country. Typical freely convertible currencies include the $US, the Euro, the British £ and the Canadian, Australian and New Zealand $s.

F

Freight forwarder

A freight forwarder is a business which handles export documentation and shipment on behalf of a domestic business. The exporter contacts the forwarder, who then makes all the necessary arrangements to ensure the safe shipment of the merchandise to its overseas destination. The forwarder deals with all the documentation which is required and completes all of this paperwork in the exporter's name. The forwarder also arranges insurance, communicates with the importing business and ensures that all labelling and marking of the merchandise is correct. For these services the freight forwarder receives a fee from the exporter and usually a percentage of the freight charge from the carrier.

Fronting loan

A fronting loan is a means by which a domestic parent company can provide a loan to a foreign subsidiary through a financial intermediary. The loan is arranged with an international bank by the parent company on behalf of the foreign subsidiary. In other cases the parent company may deposit sufficient funds with a large international bank, which in turn makes this cash available to the foreign subsidiary. This process often avoids unnecessary complications with regard to the movement of assets across international borders.

Fundamental analysis

'Fundamental analysis' is an accounting term for the investigation of a business's balance sheet, income statements, and sources and use of working capital. Fundamental analysis evaluates the balance sheet and the other financial documentation in order to assess the following:

- liquidity;
- asset quality;
- earnings quality;
- leverage;
- debt service coverage;
- profitability;
- growth;
- problems and opportunities for improvement.

Futures market

The futures markets have gradually developed over the past fifty or so years and the nature and the scope of the futures market has changed and become much more extensive. The futures market allows contracts to be bought and sold for the future delivery of a commodity, or a security. The futures market has three essential elements:

- The exchange, in which the traders or buyers and sellers meet. The exchange does not set prices, and traders (known as floor members) buy and sell contracts on behalf of clients in return for a commission.
- A clearing house, which is an independent organization that provides the mechanism for clearing transactions. Any contracts traded in the exchange must be registered with the clearing house. Floor members, or traders, are members of both the exchange and the clearing house. The members must have a solid financial backing.

F

Clients do not trade or deal directly with the clearing house, but through the members or brokers
- The traders operate on behalf of the buyers and sellers and in some cases within the exchange for themselves

F

G-5

The G-5, or group of 5, are similar to the group of 7 (**G-7**), but with the exception of Canada and Italy.

G-7

The G-7, or group of 7, are Canada, France, Germany, Italy, Japan, the United Kingdom and the United States, collectively accounting for around two-thirds of the world's economic output. These seven economic powers, through their finance ministers, seek to promote balanced economic growth and stable **exchange rates**. Their first meeting took place in Rambouillet in France in 1975. Canada joined at the 1976 Puerto Rican summit and since then the group has been known as the G-7. Each year a summit is held, the location being rotated amongst the seven countries. Since 1977 the President of the **European Commission** has been represented. The G-7 finance ministers meet quarterly to review developments both in their own economies and in the world economy, with the purpose of developing international and economic financial policies. At three of the four meetings each year the G-7 **central bank** governors are present. These are usually the first three meetings of the year, primarily to prepare for the **International Monetary Fund** and **World Bank** meetings which take place in April and September. At the end of each of the meetings the G-7 ministers issue a joint statement on economic conditions and policies. The G-7 finance ministers also meet before the **G-8** summit. When the **Euro** was launched, which would become the common currency of three of the G-7 members, France, Germany and Italy, the presidents of the **European Central Bank** and the Euro group represented the finance ministers of the 12 Euro countries.

G-7 does not have a permanent staff or a budget. The government which is hosting the summit in any given year provides facilities and support for that year.

G-8

G-8, or the group of 8, comprises of the **G-7** nations, plus Russia. From 1994 Russia began to participate in some of the meetings, notably beginning at the summit which was held in Naples that year. Russia officially became the 8th member of the group in 1997 in Denver, Colorado. Russia does not participate in financial and economic discussions, which remain the preserve of the G-7 nations. Of all of the G-8 nations, Russia currently has the smallest economy.

www.g8usa.gov

G-10

In 1962 the **International Monetary Fund** established the **General Agreement to Borrow (GAB)**. Under the terms of the GAB the 10 wealthiest nations of the IMF 'stand ready to lend their currencies to the IMF up to specified amounts when supplementary resources are needed'. The G-10 nations are Belgium, Canada, France, Germany, Italy, Japan, the Netherlands, Sweden, Switzerland, the United Kingdom and the United States. This list actually mentions 11 nations, as Switzerland joined G-10 in 1984. None the less, G-10 persists as the group's title.

G-11

The G-11 group, also known as the Cartagena Group, was established in June 1984 in order to provide a forum for the largest debtor nations in Latin America. The group comprises Argentina, Bolivia, Brazil, Chile, Colombia, the Dominican Republic, Ecuador, Mexico, Peru, Uruguay and Venezuela.

G-15

The group of 15 was created in 1990 and is comprised of nations which are comparatively prosperous, or are large, developing nations. The group meets in order to cement mutual cooperation, primarily in improving their economic position in the international world market and trade. G-15's membership consists of Algeria, Argentina, Brazil, Chile, Egypt, India, Indonesia, Jamaica, Kenya, Malaysia, Mexico, Nigeria, Peru, Senegal, Sri Lanka, Venezuela and Zimbabwe. Again, although the group currently consists of 17 countries, the name G-15 has remained. A former member was Yugoslavia until its re-designation as several separate nations following the civil war.

G-20

The group of 20 was created in 1999 at a meeting of the **G-7** finance ministers. G-20 includes the G-7 countries plus 11 other countries, including Russia, China, Australia, India and South Korea. G-20 was created to deliberate rather than make decisions, but it has a single policy focus, which is to promote international financial stability.

G-24

The group of 24 is an organization of the finance ministers of 24 developing countries who are members of the **International Monetary Fund**. The group itself represents 8 countries each from Africa, Asia and Latin America. It was formed in 1972, primarily to counteract the influence of **G-10**.

www.g24.org

G-77

The group of 77 was established in 1964 as a result of 77 developing countries signing the Joint Declaration of the 77 Countries, which was issued at the end of the first session of the **United Nations Conference on Trade and Development**. The first ministerial meeting took place in Algiers in 1967. The current membership of G-77 is 133 countries, its name having been retained for historical reasons. G-77 is the largest third world coalition in the United Nations and aims to articulate and promote collective economic interests on major issues within the United Nations' system.

www.g77.org

GATS

See **General Agreement on Trade in Services**.

GATT

This is a multilateral treaty intended to assist in the reduction of trade barriers between the signatory countries and to promote trade through concessions in tariffs.

See **General Agreement on Tariffs and Trade (GATT)**.

General Agreement on Tariffs and Trade (GATT)

GATT was established in 1947 and is a binding agreement between over 100 nations. It was considered to be an interim measure under the terms of the Havana Charter towards the establishment of the International Trade Organization. GATT discussions began in 1945, but the International Trade Organization was never ratified by the US Congress. Following the final rounds of discussions GATT was largely superseded in 1995 by the creation of the **World Trade Organization**. GATT was seen as a means by which international **free trade** could be achieved, and over the years several rounds of negotiations were required between governments of trading nations.

www.wto.org

General Agreement on Trade in Services (GATS)

GATS established a framework of rules for the international trade in services. The services area notably includes telecommunications, finance, tourism and education. The purpose of GATS was to create a more open, predictable and transparent international trading environment. GATS was adopted in 1994 as an integral part of the newly established **World Trade Organization**. In essence it is a multilateral agreement which defines restrictions on a broad range of government measures that could affect the trade in services. The restrictions are legally enforceable and can be backed up by World Trade Organization endorsed trade sanctions.

www.wto.org

General Agreement to Borrow (GAB)

The concept of a general agreement to borrow was established by the **International Monetary Fund** in 1962 in order that the fund could borrow money from the wealthier nations of the world. This group of wealthier nations includes Belgium, Canada, France, Germany, Italy, Japan, the Netherlands, Sweden, Switzerland, the United Kingdom and the United States. GAB was essential in order to supply the International Monetary Fund's ability to lend money to other countries, through loans made to the IMF when supplementary resources are required. Primarily, this occurs when lack of finance would impair the **international monetary system**.

Generalized system of preferences (GSP)

The generalized system of preferences (GSP) is a framework used by developed countries in order to provide preferential tariffs on manufactured goods which have been imported from specific developing countries. The purpose of GSP is to coordinate moves to bring developing countries into the international trading environment. Most GSPs are non-reciprocal in the sense that the preferential tariffs are one-way. Many of the developed countries, however, seek to ensure, before granting GSP, that the developing country takes steps to protect workers' rights, to work against intellectual property violations and to ensure that export practices and investments are transparent.

www.europa.eu.int/comm/trade/issues/global/gsp/index_en.htm

www.miti.gov.my/gsp.htm

Geocentric staffing

A geocentric staffing policy seeks to appoint the best individual for key roles in an organization, regardless of nationality. In the case of multinational organizations, the movement of staff from one nation to another can often be problematic, given the fact that different nations have radically different policies with regard to immigration. None the less the primary purpose of geocentric staffing is to help build a unified **culture**, throughout the organization, which stresses the opportunity of all individuals to be promoted or transferred to alternative geographic locations within the organization on the basis of ability.

Global capital market

A global capital market can be differentiated from a domestic capital market in the sense that, theoretically, there is a greater supply of funds available for borrowing and that the cost of borrowing this capital can potentially be lower for borrowers. The opportunity to invest within a global capital market also allows potential investors to diversify their portfolios and reduce the risks associated with being restricted to investment in a domestic capital market. There has been a huge increase in the scope and size of the global market in recent years, largely because funds can be electronically transferred, many financial services have been deregulated, and there has also been a relaxation of regulations regarding the flow of capital across borders. The global capital market tends to trade either in **Eurocurrencies** (which is any currency banked outside the currency of its origin) or through global bonds. Essentially,

G

global bonds are foreign bonds which are sold outside the borrower's country but which are denominated in the currency in which they were issued. A **Eurobond**, on the other hand, is underwritten by a syndicate of international banks and placed in a country other than the one which is denominated on the bond. Eurobonds are far more common.

In international business, the most important aspect of the global capital market is the opportunity to borrow funds at low cost, whilst simultaneously the market offers investors an opportunity to spread their risks.

Plender, John, *Going Off the Rails: Global Capital and the Crisis of Legitimacy*. New York: John Wiley, 2003.

Global human resource management

Increasingly, international business has recognized that staffing policy can be a key tool in the development and promotion of a clear corporate culture. Some businesses still choose to appoint parent country nationals to key management positions. This form of **ethnocentric staffing** can make the business rather myopic in its cultural understanding of the foreign markets in which it operates. A strong alternative to ethnocentric staffing is **polycentric staffing**, in which **host country** nationals manage overseas subsidiaries, whilst parent country nationals hold the key positions at home. This system can create a gap between the cultures in the host country and the home country. Businesses tend to look for a better staffing strategy which would avoid this possibility.

Increasingly, **geocentric staffing** is being implemented. This aims to place the best individuals in the key roles in the organization without regard to their nationality. Policies such as these are beginning to show that organizations can build a strong **culture** and a vital informal management network, which is ideal for international business.

One of the other key issues in global human resource management is the use of expatriates. The failure rate of these individuals, known as **expatriate failure**, has become a major concern. The other major consideration of human resource management for international businesses is providing their employees with an equivalent standard of living, no matter where they work for the business in the world. Clearly, given the fact that standards of living, or costs of living, differ from country to country, the salary and wage structure globally needs to reflect these differences. It is no longer the primary objective of a business that wishes to seek investment overseas to save money by paying less to foreign workers. Provided their equivalent standard of living is commensurate with that of the workforce at home, the human resource function of the organization is considered to be adjusted and aware of these implications.

Moran, Robert T., Harris, Philip R. and Stripp, William G., *Developing the Global Organization: Strategies for Human Resource Professionals*. Houston, TX: Gulf Publishing, 1993.

Global manufacturing

'Global manufacturing' refers to situations where international businesses choose to consider the various and alternative factors, both advantageous and disadvantageous, of various countries before deciding on where they will manufacture products. Different countries have a range of radically varying political economies, national cultures, technological expertise and other **externalities**. Technological factors, for example, could include the costs of setting up manufacturing facilities. Product factors could include transportation costs, which would be expressed in a value-to-weight ratio. Location issues revolve around decisions whether to centralize or decentralize manufacturing. All of these considerations involve trade-offs and no single location would necessarily be ideal or clearly better than any other choice. It is clear, however, that with careful and prudent management, overseas manufacturing facilities, even from a low base start, can be capable of replicating the same levels of efficiency as a home production unit. Increasingly, international businesses are looking to establish overseas manufacturing units as centres of excellence, and with the assistance of local management, factories can be upgraded over a period of time.

For international businesses which manufacture in a variety of different overseas environments, it is often a question of determining how much of the final product is actually manufactured as components and what is bought from outsourced organizations. International manufacturers will seek to be strategically flexible by subcontracting work to various foreign countries. Vertical integration through strategic alliances can also assist an international business in gaining the greatest potential benefits from its involvement with overseas manufacturing facilities.

Increasingly, information technology is providing a means whereby ever more remote cooperative manufacturing units can work together in terms of inputs, production schedules, and information flow and output targets.

Mo, John P. T. and Nemes, Laszlo (eds), *Global Engineering, Manufacturing and Enterprise Networks*. New York: Kluwer Academic Publishers, 2001.

Global marketing

Theodore Levitt was among those who argued that consumer tastes and preferences were becoming more global. He suggested that global markets, as a result of improved communication and transport, had created a demand for somewhat standardized consumer products. Levitt's argument tends to suggest a degree of standardization, but it still appears that in terms of global demand there are significant differences regarding taste and preference in different countries. Traditionally, even within a domestic market, businesses would segment their market by identifying specific groups of consumers who have shared purchasing behaviours. Global marketing takes this segmentation process to its natural conclusion and seeks not just to segment whole nations, albeit new markets, but to segment them in similar ways in order to replicate the segmentation process that has proved successful in domestic markets.

It has become clear that businesses need to customize the product attributes in the various countries in which they trade. Equally, distribution strategies which worked in their domestic market, or in long-term overseas markets, may not necessarily be appropriate. In some countries the distribution channels are difficult to penetrate; in others the retail systems are not as developed. There is also the question of traditional forms of marketing communications, which must work in accordance with the specific cultural differences in any given nation.

There have been some successful global and standardized advertising campaigns, notably when the message is simple, unambiguous and supported by clear images. In these cases standardized messages can transcend the cultural differences of different nations. For the most part, however, marketing and advertising messages need to reflect differences in culture and, in some cases, conform to different advertising regulations. In many respects the use of marketing communications in a new overseas market reflects much of the business's own **experience curve** in dealing with that nation in a more general sense. Increasingly, international businesses have recognized that they must carry out research and development in their new markets in order to ensure that new products suit these markets, and that this research and development, as well as manufacturing, needs to be integrated with the broader marketing function.

Levitt, Theodore, 'The Globalization of Markets', *Harvard Business Review*, 61(3) (May–June 1983), pp. 92–102.

Global matrix structure

A global matrix structure is essentially a **horizontal differentiation** along product divisions and geographical divisions. In other words, to visualize the organization structure, product groups are placed on a vertical axis and the foreign divisions on the horizontal axis (see Figure 2). It allows businesses to reduce costs by increasing efficiency, and to differentiate their activities with innovation and responsiveness.

The feature of the global matrix structure is that it demonstrates dual decision-making responsibility, as there is both a divisional and an area hierarchy. The system is not without its problems, as many organizations consider this form of structure to be rather clumsy and bureaucratic. There is also the question of slow decision making and a rather inflexible form of organization. Several international businesses have sought to overcome the problems by basing their organizational structure on wide networks with shared **culture** and vision, and stressing that the informal structures are more important than the formal structure itself. These forms of organizational structure are known as flexible matrix structures.

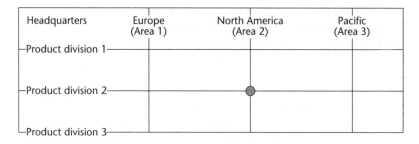

● An individual at this point in the global matrix structures is attached to the North American area and product division 2.

Figure 2   Global matrix structure

Egelhoff, W. G., 'Strategy and Structure in Multinational Corporations: a Revision of the Stopford and Wells Model', *Strategic Management Journal*, vol. 9 (1988), pp. 1–14.

G

Global strategy

A global strategy is often adopted by an international business in order to increase its profitability by taking advantage not only of cost reductions that come from **experience curve** effects, but also of economies based on the location of parts of its operations. Typically a global strategy will consider the best alternatives to concentrate research and development, marketing or production, choosing the most beneficial location for each of these key operations. In essence a global strategy can be called a multi-domestic strategy, in as much as the international business seeks to maximize its worldwide performance through maximizing any local competitive advantages, revenues or profits it can achieve. Equally, global strategies seek to maximize performance through integration and a sharing of resources.

Stonehouse, George; Hamill, Jim; Campbell, David and Purdie, Tony, *Global and Transnational Business: Strategy and Management*. New York: John Wiley, 2000.

Globalization

Globalization has many connotations, both positive and negative. In international trade the term refers to the situation we have now in the world, where individuals, businesses and governments have become increasingly dependent upon and integrated with one another.

As far as business is concerned, the opportunities are enormous, with new markets opening up, giving access to different workforces, business partners, raw materials, components, products and services. Hand in hand with these opportunities are increased competitive threats.

Marshall McLuhan suggested in his book *Understanding Media* in 1964 that electronic communications would contract the world, making it no more significant than communication in a village.

The term 'globalization' probably came into existence in the early 1980s when there was a rapid increase in the growth of international trade and the flow of capital around the world. The negative connotation with regard to globalization has been the increase in income inequality between the richest nations in the world and the poorest. The growth of globalization has also seen the diminishing power of the governments of the lesser developed nations in comparison with vast, multinational businesses. In essence, globalization implies international integration through a process of **free trade**, deregulation and liberalization of trade.

Lawson, Stephanie, *The New Agenda for International Relations: From Polarization to Globalization in World Politics*. Cambridge: Polity Press, 2001.
McLuhan, Marshall, *Understanding Media*. New York: Mentor, 1964.

Globalization of marketing

The term 'globalization' in a marketing sense relates to the rolling out of products and services across the world. It has been a considerable feature of the development of world trade that brands can now enjoy similar levels of success, no matter which country they are offered in. Clearly there are regional differences in both the needs and wants of overseas customers, coupled with the requirement to adapt the brand to meet the tastes of those different markets. None the less, global branding has become a major feature in international marketing.

The development of globalization has taken place as businesses have sought to find a competitive advantage in overseas markets to compensate for the fact that they do not enjoy this advantage in their home market. Customers have been receptive to the globalization of brands for the following reasons:

- Consumers in the majority of markets have become more sophisticated and are now willing to experiment with non-domestic products and services, as well as demanding products and services which they have consumed while abroad.
- This has been enabled by the gradual elimination of trade and travel barriers, coupled with a strong political resolve to open most markets to competition.
- The globalization of brands has been coupled with the internationalization of both print and broadcast media, which carry advertisements for global brands.
- Given the fact that a domestic market may be saturated, businesses increasingly look for markets in which their products and services can continue to grow.

Keegan, Warren J. and Mark C., *Global Marketing Management* (7th edition). New York: Prentice-Hall, 2001.

Globalization of markets

The term 'globalization of markets' is in stark contrast to more familiar views of **global marketing**. The globalization of markets implies that many international businesses no longer consider individual national markets to be distinct entities. Given that many nations until recently were closed by virtue of the fact that it was difficult to trade there, now that trade barriers have been removed these national markets are merging and can be treated in a very similar manner. Concerns regarding transportation, distance to market and even **culture** are being subsumed as international businesses increasingly treat new national markets in a similar manner to markets in which they already trade.

See also **Globalization**.

Globalization of production

The term 'globalization of production' refers to the trend of international businesses, notably multinationals, that have increasingly chosen to disperse their production processes across the world. In essence these multinationals take full advantage of specific countries' **factors of production** in order to frame their **global manufacturing** policy.

Weiss, John, *Industrialization and Globalization: Theory and Evidence from Developing Countries*. London: Routledge, 2002.

Gold par value

Gold par value is simply the amount of any given currency which is required to purchase an ounce of gold.

Gold standard

In the past a nation's currency was backed by a reserve of gold, which, in theory, would allow currency holders to exchange their notes and coins for gold. In the period up to 1914 most of the world's leading currencies determined their exchange rates by the gold standard. Many countries abandoned this linkage as a result of the economic disruption caused by the First World War. The UK returned to the gold standard in 1925, but again abandoned it in 1931.

The majority of countries abandoned the gold standard during the global depression of the 1930s; the US, for example, left in 1933, returning to it the following year. Following the Second World War a version of the gold standard continued, applying just to the US dollar, whilst other currencies fixed their exchange rates to the dollar under the terms of the **Bretton Woods** Agreements. The dollar finally left the gold standard in 1971.

Remarkably, however, in recent years, with the exception of 1999, the value of gold has steadily risen. Following the terrorist attack on the United States in 2001, gold has become once again one of the best performing assets in any type of investment.

Eichengreen, Barry, *Globalizing Capital: A History of the International Monetary System*. Princeton, NJ: Princeton University Press, 1996.

Grandfather clause

The grandfather clause was a provision of the **General Agreement on Tariffs and Trade (GATT)**. It allows the original contracting parties to GATT to be exempt from GATT obligations if domestic legislation that already existed prior to the signature is inconsistent with the GATT provisions. The newer GATT members were also allowed to use the grandfather clause provided this was negotiated before accession to GATT.

Green-field investment

When an international business considers **foreign direct investment (FDI)** it can choose to invest in the establishment of a completely new operation in a **host country**, known as a green-field investment, or it can merge with or acquire an existing operation. Many governments earmark specific areas of their country in which foreign green-field investment can be made. These restrictions, which were once rigid and widespread, are now far more relaxed. The primary advantage of green-field foreign direct investment is that it adds to the stock of domestic capital investment and, of course, it expands the productive capacity of the host country.

Developing countries, in particular, are keen to attract green-field FDI as it brings new technology to the country, together with different organizational structures and management ability. This inflow of knowledge is far more limited in the case of **acquisition**. Green-field investment is also advantageous in the sense that it increases competition, whilst acquisitions concentrate ownership and reduce competition. Above all, green-field investments provide an inflow of foreign currency, whilst acquisitions may be funded by internally borrowed funds.

In the case both of green-field investment and of acquisitions and mergers, they are seen as a means by which international businesses can strengthen their market position in new countries.

Gross domestic product (GDP)

Gross domestic product is the sum of the market value of all goods and services which were produced within the boundaries of a particular nation, regardless of who owns those assets. GDP excludes earnings from business operations in foreign countries and also excludes re-invested earnings in foreign **affiliates**.

Gross domestic product, therefore, is equal to the private consumption + investment, public spending, change in inventories + the balance between exports and imports.

Labonte, Marc and Makinen, Gail E., *The Economic Expansion of the 1990s*. Hauppauge, NY: Nova Science Publishers, 2003.

Gross fixed capital formation

Gross fixed capital formation relates primarily to the investment in tangible fixed assets, such as plant, machinery, buildings, transport equipment and other structures. It can also include investment in intangible fixed assets, such as improvement to land and any costs associated with the transfer of assets.

Gross national product (GNP)

Gross national product is a measure of the market value of goods and services which are produced by a nation. It includes receipts from the nation's business operations in overseas countries, as well as the share of reinvested earnings in foreign **affiliates**. It is prime measure of a country's economic performance. It is calculated by adding the **gross domestic product** to the income earned by the country's nationals from investments abroad, less the income earned by foreigners from investments made in the country, but sent home.

Shaikh, Anwar M. and Tonak, E. Ahmet, *Measuring the Wealth of Nations: The Political Economy of National Accounts*. Cambridge: Cambridge University Press, 1997.

Gulf Cooperation Council (GCC)

The Gulf Cooperation Council was established in 1981 and consists of Bahrain, Kuwait, Oman, Qatar, Saudi Arabia and the United Arab Emirates. Its primary aim was to coordinate resistance to intervention in the Gulf area, but it was also concerned with the movement towards economic integration. This latter priority has barely moved in the intervening years. The six members of the GCC have made attempts to strengthen their cooperation, primarily in the areas of agriculture, industry, investment, security and trade. One of the major reasons for the creation of the GCC was the outbreak of the Iran–Iraq War. Since then it has established the Gulf Standards Organization (1982) and the Gulf Investment Corporation (1984). The presidency of the GCC rotates on a yearly basis amongst its members, but its headquarters are in Riyadh, Saudi Arabia.

www.europa.eu.int/comm/external_relations/gulf_cooperation/intro

Hard currency

Hard currency is also known as 'convertible currency'. It has a sound value and, above all, it is generally accepted internationally on the open market. Hard currency is expected, by its definition, to retain its value to a great degree. As it is a far more reliable currency than most, it has become the currency of choice for many businesses involved in international transactions. Typically, hard currencies include the dollar, the pound sterling and the Swiss franc.

Harmonized system

Under the guidance of the **Customs Cooperation Council**, the harmonized commodity description and coding system, which is also known as the harmonized system (HS), is a way in which goods can be classified for international trade. Prior to January 1989 there were innumerable different schedules and coding systems which described various goods. HS now incorporates over 50 countries. All other forms of commodity code classifications are simply transformations of original HS numbers. The code is hierarchically structured, with a produce nomenclature which contains around 5,000 headings and sub-headings, organized into 99 chapters, arranged in 22 sections. Each of the basic codes contains 4-digit headings and 6-digit sub-headings. Some countries will add digits for customs tariff and statistical purposes.

Heckscher–Ohlin Theory

The Heckscher–Ohlin Theory states that countries will export products or services in which they have a **comparative advantage**. They will use their most advantageous **factor endowments** as integral parts of their **factors of production**. It is based on the Rybczynski Theorem, which states that if two countries have, to all intents and purposes, similar product preferences, technologies and factor endowments, their relative prices will be the same. If one country has more capital and the other has more labour, then food production will go up in the first country, which will depress the price of food there. Simultaneously, clothing, for example, may expand in the second country, which depresses the relative price of clothing there and raises the relative price of food. Using the Heckscher–Ohlin Theory, when trade then takes place between the two countries, the first will export food and the second will export clothing.

Leamer, Edward E., *The Heckschler–Ohlin Model in Theory and Practice*. Princeton, NJ: Princeton University International Economics, 1995.

Hedge/hedging fund

In financial markets individuals and businesses will seek to maximize their absolute returns and concentrate on generating profits. A hedge fund allows these individuals and businesses to reduce their risks by taking a new risk which offsets an existing one. In the majority of cases hedge funds are used to make an investment on an adverse position to the original investment.

In international business an organization may choose to hedge its financial risks by financing the construction of a new factory in a particular country by borrowing the currency of that country. This means that should the economic situation in that country deteriorate, the value of that country's currency will also deteriorate, thereby reducing the organization's overall **economic exposure**.

Barham, Sarah and Hallsworth, Alan (eds), *Starting a Hedge Fund – A European Perspective*. Tunbridge Wells, Kent: ISI Publications, 2002.

Helmes–Burton Act

H

In the period 1959 to 1960, the Cuban government, led by Fidel Castro, nationalized all foreign corporate and individually owned properties. In response, the US demanded $1.8 billion in compensation; Cuba failed to pay and since then the US has imposed several different forms of economic embargo against Cuba. In 1996 two Miami-based civilian aircraft, owned by a humanitarian organization, were shot down by the Cuban air force. This triggered the Helmes–Burton Act, which is otherwise known as the Cuban Liberty and Democratic Solidarity (Libertad) Act (1996).

In essence it proposed to increase Cuba's economic isolation by imposing penalties on individuals or businesses that engaged in certain economic relations with the country. The Act specifically directs the President to instruct both the Secretary of the Treasury and the Attorney-General to enforce all existing regulations against Cuba. The Act is somewhat draconian as even the renting of a room for the purposes of a meeting in a building which is a registered and certified confiscated property means that the person renting can fall foul of the Act, being considered to have trafficked in confiscated property and thus to be eligible for the imposition of a treble damage charge penalty.

Helsinki accord

The Helsinki accord was signed in 1975 and is concerned with the rights of individuals to migrate. It sought to lower the fees and the volume of documentation required for international travel. It also had considerable implications in terms of international trade, in as much as the accord officially recognized the new territorial borders which had been created in Europe since 1945.

Historical cost principle

The historical cost principle is based on the assumption that asset and liability measurements should be based on the amount that was given or received during an exchange transaction. Historical cost measurement is considered to be an important piece of cash-flow information as it is verifiable. It is primarily used for accounting for plant assets. In this instance the recorded costs of the plant assets are equal to the cash equivalent price, the value of which does not change unless the asset has suffered an impairment. In using the historical cost principle it is possible to value an asset over its lifespan on the more reliable basis of past transactions. The value of the plant assets is derived through their use and not their disposal at the end of their useful economic life.

Home country

In essence the term 'home country', as far as international business is concerned, is an identification of the country in which the parent business operates, or largely operates, or where it was founded. The other major use of the term 'home country' refers to the source country of **foreign direct investment**.

See also **host country**.

Horizontal differentiation

Horizontal differentiation involves the division of a multinational business into a series of sub-units, usually on a nation-by-nation basis.

Horizontal foreign direct investment

Horizontal **foreign direct investment** is a form of investment from an overseas business into a similar industry, in an overseas country, to the type of business activity it operates at home.

Host country

The term 'host country' as far as international business is concerned can refer to a nation in which the business has established a presence either by means of **foreign direct investment** or via an **acquisition** or merger. The term is also used to describe a recipient country which has had inward investment by a foreign business.

H

Import quota

An import quota is a means by which a government seeks to restrict the volume or value of imports. It achieves this by issuing licences to importers by assigning a quota to each importer based on the total amount of any specific commodity which will be imported over a period of time. These import licences may also specify from which countries importers may purchase goods.

Import restriction

An import restriction may be applied by a government which has an adverse **balance of payments**. It may also restrict imports in order to control the volume of commodities coming into the country, by imposing **import quotas** or **tariffs** or even by restricting the amount of foreign currency available to purchase imports. In some cases surcharges may be levied, or indeed whole categories of imports may be prohibited.

Import substitution

Import substitution is a government strategy which seeks to replace imports with domestically produced products. It will offer domestic manufacturers an incentive to produce these substitute goods in an attempt to dissuade them from producing products which would normally be destined for export. The strategy is primarily designed to develop the range of products produced by the domestic industry and reduce the country's reliance on imported goods.

Importer

An importer is an individual or business which is primarily responsible for the payment of duties on merchandise which has been brought into a country. Typically, importers will have trade links with foreign manufacturers or suppliers and will organize the delivery of various products to their **home country**. The importers can either be the **consignee**, the importer of record or the actual owner of the merchandise.

Incoterms

Incoterms are a set of 13 standard trade definitions which are used in international sales contracts. They were devised by the **International Chamber of Commerce**. Amongst the best known terms are **FOB (free on board)**, **cost, insurance and freight (CIF)** and **carriage paid to (CPT)**. The first version of the Incoterms, which is short for 'international commercial terms', was introduced in 1936; since then they have been updated six times. The latest version is known as Incoterms 2000. Incoterms have been endorsed by the **United Nations Commission on International Trade Law (UNCITRAL arbitration rules)** and have been translated into 31 languages.

www.iccwbo.org

Incumbent advantage

'Incumbent advantage' refers to businesses which have a **competitive advantage** over other businesses that wish to enter a specific overseas market. Incumbent advantage is a feature of businesses which are **first movers** into a new market in as much as they have the opportunity to begin to erect **barriers to entry** against the competition.

Independent European Programme Group (IEPG)

The IEPG was established in 1976 and its membership includes the members of the **European Union** in addition to Norway and Turkey. Its purpose is to promote European cooperation in research, development, defence, and trans-Atlantic armaments.

Inefficient market

Inefficient markets take place when the market is manipulated in some way to affect prices. In accordance with free market theory, where there is no form of intervention in the market, prices and output are determined purely by supply and demand. In an inefficient market a circumstance has arisen whereby this normal relationship has been manipulated.

Infant industry

An infant industry is an area of economic activity which is considered to be fragile. In other words, these are industries which are at an early stage in their development. The term is usually used in connection with the concept that a temporary form of protection, in the form of tariff or non-tariff barriers, needs to be established so as to enable these fragile industries to establish themselves and become competitive in the world market. Under the terms of the **World Trade Organization** rules, countries are allowed to protect their infant industries provided they compensate other countries that may be adversely affected by this protection.

www.wto.org

Inflow of FDI

'Inflow of **foreign direct investment**' describes the level of overseas involvement in a domestic market. The inflow not only increases the capital stock, but is also a vital channel of international technology transfer. Given the fact that the majority of businesses that involve themselves in FDI are technologically advanced, these investments not only provide more efficient technologies, but also generate technological spill-overs for local businesses. The most accurate figures regarding capital inflows are provided by both the **International Monetary Fund** and the **Organization for Economic Cooperation and Development** (although the latter only covers flows from OECD members). The complete figures for inflows of FDI are combined in the World Investment Reports of the **United Nations Conference on Trade and Development**.

Agarwal, S. and Ramaswami, S. N., 'Choice of Foreign Market Entry Mode: Impact of Ownership, Location and Internalization Factors', *Journal of International Business Studies*, 23(1) (1992), pp. 1–27.

Initial negotiating right

The initial negotiating right (INR) is a right of one **World Trade Organization** country to demand compensation from another World Trade Organization country for the infringement of a bound tariff. The concept of INR stems from negotiating concessions which allow the INR holders to require compensation should they suffer an impairment of tariff concessions.

www.wto.org

Initial rate

An initial rate is an interest rate, paid on a loan, which is normally lower than the average variable rate. At the end of the initial period the business which has taken out the loan will pay the normal variable rate of interest.

Inland bill of lading

An inland **bill of lading** is used when transporting goods over land to an exporter's international carrier. In some cases a **through bill of lading** can be used, but in most cases it is necessary to have both an inland bill of lading and an **ocean bill of lading** for export shipments.

Insurance

In the context of international business, insurance is essential as it covers potential losses or damage to cargo while goods are in transit. Depending upon the terms of the sale, the seller will include an insurance premium as part of the price, up to a specified point in the journey of the goods. In some cases the insurance is then picked up by the buyer for the onward movement of the goods.

Integrating mechanisms

For international businesses a well planned and considered means by which they can integrate their operations across several countries has become essential. Businesses that are involved in multi-domestic, international, global or trans-national business will seek to integrate their systems, usually through a more complex form of **organizational structure**. There are various different forms of integrating mechanisms: perhaps the most obvious is to have individuals from the parent company in direct contact with, or posted to, new overseas ventures in order to gradually integrate the new business enterprise into the overall organizational system. Other international businesses prefer inter-departmental liaison, in which selected individuals from key functional departments of the parent company are available to assist the new overseas enterprise in integrating its systems into the parent's mechanisms. Other international businesses choose to create temporary task forces to speed up the integration process. They may well choose to site permanent teams with the new overseas enterprise, with a view not only to integrate the overseas business, but to learn best practice from that overseas business, which can then be fed back to the parent company.

One of the most common forms of integrating mechanism is to create a **global matrix structure**, which effectively makes key functional departments in the parent company responsible for certain aspects of the overseas business's activities and helps ensure clearer integration and permanent liaison.

Intellectual property rights (IPR)

The term 'intellectual property rights' refers to intangible products such as **patents**, **copyright** and trademarks. With the massive increase in international trade, the right to possess, use or dispose of these intangible assets has become an increasingly important aspect not only in trade itself, but in policing the use of these assets across the world. There have been innumerable examples of violation of intellectual property rights and increasingly steps are being taken to prevent piracy, passing off and other means by which businesses seek to benefit illegally from the use of IPRs owned by others. The World Intellectual Property Organization's main function is to protect intellectual property rights across the world.

www.wipo.org

Internal forward rate

The internal forward rate is a forecast generated by a business which suggests the probable exchange rate of currencies at some point in the future. The business will use this internal forward rate to make an estimate as to the true value of a business transaction with a foreign business, as a means of predicting future cash flows.

Andersen, Torben Juul, *Currency and Interest-rate Hedging: A User's Guide to Options, Futures, Swaps and Forward Contracts*. New York: NYIF, 1994.

Internalization

'Internalization' refers to a situation where an international business has seen an increasing demand for its products in overseas markets in a given country over a period of time. The organization may choose to continue to export the products through existing channels and with existing business partners abroad. However, it may view the situation as being ideal to make a **foreign direct investment** in that country. It will do this in order to acquire the primary importer, or distributor, of the products which it has been historically exporting to that country. The exporting business will therefore bring that overseas distributor into its own organizational structure, thereby internalizing both the export and import functions of that foreign trade. It will seek to do this in order to enjoy greater profits from the exports and maintain a tighter control over that overseas market, thus preventing competitors from establishing a business relationship with the overseas importer.

International Accounting Standards Committee (IASC)

The IASC was established in 1973 as a standard-setting board which aimed to require businesses to produce quality, transparent and comparable information in their financial statements and reporting. In 2000 the IASC became the International Accounting Standards Committee Foundation, which appointed the International Accounting Standards Board (IASB) to develop and approve both international accounting standards and international financial reporting standards.

Since 2001 the standards-setting work has been conducted by the IASB and they have sought to bring international businesses into compliance with their standards – 'an enterprise whose financial statements comply with international accounting standards should disclose that fact. Financial statements should not be described as complying with international accounting standards unless they comply with all the requirements of each applicable standard and each applicable interpretation of the Standing Interpretations Committee.'

www.iasc.org.uk

International agreements

International agreements are broad classifications of legally binding arrangements between different nations. Typically, these international agreements will include accords, annexes, conventions, memoranda of understanding, protocols and treaties. They may also include declarations, pacts and statutes. Most of these terms are synonyms of one another and they have very little differentiation. A treaty, for example, as defined by the Vienna Convention on the Law on Treaties, is 'an international agreement concluded between states in written form and governed by international law, whether embodied in a single instrument or in two or more related instruments and whatever its particular designation'.

Many nations will sign several dozen, if not more, international agreements each year. Some will be treaties whilst others will simply codify existing arrangements between two nations. Protocols can be stand-alone arrangements, but are usually supplementary agreements or amendments. Annexes are usually subsidiary agreements to already established relationships. Accords are usually non-binding agreements, whilst memoranda of understanding are very detailed and take into account the practices and requirements of both governments.

International Bank for Reconstruction and Development

The International Bank for Reconstruction and Development (IBRD) is more commonly referred to as the **World Bank**. The IBRD is, in effect, an inter-governmental financial institution which seeks to promote economic growth in developing countries and raise living standards. Primarily it grants loans to governments of **lesser developed countries**, with the proviso that the funds be used to promote long-term development. The IBRD tends to loan funds for specific development projects, such as infrastructure, agricultural and rural development, or education. Any loans which are granted must be guaranteed by the government of the country concerned. The IBRD is based in Washington, DC, and was established in 1945, initially to help countries reconstruct their economies after the Second World War.

www.worldbank.org

International Banking Act

The International Banking Act is a US Federal framework which was passed in 1978 in order to govern the activities of foreign banks which had previously only been controlled by State law. In essence the Act established a policy detailing how the US would treat foreign banks. The key elements are:

- Limiting branching activities so that they are more comparable to US banks.
- Requiring that the foreign banks have the same reserve requirements as US banks.
- Limiting the degree to which foreign banks can be involved in US securities.
- Opening Federal deposit insurance to US officers of foreign banks if they are involved in retail banking.

International business

'International business' is a generic term which is used to describe any form of business transaction, whether undertaken by an individual or a company, which involves at least two countries. The term suggests that the business world is no longer limited by national boundaries. The vast improvements in communication, transport and information technology have enabled businesses to operate in radically new environments, whilst simultaneously making many nations wholly interdependent on one another.

Increasingly, businesses are as concerned with the international environment as they are with their local environments. Huge numbers of businesses carry out international operations and increase their opportunities through diversifying their markets and obtaining supplies of raw materials and components at lower cost. Alongside this, these international businesses are facing greater risks, in many cases, with an incomplete knowledge of the markets in which they are now operating. These new risks include political or economic instability together with volatile exchange rates.

International business is not simply concerned with the exporting of products or services to overseas markets. It has an equal relevance for the sourcing of goods and raw materials and, indeed, making direct foreign investments into nations which hitherto were rather closed and misunderstood.

Morrison, Janet, *The International Business Environment*. Basingstoke: Palgrave Macmillan, 2002.
Woods, Margaret, *International Business*. Basingstoke: Palgrave Macmillan, 2001.

International Business Opportunities Service

The International Business Opportunities Service (IBOS) is provided by the **World Bank**. Businesses can subscribe to this service and receive information regarding imminent projects and business opportunities. The IBOS provides the following:

- A listing of all projects which are being considered, known as the Monthly Operational Summary (MOS).
- A series of technical data sheets (TDS) for each approved loan.
- Procurement notices, which are used for international competitive bidding.
- Specific procurement notices describing items which need to be procured, and bidding requirements.
- Contract award notices which identify successful bidders.

www.worldbank.org

International Center for Settlement of Investment Disputes (ICSID)

The International Center for Settlement of Investment Disputes was created in 1966 in order to mediate or conciliate in cases of investment disputes between private foreign investors and governments. The centre itself does not engage in conciliation or arbitration, but insists on the initiation of such proceedings. Provided both parties consent, they are bound to carry out the undertakings of future deliberations.

The ICSID is an autonomous organization with close links to the **World Bank**. The number of cases which have been submitted to the centre has increased significantly in recent years and since 1986 the centre has published a law journal. Since 1983 it has sponsored the International Court of Arbitration.

www.worldbank.org/icsid

International Chamber of Commerce (ICC)

The ICC was created in 1919, primarily to promote **free trade** and private enterprise, and to represent the interests of businesses at both national and international levels. The ICC is involved in virtually every area of international business, from anti-corruption through customs and trade regulations, **intellectual property rights** and trade and investment policy.

After the creation of the United Nations in 1945 the ICC was granted consultative status with the United Nations. The ICC vigorously resists any form of protectionism in international trade and has built a strong presence across the world, including most of the emerging economies. It has national committees in some 84 countries and keeps in touch with its membership through local, national and international conferences.

www.iccwbo.org

International Commodity Agreement

The International Commodity Agreement (ICA) is an international understanding relating to trade in a particular commodity. It is based on terms which have been negotiated and accepted by most of the countries which either export or import significant quantities of that commodity. There are existing commodity agreements for products such as coffee, cocoa, rubber and sugar. The purpose is to stabilize the market price with a negotiated price range for the commodity by using buffer stocks or **export quotas**, or a combination of the two. There are other commodity agreements for jute, olive oil and wheat. The ICA seeks to promote cooperation between both producers and consumers through consultation, an exchange of information, research and development, and the promotion of exports.

International competitive bidding (ICB)

International competitive bidding is a form of procurement which is made with **World Bank** financing. The ICB code requires the following:

- All goods or works which are procured through ICB are internationally advertised through the United Nations' *Development Business* publication and in one major local newspaper.
- Bids must be made in either the bidder's or an international currency specified by the borrower.
- Payments must be made in the currency in the bid, with no requirement for **counter-trade**.
- Documents must be in an international language (English, French or Spanish).
- Bids must be openly reviewed.
- Contracts will be awarded to the lowest evaluated bid, but under certain circumstances a preference can be given to domestic bids for domestic contracting services in developing countries.

www.worldbank.org

International Confederation of Free Trade Unions (ICFTU)

The International Confederation of Free Trade Unions was established in 1949. Its primary purpose is to promote the Trade Union movement through the recognition of workers' organizations and to support the rights of workers to bargain with employers. The ICFTU now has 231 affiliated organizations in 150 countries and a nominal membership of 158 million.

There are three regional organizations, APRO (Asia and the Pacific), AFRO (Africa) and ORIT (the Americas). The ICFTU has close links with the **European Trade Union Confederation** and the Global Union Federations. It also operates closely with the International Labour Organization, the United Nations Economic and Social Council, the **International Monetary Fund**, the **World Bank** and the **World Trade Organization**.

www.icftu.org

International Convention on the Simplification and Harmonization of Customs Procedures

The International Convention on the Simplification and Harmonization of Customs Procedures states that its mission is:

1 Endeavouring to eliminate divergence between the customs procedures and practices of contracting parties that can hamper international trade and other international exchanges.
2 Desiring to contribute effectively to the development of such trade and exchanges by simplifying and harmonizing customs procedures and practices and by fostering international cooperation.
3 Noting that the significant benefits of facilitation of international trade may be achieved without compromising appropriate standards of customs control.
4. Recognizing that such simplification and harmonization can be accomplished by applying, in particular, the following principles:

- the implementation of programmes aimed at continuously modernizing customs procedures and practices and thus enhancing efficiency and effectiveness;
- the application of customs procedures and practices in a predictable, consistent and transparent manner;
- the provision to interested parties of all the necessary information regarding customs laws, regulations, administrative guidelines, procedures and practices;
- the adoption of modern techniques such as risk management and audit-based controls, and the maximum practicable use of information technology;
- cooperation wherever appropriate with other national authorities, other customs administrations and the trading communities;
- the implementation of relevant international standards;
- the provision to affected parties of easily accessible processes of administrative and judicial review.

5 Convinced that an international instrument incorporating the above objectives and principles that contracting parties undertake to apply would lead to the high degree of simplification and harmonization of customs procedures and practices which is an essential aim of the Customs Cooperation Council, and so make a major contribution to facilitation of international trade.

The International Convention on the Simplification and Harmonization of Customs Procedures (Kyoto Convention) is the full name of the

International Instrument on the Harmonization of Customs Techniques. It entered into force in 1974, since which time the growth in international transactions, the development of information technology and the increasingly competitive international business environment have created conflict with this harmonization attempt. In June 1999 the World Customs Organization adopted a revised version of the Kyoto Convention with the objective of creating an international understanding which would still be relevant in the twenty-first century.

International Court of Justice

The International Court of Justice (ICJ) was established in 1945 as the principal judicial organ of the United Nations. The court is composed of 15 elected judges from a list of individuals nominated by national groups which are members of the Permanent Court of Arbitration. Submitted cases are heard in The Hague, Netherlands. The ICJ began its work in 1946 when it replaced the Permanent Court of International Justice, which itself had been in operation since 1922.

www.icj-cij.org

International database

The international database (IDB) is maintained in the United States by the Center for International Research. The IDB is an automated databank containing demographic, economic and social data for all countries. Typical data categories are population, health, fertility, migration, literacy, education, labour force statistics, employment, **gross national product** and housing indicators. The IDB is used by many different international organizations, as well as private businesses, research institutes and the US government.

International Finance Corporation

The International Finance Corporation (IFC) is part of the **World Bank**. It was established in 1956 and is based in Washington, DC. It has a similar objective to that of the World Bank in as much as it aims to improve the quality of lives of individuals in developing member countries. The IFC is the largest multilateral source of loan and equity financing. It primarily focuses on private sector projects in developing nations. It assists private companies in finding finance on the international financial markets and also provides technical assistance and advice to both businesses and governments. The IFC uses its 175 member countries to collectively approve investments and determine policy. All IFC members are also members of the **International Bank for Reconstruction and Development (IBRD)**. The IFC has an authorized capital of $2.45 billion. It is independent and therefore financially and legally autonomous, with its own share capital and management. The IFC charges market rates for loans and reinvests its profits in new projects.

www.ifc.org

International Fisher effect

The international Fisher effect states that for any two particular countries, spot exchange rates should change by an equal amount, but in the opposite direction to the difference in nominal interest rates.

International Labour Organization (ILO)

The International Labour Organization is a United Nations specialized agency which was founded in 1919 and seeks to promote justice and internationally recognized human and labour rights. The ILO formulates international labour standards, sets minimum standards for basic labour rights, including freedom of association, organization and collective bargaining, the abolition of forced labour, equal opportunity, and other standards related to working conditions.

www.ilo.org

International marketing

'International marketing' is a collective term used to describe **global marketing** activities undertaken by certain businesses. International or multinational businesses will have identified target markets in different countries across the world. International marketing is designed to impose some kind of coordination between these disparate activities. It is not always appropriate to run either a simultaneous, or indeed a similar, advertising and marketing campaign in different markets. Given the fact that each market has its own peculiarities, seasonal fluctuations and specific customer needs and wants, the imposition of a standardized marketing system, incorporating identical advertising, is not always appropriate. None the less, international marketing can offer a business the opportunity to compare like with like in different overseas markets. It may be possible, for example, to compare response rates against costs, running similar advertisements or sales promotions in different countries. The purpose of coordination and planning is to establish the

correct mix of activities for each overseas market and to learn lessons
from similar markets when first entering a new overseas market.

Doole, Isobel and Lowe, Robin, *International Marketing Strategy: Analysis, Development
and Implementation*. London: Thomson Learning, 2001.

International Monetary Fund (IMF)

The International Monetary Fund was established in 1945 in order to
promote international monetary harmony, monitor exchange rates and
monetary policies and provide credit for countries that were experiencing problems in terms of deficits in their **balance of payments**. All
members of the IMF have a quota, known as the Special Drawing Rights.
This reflects the relative size of their economy and their relative voting
power. The quotas also determine each member's access to financial
resources. The IMF itself is funded through quotas paid by members.
Currently the IMF has approximately 175 members.

The IMF came into being as a result of the **Bretton Woods** meeting
and together with the **World Bank** it helps supervise the exchange rate
system. There was an abrupt change of policy in the early 1970s when it
became increasingly difficult to regulate fixed exchange rates. As a
result, the IMF is now more concerned with its members' economic policies. During the 1980s it became involved in trying to deal with the
foreign debt crisis of many of the developing countries. During the
1990s it was engaged in trying to deal with the innumerable **currency
crises**.

Many commentators believe that the IMF has outlived its usefulness
and should now be abolished, whilst others believe that it should simply
become a lender of last resort.

www.imf.org

International monetary system

The international monetary system used to be based on the concept of
pegging currencies to the value of gold. This was known as the **gold
standard** and guaranteed that a currency could be converted into gold.
During the 1930s the system of the gold standard broke down and many
currencies were devalued. In 1944, however, the **Bretton Woods**
system set fixed exchange rates, with the $US (still pegged to the gold
standard) being at the centre of this new system, in as much as every
other currency was pegged to its value. Significant changes in exchange
rates were only allowed provided the **International Monetary Fund**
agreed. At that time the IMF's main purpose was to maintain order in the

international monetary system by effectively disallowing the competitive devaluations which had been seen in the 1930s, and to impose monetary discipline on countries in order to control price inflation. Also at that time the IMF provided loans to countries to bail out their currency on the **foreign exchange market**, primarily in situations where there had been widespread **currency speculation**. Loans were also available in order to rebalance a fundamentally unbalanced **balance of payments**.

The fixed exchange rate system effectively collapsed in 1973. There were two main reasons for this: first there was a huge **balance of trade** deficit in the US, and secondly, as a result of the rise in inflation in the US, there was enormous speculative pressure on the dollar. Since that time the **fixed exchange rate** system has been replaced by a **floating exchange rate** regime. As a result, exchange rates fluctuate far more violently. However, the floating exchange rates give many countries more control over their own monetary policy and it also helps smooth out imbalances in trade. Fixed exchange rates, on the other hand, imposed a strong monetary discipline on each of the countries, whereas floating exchange rates are very vulnerable to currency speculation.

The argument with regard to international trade and investment is that the potential volatility of floating exchange rates makes overseas investment far more risky. Most countries have adopted a form of floating exchange rate, whilst others have pegged their currency to what they perceive to be a strong currency, such as the US dollar. In order to work around the potential volatility of exchange rates, many international businesses have chosen to build in their own strategic flexibility by dispersing their production and other operations around the world. This has been an important side effect and has undoubtedly contributed to widespread **foreign direct investment** in a number of countries which would otherwise have been overlooked.

www.imf.org

International Organization for Standardization (ISO)

The International Organization for Standardization (ISO) is the source of **ISO 9000** and over 14,000 international standards designed for business, government and society in general. The ISO is, in fact, a network of some 147 national standards institutes from various countries around the world, who work in partnership with international businesses, governments and consumer organizations. The ISO is a non-governmental, worldwide federation, which was established in 1947.

www.iso.org

International Petroleum Exchange (IPE)

The International Petroleum Exchange is Europe's most important energy futures and options exchange, trading $2 billion each day. The IPE was founded in 1980, and was initially concerned with the trading of gas oil futures, since when it has been extended to deal with other forms of energy, including natural gas.

www.ipe.uk.com

International strategy

Whilst strategy can be defined as being actions which the management of a business takes in order to meet the objectives of the organization, international strategy requires a more complicated and holistic view. International businesses which operate in different countries need to be aware of national differences, in terms both of the markets in which they operate and of the potential advantages and disadvantages of establishing operations in those countries. They will often make a judgement as to the various factors which can affect the performance of their activity in any given country. In each specific nation the strategy needs to be adapted in order to match the different location economies.

One specific strategy could be the production or the offering of standardized products, but ultimately international expansion requires a business to attain specific competences in relation to each market. Multinational organizations can have a considerable advantage if they set up foreign subsidiaries and use the skills inherent in the marketplace in pursuit of their global strategy and objectives. Businesses will often look to find areas in which they can reduce costs and produce specific commodities where price is the main competitive weapon. Part of the success of a strategy revolves around being locally responsive and reflecting consumer tastes and preferences whilst working within the peculiarities of an overseas nation's infrastructure and mirroring their traditional practices, using their distribution channels and being cognizant of the host government's policies and regulations.

Many multinational businesses will also consider that an integral part of their international strategy is the transference of skills and products into foreign markets which have been customized for local consumption. This means that the strategy aimed at customizing their products must include their overall business strategy in relation to that nation and the framing of appropriate marketing strategies.

International businesses no longer consider simply replicating their domestic strategy in overseas markets. Indeed, to remain competitive and successful, they adopt a trans-national strategy which focuses upon cost reduction, the transference of skills and products, and stimulating local responsiveness.

Stonehouse, George, Hamill, Jim, Campbell, David and Purdie, Tony, *Global and Trans-national Business: Strategy and Management*. New York: John Wiley, 2000.

International trade

The term 'international trade' is usually used as a means of introducing the various theories with regard to worldwide business transactions. In essence, there are some six different ways of approaching the concept of international trade in theoretical terms:

- The theory of **comparative advantage** suggests that different nations' productivity differences are crucial, in as much as particular countries specialize in producing products which they can manufacture in the most efficient manner. They then buy products which they can produce relatively less efficiently. The theory also suggests that each time a new country is opened to **free trade**, there is a stimulation of worldwide economic growth; in other words, dynamic gains are created from the trade.
- The **Heckscher–Ohlin Theory** suggests that each country has important **factor endowments** and as a result will tend to export products which make use of factors that are abundant there. It will import products that make use of factors which are locally scarce.
- The **product life cycle theory** suggests that of vital importance is where new products are introduced. The suggestion is that products need to gain a general acceptance in the market into which they have been introduced before they can be rolled out to other countries. With the development of a more integrated global economy, this has become a less valuable means by which to look at international trade.
- The new trade theory suggests that the two most important factors are increasing returns on specialization and **first-mover advantage**. The suggestion is that if a particular industry can obtain substantial **economies of scale**, then only a handful of businesses will be able to exist comfortably in any given market. The theory also suggests that businesses which have moved into a particular market and have been the first to produce a specific product will be able to dominate the market simply because they were first and can protect their **market share** from a position of strength.
- **Michael Porter**'s theory of national competitive advantage

suggests that the two key factors of the new trade theory are, indeed, important, but only in respect of the four key attributes he ascribes to each nation. These are factor endowments, domestic demand conditions, related and supporting industries and the business's strategy, structure and rivalries.

- The theory of **absolute advantage** suggests that countries differ in their ability to produce different goods. It goes on to suggest that each country should specialize in producing and exporting goods for which it has an absolute advantage and not bother to compete with other countries that have absolute advantages for other products, in which case it should import these.

The various theories of international trade are of vital importance to international businesses as they can provide useful pointers as to how to frame their strategies and decide exactly where to locate either their production facilities or strategic alliances.

International Trade Administration

International Trade Administration is a portal for information about international trade.

www.ita.doc.gov

International Trade Commission

The International Trade Commission is an independent US government agency which is primarily concerned with the impact of imports on US industries. It is also concerned with taking actions against unfair trade practices, particularly **intellectual property rights** violations. The International Trade Commission was formerly known as the US Tariff Commission before its range of responsibilities was increased and codified by the US Trade Act (1974). The commission, operating through six commissioners, reviews **countervailing duties** and **anti-dumping** petitions submitted by US industries.

www.usitc.gov

Invisibles

'Invisibles' is a generic term used to describe non-merchandise trade. Invisibles therefore include trading in services, investments, freight costs and insurance.

Islamic Development Bank

The Islamic Development Bank, or the IsDB, was created in 1973 and began operations in 1975. Its primary aim is to provide equity capital and grant loans for projects, and to provide financial assistance to its member countries in the form of economic and social development. It has a membership of some 54 countries, all of which are members of the Islamic Conference. Each country pays a contribution to the capital of the bank, which is currently some 6 billion Islamic Dinars. The bank's main offices are situated in Jeddah, Saudi Arabia, although it has regional offices in Morocco, Malaysia and Kazakhstan.

www.isdb.org

ISO 9000

This is a certification standard which was created by the **International Organization for Standardization** (1987). ISO 9000 plays a major part in establishing the documentation standards for global manufacturers.

The standards are recognized in many countries around the world, and ISO standards can be summarized as being an externally driven methodology which aims to persuade organizations to 'document what you do – and do what you document'.

As far as many countries are concerned, the ISO standards are seen as only seeking to bar them from markets (notably Europe), whilst others see the system as being a benchmarking process by which overseas business can aspire to match the best standards of the leading European and North American organizations.

The latest versions of the ISO 9000 importantly focus on ongoing improvements rather than striving for a specified goal and then remaining there.

www.iso.ch

ISO 9002

ISO 9002:1994, together with ISO 9001:1994 and ISO 9003:1994, have all been replaced by ISO 9001:2000. The original ISO 9002 pertained to quality and management systems.

www.iso.ch

ISO 14001

ISO 14001 contains certification standards created by the **International Organization for Standardization** that are related to environmental impacts of business. The standards require organizations to have an environmental management system as a driver to formulate a policy (and objectives) on their environmental impacts. The standards also require the organization to take into account any relevant legislative requirements derived from countries and/or areas in which the organization operates.

The certification is reliant on the organization effectively controlling the environmental aspects over which it can reasonably be expected to have a degree of control.

www.iso.ch

J curve

The j curve is a phenomenon related to the **current account**. A current account may initially worsen before it improves in response to a depreciation in exchange rates, as it takes time for the growth of imports to decline in response to higher import prices. This phenomenon is known as the j curve effect as the downward movement is followed by an upward movement which resembles the letter 'j'. It is, in effect, the shape of the trend of a country's trade balance following devaluation. Initially the lower exchange rates mean cheaper exports and more expensive imports; this makes the current account worse. After a period of time, however, the volume of exports will start to rise because of their lower price to foreign buyers. Domestic consumers will simultaneously buy fewer of the costlier imports. In due course the trade balance will improve compared with how it was before the devaluation.

In cases where there is a currency appreciation, an inverted j curve effect may be the outcome.

Joint venture

A joint venture implies a long-term agreement by two or more separate business entities to cooperate and jointly control a separate business entity. Typically, a joint venture would involve a manufacturer and, perhaps, a distributor, in developing a new business venture which affords both parties the potential for profit and a more secure share of the market. A contractual arrangement, setting out the terms of the joint venture, forms the basis of the association between the two separate founding businesses.

The term 'joint venture' is also applicable to international business deals which see collaboration between organizations based in two different countries. Both will contribute to the new business enterprise, in which, in one way or another, ownership and control is shared.

Joint ventures may be characterized as being either populated or unpopulated. A populated joint venture is a legally independent business, with its own management and staff. An unpopulated joint venture is one which is typified by the concept of a shell company in which the partner companies temporarily loan their management and staff to the joint venture.

Vermeulen, Erik, *The Evolution of Legal Business Forms in Europe and the United States: Venture Capital, Joint Venture and Partnership Structures.* New York: Kluwer Law International, 2003.

Jurisdiction

'Jurisdiction' refers to a geographical area in which a specific country has legislative control. In other words, the country's laws are applicable to the formation of businesses, their management and their taxation. In effect there are two different forms of jurisdiction:

- An offshore or location jurisdiction is a special area within a country, in which the legislation is geared towards international business rather than being concerned directly with the domestic business of the country. In these areas both legislation and taxation are more favourable to companies who are located there.
- An onshore jurisdiction is a normal state of affairs where the legislation pertaining to businesses is geared towards the domestic economy. In most cases the legislation and taxation is less favourable than in offshore jurisdictions.

Just-in-time (JIT)

JIT is a philosophy which was developed in Japan, emphasizing the importance of deliveries in relation to the processing of small lot-sizes. The philosophy emphasizes the importance of set-up cost reduction, small lot-sizes, pull systems, level production and importantly, the elimination of waste (*muda*).

JIT is designed to allow the achievement of high-volume production, whilst ensuring that minimal inventories of raw materials, work-in-process and finished goods are held by the business. Parts arrive at the manufacturing plant from suppliers, just in time to be placed into the manufacturing process, and as the products progress along the line they arrive at the next work station just in time, thereby moving through the whole system very quickly.

JIT relies on the management ensuring that manufacturing waste is kept to a minimum and that nothing is made or brought onto the premises that is not immediately required. JIT requires precision as the right part needs to be in the right place at the right time. Waste is described as being the results from any activity that adds cost without adding value (which includes moving and storing).

JIT is also known as 'lean production' or 'stockless production' and the theory is that it should improve profits and the returns on investment by the following means:

- reducing inventory levels;
- increasing the inventory turnover rate;
- improving product quality;
- reducing production and delivery lead times;
- reducing other costs (machine set-ups and equipment breakdown).

JIT also recognizes that any under-utilized capacity can be used to build up a small stock of products or components (buffer inventories) in order to ensure that in the event of a problem the production process will not be interrupted.

JIT is primarily used in manufacturing processes which are repetitive in nature and where the same products and components are used and produced in relatively high volumes. Once the flow has been set up, there should be a steady and even flow of materials, components and finished products passing through the facility. Each work station is linked in a similar way to an assembly line (although the exact layout may be a jobbing or batch process layout). The goal is to eliminate queuing and to achieve the ideal lot-size per unit of production.

Delbridge, Rick, *Life on the Line in Contemporary Manufacturing: The Workplace Experience of Lean Production and the 'Japanese' Model.* Oxford: Oxford University Press, 2000.
Gross, John M. and McInnis, Kenneth R., *Kanban Made Simple: Demystifying and Applying Toyota's Legendary Manufacturing Process.* New York: Amacom, 2003.

J

Keidanren

Keidanren was established in 1946 in the aftermath of the Second World War, which had devastated the Japanese economy. Two years later *Nikkeiren* was created as an umbrella organization of employers' associations designed to create good labour and management relations.

Keidanren, or the Japanese Federation of Economic Organizations, is a non-profit-making economic organization which represents various branches of the Japanese economy. It has been involved in the promotion of Japan's economic development through liberalizing trade, enhancing competition, demanding administrative and fiscal reforms and tackling environmental issues. Its members are encouraged to adhere to a Charter of Corporate Behaviour and a Global Environment Charter, primarily to recover 'public confidences in businesses'.

www.keidanren.or.jp

Keiretsu

Keiretsu was formerly a unique Japanese type of corporate organization, but increasingly other countries have been moving towards this form of organizational typology.

The key aspect of a *keiretsu* is that a group or a family of affiliated trans-national organizations operate together (both vertically and horizontally) in an integrated manner. Importantly, the *keiretsu* has its own trading entities and banks, thereby allowing it to control each part of the economic chain in a major industrial or service-based sector.

Therefore, not only can a *keiretsu* research and develop a technology and products, but it can also plan the production, secure the finance, cover the insurance implications and then find the resources (wherever they are) in order to process them. The purpose of the exercise is to maintain control and production in Japan, where the resources will be turned into finished products, packaged and then distributed across the world.

Keiretsu use **just-in-time (JIT)** and specific forms of supply-chain management:

- They apply pressure to suppliers to reduce price.
- They encourage supplier involvement in *kaizen*.
- They involve suppliers at the earliest stage of the development of new products, in as much as they ask for comment on designs and do not merely supply the designs prior to commencement of production.
- They commit suppliers to the notion that they will only supply quality parts and components.
- They use a two-vendor policy, a means of ensuring that suppliers remain competitive as they risk losing a portion or all of their contracts to the better supplier.
- They encourage suppliers to use just-in-time.
- They use a monthly master schedule using *kanban* as a signal for the adjustment of this schedule.
- They are committed to a levelled production.

Burt, David, *American Keiretsu: A Strategic Weapon for Global Competitiveness*. Boston, MA: Irwin Professional, 1993.

Miyashita, Kenichi and Russell, David, *Keiretsu: Inside the Hidden Japanese Conglomerates*. New York: McGraw-Hill Education, 1993.

Kyoto Convention

See **International Convention on the Simplification and Harmonization of Customs Procedures.**

K

Lag strategy

Based on the premise that capacity expansion can either lead demand, lag behind demand, or meet average demand, a capacity lag strategy is said to produce a higher return on investment. Although it can lose customers in the process, it is used in many industries which have standard products and weak competition.

A capacity lead strategy, on the other hand, is used to take customers away from competitors on the basis that competitors have capacity constraints. Average capacity strategy is used when a business knows that it will be able to sell at least the majority of any additional output. The ideal solution is to consider an incremental expansion of capacity, which offers less risk but can potentially be more expensive.

In essence, a lag strategy seeks to satisfy demand for products once the increased demand has already been created.

Late-mover advantage

The concept of the late-mover advantage suggests that businesses that enter a market late have a competitive advantage. This is based on the assumption that not only can late movers replicate the technological advances of businesses that have already entered the market, but they can also reduce risk by not only waiting until the market is established, but ensuring that they do not make the same mistakes as are made by the existing businesses.

The late-mover advantage also suggests that consumers will already be familiar with the product and that there is less resistance, or misunderstanding, regarding the late-mover business's products.

See also **first-mover advantage**.

Law of one price

The law of one price is a theory which suggests that in competitive markets which are relatively free of transportation costs and **trade**

barriers, identical products which are sold in different countries must sell for broadly the same price when that price is expressed in the same currency. The law of one price (LOOP) is also based on the idea of perfect goods **arbitrage**. This takes places when commodity arbitrages exploit price differences to make a risk-less profit.

See also **purchase power parity**.

Jain, Arvind, *Commodity Futures Markets and the Law of One Price*. Ann Arbor, MI: University of Michigan Press, 1980.

Lead market

A lead market is either a home or an overseas market in which products or services are first introduced. In many respects international businesses will seek to identify any problems related to the production, distribution and marketing of particular products and services in this lead market before they are rolled out to other markets. By making careful adjustments to the strategies which were employed in the lead market, the international business should be able to make amendments to the ways in which it performs certain aspects of its operations to match the peculiarities or requirements of other markets.

McDonald, Malcolm, Christopher, Martin, Knox, Simon and Payne, Adrian, *Creating a Company for Customers: How to Build and Lead a Market Driven Organisation*. London: Financial Times, Prentice-Hall, 2000.

Lead strategy

Lead strategy involves the collection of foreign currency receivables before they are due in cases where that foreign currency is expected to depreciate. It also involves the paying of foreign currency payables before they are due when a currency is expected to appreciate.

Lean production

Lean production/manufacturing is an approach based on the Toyota Production system. An organization takes a number of steps to assist in ensuring that its manufacturing activities focus on five key concepts:

- Value centred on customer needs by creating activities as and when customers demand them.
- Value creation – which occurs along a series of steps and is known as the 'value stream'. This is achieved through a closely synchronized flow of the organization's activities.

● Continually making improvements within the production process in order to maintain customer service and strive for perfection.

Central to an organization adopting the lean production/manufacturing approach is the question of waste reduction and a high level of engagement of all company personnel in implementing and improving the manufacturing process.

The benefits available to an organization adopting the lean production/manufacturing process are high. It is claimed that organizations have achieved benefits of 80% reduction in cycle time, 50% reduction in lead times, 50% reduction in the levels of their inventory, and an increase in customer response rates, as well as an increase in quality.

Lean Enterprise Institute www.lean.org/

Learning effects

'Learning effects' refers to cost savings which are achieved as an international business moves along an **experience curve**. By continuing to operate and learn from their experiences, businesses will be able to make considerable cost savings by adjusting their operating procedures.

Legal risk

A legal risk in international business terms is considered to be the likelihood that an overseas trading partner will opportunistically break a contract. It can also refer to situations where a trading partner may take the opportunity to seize **intellectual property rights** and profit from them without reference to the owner of that intellectual property.

Leontief paradox

The Leontief paradox seems to prove the exact opposite of the **Heckscher–Ohlin Theory** as it suggests that US exports are less capital-intensive than US imports. The Russian-born US economist Wassily Leontief, who won the Nobel Prize for Economics in 1973, suggested that the US was relatively replete with capital compared with many other nations. He therefore assumed that the US should be an exporter of capital-intensive goods and an importer of labour-intensive goods. His findings, however, discovered the reverse, in as much as US exports were less capital-intensive than US imports. This became known as the Leontief paradox.

Possible explanations include the fact that the US may have a special advantage in producing new products with innovative technology. These products are less capital-intensive than other products whose technology makes them more suitable for mass production. The US, therefore, exports goods which have used skilled labour and innovation, whilst importing goods which have used large amounts of capital. A prime example of this would be the US exportation of commercial aircraft, as the country is more efficient at producing aircraft than many other nations. On the other hand, the US imports vast numbers of automobiles, which are capital-intensive products, leading to the assumption that the US is not as suited to automobile manufacture as some other nations.

Lesser developed country

A lesser developed country is a country which has a low **gross domestic product** per capita and usually has a comparatively poorly developed infrastructure. These countries, therefore, rely more heavily on primary industries, such as agriculture, fishing, forestry and mining. Lesser developed countries can be differentiated from the three other broad definitions of the development of specific nations, which are:

- *Early developed countries* – which have a primary industry base with a developing secondary industrial sector. They have a low, but growing, gross domestic product and a developing infrastructure.
- *Semi-developed countries* – these countries have a significant secondary industrial sector, with rising levels of education and affluence and, perhaps, the emergence of what could be described as a middle class. Their infrastructure is quite well, but not fully, developed.
- *Fully developed countries* – in these countries the primary sector of industry accounts for very little of the country's gross domestic product. The secondary sector is still strong, but the big earner for the country is the service centre. These countries have a highly sophisticated infrastructure.

Letter of credit

A letter of credit is issued by a buyer's bank in favour of a seller. It undertakes to pay an agreed amount of money on receipt, by the bank, of conforming documents within a specified period of time. An irrevocable letter of credit is issued in cases where the issuing bank waives the rights to cancel or amend the payment without the consent of the seller. A confirmed irrevocable letter of credit involves the added responsibility of a bank other than the issuing bank. A revocable letter of credit allows the issuing bank to cancel or amend part of the amount owing.

A typical letter of credit transaction, using an irrevocable letter of credit, would be carried out as follows:

- Once the buyer and seller agree on the terms of a sale the buyer arranges for its bank to open a letter of credit which specifies the documents required for payment.
- The buyer's bank issues or opens an irrevocable letter of credit, including all instructions to the seller relating to the shipment.
- The buyer's bank sends its irrevocable letter of credit to the seller's bank and requests confirmation.
- The seller's bank then prepares a letter of confirmation, which is forwarded to the exporter, along with the irrevocable letter of credit.
- The exporter then checks the letter of credit and, if relevant, contacts a **freight forwarder** and confirms shipping dates. If the exporter has a problem with any of the conditions on the letter of credit at this stage, the buyer is contacted.
- The exporter then arranges for the delivery of the goods to the appropriate port.
- Once the goods are loaded, the freight forwarder completes the necessary documentation.
- The exporter, or the freight forwarder acting for the exporter, presents the documents which prove compliance with the terms of the letter of credit, to their bank.
- The bank then reviews the documents. If everything is in order these are then sent to the buyer's bank for review.
- The buyer then uses the documents at their end to claim the goods.
- A draft, which would accompany the letter of credit, is then paid by the buyer's bank to the exporter's bank.

L

Leveraged buy-out

Leveraged buy-outs are an alternative means by which a business can seek to acquire another company. The business which is buying another company borrows money to pay for the majority of the purchase price. The debt which has been incurred is secured against the assets of the business being purchased. Interest payable on the loan will be paid from the acquired company's future cash flow.

During the 1980s leveraged buy-outs became very much a trend and businesses were able to raise loans of millions of dollars to purchase other businesses, which were often unwilling to sell. Many of these purchases ended in disaster, with the borrowers being declared bank-rupt, as they could not meet the interest demands. However, many other businesses recognized that once having purchased another business on this basis they would need to run the acquired business far more effi-ciently than the previous owners in order to ensure that sufficient funds were available to pay the interest.

Theoretically, of course, leveraged buy-outs can be, and are, used by international businesses to acquire overseas companies. In practice the approach is dependent upon the prevailing regulations which apply to different nations.

Levitt, Theodore

In 1983 Theodore Levitt of the Harvard Business School wrote an article which suggested the gradual emergence of **globalization**. Bearing in mind that he was writing some 20 years ago, when there were only feint glimpses of what new technology, and in particular, communications, could do to international trade, he prophesied many of the global trends which have since taken place.

Levitt suggested that the global media and the reduced cost of communication would lead to a convergence of consumer tastes across the world, which would, in effect, create a global market for **standard-ized** products. It should be remembered that in 1983 around 30 per cent of the world's population lived in Communist countries, but by the 1990s Levitt's predictions of global brands dominating the world economy seemed to have begun, notably with McDonald's, Coca-Cola and Walt Disney dominating the world marketplace.

Levitt did not predict that technology would actually change produc-tion itself, which in turn would allow international businesses to offer consumers a broad choice; in effect they would be able to offer special-ized rather than standardized products. Increasingly, large multination-als, having achieved global dominance, have begun to adapt their standardized products for local tastes.

L

Levitt, Theodore, 'The Globalization of Markets', *Harvard Business Review*, 61(3) (May–June 1983), pp. 92–102.

Licensing

Licensing involves giving either legal or official permission for a third party to use, or own, the intellectual property of another business. This could include trademarks, technology, or the understanding of how to deliver a specific service. Innumerable international licensing agreements exist between businesses in different countries, all of which are subject to laws applicable in each country, which often differ in terms of their enforcement and the rights and liabilities of the parties which have entered into the agreement. In effect, licensing is a business arrangement by which a manufacturer or owner of a product can grant permission to another business, or individual, to manufacture a product or offer a service (sometimes making use of proprietary material) in return for a payment, often in the form of royalties.

Limited international bidding

Limited international bidding (LIB) is a procurement method which is used for **World Bank** financing. It is used in situations where either there is an urgent need, or there are few suppliers, and, in some cases, for small purchases. Contractors or suppliers are invited to participate in the bidding process, rather than the offer being advertised.

> See also **International Business Opportunities Service, international competitive bidding, local competitive bidding.**

> www.worldbank.org

Link contract

A link contract is a document which links the import and export components of a **counter-trade** transaction. The link contract specifies the supplier's commitment to purchase, or cause to be purchased, products and services which are designated by the buyer. It usually includes penalties and procedures in cases of non-compliance. The link contract is also known as a 'letter of undertaking', or a 'counter-trade contract'.

Lloyds of London

Lloyds of London provides services to the insurance market and is active in over 120 countries. Lloyds is the second largest commercial insurer and the sixth largest reinsurance group in the world. In 2003 Lloyds accepted insurance premiums of £14.4 billion. Some 71 syndicates underwrite the insurance at Lloyds and 150 brokerage companies operate there. Lloyds offers insurance for specific risks, including 96 per cent of the FTSE 100 companies and 93 per cent of the Dow Jones Industrial Average companies.

> www.lloyds.com

Local competitive bidding (LCB)

Local competitive bidding is a procurement methodology required by the **World Bank** financing. LCB tends to be used for a contract which involves the following:

- labour-intensive activities;
- small-value projects;
- locally available products or services which are priced lower than those on the world market;
- intermittent work;
- work which needs to be carried out at various different sites.

The competitive bidding process is primarily aimed at domestic businesses, although overseas bidders can participate; but the bid offers are only advertised locally.

See also **International Business Opportunities Service, limited international bidding, international competitive bidding.**

www.worldbank.org

Local content requirement

A local content requirement (LCR) is a requirement that a specified amount of a particular product is produced in the domestic market. This is often imposed in order to reap the benefits of employment and technology transfers into developing countries. LCR policy requires that a multinational business uses a proportion of locally made parts or components, thus employing directly, or indirectly, the local workforce or industries. In order to maintain the quality of the multinational's final products, it is also necessary for the multinational business to transfer some technology to the local industries. LCR has become an integral part of many countries' regulation of **foreign direct investment**.

LCR policy does push up the cost of production for multinational businesses, as parts or components which are produced in the domestic market are often of lower quality and higher cost. The relative cost increase for more efficient multinational businesses is higher than the increase in costs for less efficient multinational businesses.

As a result of LCR, the more efficient multinational organizations choose to export, whilst less efficient ones choose foreign direct investment. Given that multinational businesses may choose the foreign direct investment mode, LCR policy allows the **host country** to capture the full benefits of employment and technology transfers.

L

Whilst LCR policy adversely affects the consumer surplus, it raises the cost of production.

Lahiri, Sajal and Ono, Yoshiyashu, 'Foreign Direct Investment, Local Content Requirement and Profit Taxation', *Economic Journal*, 1998, pp. 444–57.

Location economies

Location economies are essentially cost advantages which an international business may enjoy by carrying out value-creation activities in optimal locations. In terms of international business, 'location economies' refers to specific countries which may have a particular blend of **factor endowments** which make a particular form of production, or business operation, more attractive in that region than in other areas of the world.

Location-specific advantages

Location-specific advantages differ from **location economies** in as much as they are a blend of the **factor endowments** of a particular foreign location, combined with an international business's own unique assets. The combination of the two aspects, which, as far as the international business is concerned, would include their technological abilities, marketing expertise and management experience, often proves that the sum total of the two sets of advantages is more than the sum of the parts independently.

Lal, Deepak, *Unintended Consequences: The Impact of Factor Endowments, Culture and Politics on Long-Run Economic Performance.* Cambridge, MA: MIT Press, 1998.

Logistics

Logistics incorporates the planning and control of all materials and products across the entire production and supply-chain system. Logistics is, in effect, a managerial function which deals with the flow of materials, including the purchasing, shipping and distribution issues before, during and after the completion of the finished product.

In international business, logistics can be far more complex as it may require particular elements which will be needed in the manufacture of products to be coordinated regarding shipment and delivery from various parts of the world. Increasingly, raw materials and components are sourced from overseas locations and delivered either to a single nation, or a series of manufacturers within a multinational, for onward processing. Logistics therefore includes the shipment of raw materials, components, finished goods, machinery, packaging materials and innumerable other inputs into a manufacturing and packaging service.

Clearly it is advantageous for multinational businesses to reduce the movement of heavy or bulky raw materials and components, but often the associated transportation costs are offset by the fact that these materials can be sourced at radically lower prices then could be achieved in the domestic market. This means that the logistical task of multinationals has become increasingly complex, particularly in cases where the business has chosen to locate parts of its manufacturing process across the world. Increasingly, multinationals have sought to acquire businesses which had hitherto been their suppliers, in order to have a firmer grasp and control of the logistics chain.

Christopher, Martin, *Logistics and Supply Chain Management.* London: Financial Times, Prentice-Hall, 1999.

Lomé Convention

The Lomé Convention was a product of European de-colonization of Africa. In the Second World War period, the former colonial powers, notably Britain, France and Belgium, desired to continue their relationships with the newly independent countries. They also wanted to ensure that trade between these countries continued. In 1957 France had already signed an agreement with its former African colonies. The Lomé Convention was signed in 1975 and linked aid with trade concessions. During that time the former colonies were given preferred access into Europe for their raw materials in return for aid. Indeed, the aid programme set up two stabilization funds, one to ensure agricultural exports and the other for mineral exports.

The agreement covered 71 African, Caribbean and Pacific countries and between 1981 and 1999 it was amended (Lomé II, Lomé III and Lomé IV). In 1993, however, the **European Union** introduced preferential imports for bananas from former French and British colonies (which effectively gave them 30% of the market). This agreement was challenged by the US in the **World Trade Organization** and it was finally agreed that the arrangement would be phased out over a 15-year period.

Under the terms of the Lomé Convention, however, many of the countries involved have found that they have been left behind as the global world trade has developed. A new agreement, known as the Cotonou Agreement, covers the period 2000 to 2007. Effectively it replaces the Lomé Convention and is a new trade and aid agreement between the European Union and 71 developing countries. The new deal transforms the systems of trade and cooperation pacts. Many of the poorer states will continue to have free access to European markets. In addition to this there will be regional **free trade agreements** between the European Union and some of the more developed nations amongst the 71.

The European Union has undertaken to provide some 20 billion euros, provided the nations uphold their basic principles of good governance.

London Club

The London Club came into existence during the early 1980s and is essentially a cartel of commercial banks. Its primary function is the rescheduling of debt. In many respects the **Bank Advisory Committee** has replaced the London Club.

See also **Paris Club.**

London International Financial Futures and Options Exchange (LIFFE)

In 2002 LIFFE was purchased by Euronext. It has evolved into an electronic trading exchange, currently dealing with over £550 billion worth of business. Each day some £4,000 billion is traded in the London markets. LIFFE provides a central exchange for investment and risk transfer. The LIFFE system allows traders to participate in around 60 cities in the world.

www.liffe.com

L

Maastricht Treaty

The Maastricht Treaty, named after the Dutch town in which it was signed, is also known as the Treaty of the **European Union**. In effect, the Maastricht Treaty created the European Union in the following way:

- It committed the then 12 member states of the European Economic Community to European monetary union and political union.
- It introduced a single currency, then known as the European Currency Unit or **Ecu** (which has since been replaced by the **Euro**).
- It established a European system of **central banks**.
- It created the **European Central Bank**.
- It broadened integration by including common foreign and security policies and cooperation in justice and home affairs.

The treaty itself, which was negotiated during 1991, was signed in February 1992, coming into force on 1 November 1993.

The Maastricht Treaty saw European monetary union as moving forward in three distinct phases. These were:

1 The ratification of treaty amendments which were required to establish the European monetary union, and the participation of the 12 states in the **Exchange Rate Mechanism** (it was suggested that this would last until 1 January 1994).
2 The establishment of a **European Monetary Institute** in order to support the single currency, and the creation of the European Central Bank (this was to be completed by 1 January 1999).
3 The fixing of irrevocable exchange rates and the transfer of powers to the European Central Bank (to be begun by 1 January 1999).

The Maastricht Treaty was the blueprint for what was to become the most fundamental change in Europe for centuries. Not only did it call for economic and monetary union, the creation of a single currency and the convergence of economic policy, but it also introduced the integration of employment and social issues. At the same time it introduced the concept of subsidiarity, which states that the European Union will not take action unless it would be more effective than action taken either at local, regional or national level.

www.europa.eu.int/en/record/mt/top.html

Maker

A maker is an individual or a business which initiates a draft **bill of lading**.

Managed-float system

A managed-float system is a system in which the exchange rates between various currencies are determined purely by supply and demand. Literally, those currencies are allowed to float freely, whereas other currencies may be pegged to another currency, or managed by government intervention. Even in a managed-float system, governments may sometimes intervene in order to prevent a currency's value from radically changing.

Market forces can drive up the value of one particular currency and drive down the value of another currency in relation to the first currency. These fluctuations are of considerable concern for international businesses, since it is in the inherent nature of international business that its transactions require the conversion of funds from one currency to another. Indeed, considerable fluctuations within a managed-float system over a relatively short period of time can adversely affect the profitability of any given business transaction. International businesses, therefore, will seek the best means by which they can avoid any detrimental impacts that exchange rate volatility may present, whilst looking for opportunities to make an additional profit from a positive move in an exchange rate.

M Management network

A management network is simply a series of informal contacts and channels of communication between individual managers in a multi-national organization.

Market

'Market' is a generic term which is used to describe a group of potential customers who have similar needs. These potential customers are willing to purchase various products and services in order to satisfy their needs. The term 'market' can be used to describe both consumers and other businesses, either as specific segments or target audiences, whether they are part of a population in a given country, or more widely spread across the world. The term can equally be applied, therefore, to UK home-owners and to airline operators. Both are markets: one is focused primarily in a single country, with specific criteria; the other is a more global target, which includes operators, large and small, often located in other countries.

Market economy

A market economy is a decentralized, flexible, essentially practical, but changeable environment in which businesses can operate. A market economy is based on the assumption that consumers can choose between competing products and services, whilst simultaneously there is freedom for businesses to begin, or expand, their operations and take responsibility for their own risks and rewards.

In essence, market economies are deemed to be the assertion of freedom, risk and opportunity and are typified by political democracies. Market economies are not without their own abuses and iniquities, but theoretically consumers play an important role in the overall working of a market economy. While consumers have limited budgets, they have to make careful considerations as to which products and services they will purchase. Businesses, meanwhile, depend on being able to satisfy customers by producing products and services which they wish to purchase. Businesses must also get the greatest value of outputs from their inputs in order to be profitable. In a market economy, if a business does not keep its production costs down it will have to charge higher prices for its products. This is against a backdrop of other businesses producing goods of similar quality but being able to sell them at a lower price because their costs are lower. Theoretically, at least, consumers then benefit from this competition between businesses; the higher the degree of competition, the lower the prices. Therefore consumers can actually purchase more and stay within their budget.

International trade makes a vital contribution to this productivity and prosperity as businesses not only need to be aware of domestic competitors, but also need to consider overseas competitors, who may be operating in completely different sets of circumstances. Undoubtedly, wage costs in certain countries are considerably lower, which is one part of the equation in being able to drive down relative costs and thus offer products and services at lower prices. High-wage industries, assuming that they have equivalent competitors in lower-wage countries under the market economy model, are under considerable threat.

M

One primary means by which domestic businesses, no matter how uncompetitive they may be, are protected is via taxation on imported goods, or some form of restriction as to how much can be imported. By imposing **tariffs** or **quotas**, a country in effect protects its manufacturers and its workforce, but on the negative side, ensures that prices of products and services remain artificially high.

As far as employees are concerned, a market economy in theory should offer them opportunities in accordance with their education and expertise. In reality, however, the more competitive a specific market may be, the more demanding the businesses are with regard to employee productivity. Whilst businesses have to offer competitive terms of both employment and remuneration, they will also demand a minimum level of productivity and only the most productive can command the highest wages. Again in terms of international trade, businesses have to be able to compete successfully in order to export to foreign markets: both domestically and internationally they will then be able to offer more career opportunities. By exporting goods, they give consumers a wider choice of products at competitive prices, but this also means that in that overseas market domestic producers will demand ever-greater levels of productivity from their own employees. Theoretically, a series of countries all connected by market economies should continually drive up productivity, whilst ensuring that prices remain competitive. Each new addition in the form of a new nation adds to those competitive forces, whilst offering existing businesses within the market system more opportunities to sell their products.

If a market economy is so efficient, then why do governments often interfere? Historically it has been shown that market economies are periodically affected by rapidly rising price levels. At other times they have high unemployment or high inflation. Governments therefore step in to attempt to re-stabilize their economies by making either more or less money available in order to drive or retard the flow of money in the economy.

Gillingham, John, *European Integration, 1950–2003: Superstate or New Market Economy*. Cambridge: Cambridge University Press, 2003.

Market makers

Market makers are financial business services which connect potential investors and borrowers seeking finance. The financial service businesses either continue to act as intermediaries, or introduce the investor to the borrower so that the two parties can discuss the opportunities for the potential transfer of funds.

Market power

Market power exists when a single seller or buyer in a particular market has the ability to significantly influence the quantity of products or services which are being traded in that market. They may often be able to manipulate the prices at which those products and services are sold.

The market power situation can often occur when a single business has a **monopoly** in that market or is part of an **oligopoly**.

Market segmentation

Market segmentation involves the identification of specific target markets for broader-based products and services, in order to enable a business to develop a suitable **marketing mix** for each of its target segments.

Market segmentation probably came into existence in the 1950s when product differentiation was a primary marketing strategy. By the 1970s, however, market segmentation had begun to be seen as a means of increasing sales and obtaining a competitive advantage. In recent years more sophisticated techniques have been developed to reach potential buyers in ever more specific target markets.

Businesses will tend to segment the market for the following reasons:

- To make marketing easier in the sense that segmentation allows a business to address the needs of smaller groups of customers which have the same characteristics.
- To find niches, typically unserved or under-served markets, and be able to target these buyers in a less competitive environment.
- To increase efficiency in being able to apply resources directly towards the segments which have been identified by the business as being the best.

There are some common rules regarding market segmentation which determine whether the identified segments are significant enough or measurable. These are listed in Table 3.

In effect, there are two ways of segmenting a market. These are known as either *a priori* or *post hoc*. These two approaches are typified in the following manner:

- *A priori* segmentation is based on a mixture of intuition, the use of secondary data and analysis of existing customer database information. *A priori* segmentation takes place without the benefit of primary market research and may well produce relatively simplistic segmentation, such as male or female, young or old, regional segments or buyers and non-buyers.

M

Table 3   Market segmentation

Segmentation criteria	Description
Size	The market itself needs to be large enough to warrant segmentation. Once a market has been segmented, it may be revealed that each of the segments is too small to consider.
Differentiation	There must be measurable differences between the members of a segment and the market in general.
Responsiveness	Having segmented the market, marketing communications need to be developed to address the needs of each segment. If a business cannot develop marketing communications which can contact a segment and have an impact upon it, there is little value in knowing about the segment in the first place.
Reachability	Marketing communications need to be able to get through to the segments in order to be effective. There may well be a single best advertising medium or promotional device which can reach the individual segments and tell them the business's message.
Interest	Having established what benefits a segment is looking for, the business needs to be assured that this is precisely what the potential customers require and that the product or service matches these needs.
Profitability	A decision needs to be reached as to whether it is cost-effective to reach these segments, considering the cost which may be incurred in running multiple marketing programmes alongside one another. Existing products or services may need to be redesigned in order to match the specific needs of particular segments.

- *Post hoc* segmentation uses primary market research to classify and describe individuals within the target market, but segments are not defined themselves until after the collection and analysis period. The definition of each segment requires the placing of all members of the target market into specific segments.

There are a number of different types of information which are used extensively in market segmentation. These can be best described by category as in Table 4.

Table 4 Segmentation categories

Measured variable	Description
Classification	Broadly speaking, classification actually encompasses demographic, geographic, psychographic and behavioural variables. It requires a system of classifying individuals and placing them into segments by using a mixture of these variables.
Demographic	Demographic variables feature age, gender, income, ethnicity, marital status, education, occupation, household size, type of residence and length of residence, amongst many other demographically based measures.
Geographic	This broad range of variables includes population density, climate, zip or postcode, city, state or county, region, or metropolitan/rural area.
Psychographic	Another broad range of variables which include attitudes, hobbies, leadership traits, lifestyle, magazines and newspapers read, personality traits, risk aversion and television or radio programmes watched or listened to.
Behavioural	These variables encompass the current ways in which the target market views, buys and responds to products, services and marketing. The category includes brand loyalty, benefits sought, distribution channels used and level of use.
Descriptor	Descriptor variables actually describe each segment in order to distinguish it from other groups. The descriptors need to be measurable and are usually derived solely from primary research, rather than secondary sources of information. Descriptors will typically explain in shorthand the key characteristics of each segment and the members of that segment, so that these characteristics can be more readily exploited by subtle changes in the marketing mix. A descriptor variable may be featured as 'under 30, single, urban dweller, rented accommodation, medium to high income', etc.

Wedel, Michel and Kamakura, Wagner A., *Market Segmentation: Conceptual and Methodological Foundations*. New York: Kluwer Academic Publishers, 1999.

McDonald, Malcolm and Dunbar, Ian, *Market Segmentation*. Basingstoke: Palgrave Macmillan, 1998.

Market share

Sales figures do not necessarily indicate how a business is performing relative to its competitors. Changes in sales may simply reflect changes in the market size or changes in economic conditions. The business's performance relative to competitors can be measured by the proportion of the market that the firm is able to capture. This proportion is referred to as the business's market share and is calculated as follows:

Market share = Business's sales ÷ Total market sales

Sales may be determined on a value basis (sales price multiplied by volume) or on a unit basis (number of units shipped or number of customers served). While the business's own sales figures are readily available, total market sales are more difficult to determine. Usually, this information is available from trade associations and market research firms.

Market share is often associated with profitability and thus many businesses seek to increase their sales relative to competitors. Businesses may seek to increase their market share using the following:

- Economies of scale – higher volume can be instrumental in developing a cost advantage.
- Sales growth in a stagnant industry – when the industry is not growing, the business can still increase its sales by increasing its market share.
- Reputation – market leaders have power, which they can use to their advantage.
- Increased bargaining power – a larger market share gives an advantage in negotiations with suppliers and distributors.

The market share of a product can be modelled as:

Share of market = Share of preference × Share of voice × Share of distribution

According to this model, there are three drivers of market share:

- Share of preference – can be increased through product, pricing, and promotional changes.
- Share of voice – the business's proportion of total promotional expenditures in the market. Thus, share of voice can be increased by increasing advertising expenditures.
- Share of distribution – can be increased through more intensive distribution.

From these drivers market share can be increased by changing the variables of the **marketing mix**.

- Product – the product attributes can be changed to provide more value to the customer, for example, by improving product quality.
- Price – if the price of demand is elastic, a decrease in price will increase sales revenue. This tactic may not succeed if competitors are willing and able to meet any price cuts.
- Distribution – adding new distribution channels or increasing the intensity of distribution in each channel.
- Promotion – increasing advertising expenditures can increase market share, unless competitors respond with similar increases.

Miniter, Richard, *The Myth of Market Share*. London: Nicholas Brealey Publishing, 2002.

Marketing mix

The major marketing management decisions can be classified in one of the following seven categories:

- product
- price
- place (distribution)
- promotion
- physical evidence
- processes
- people

These variables are known as the marketing mix, or the 7 Ps of marketing. They are the variables that marketing managers can control in order to best satisfy customers in the target market. The marketing mix is portrayed in Figure 3.

The business attempts to generate a positive response in the target market by blending these seven marketing-mix variables in an optimal manner.

M

- *Product* – The product is the physical product or service offered to the consumer. In the case of physical tangible products, it also refers to any services or conveniences that are part of the offering. Product decisions include aspects such as function, appearance, packaging, service, warranty, etc.
- *Price* – Pricing decisions should take into account profit margins and the probable pricing response of competitors. Pricing includes not only the list price, but also discounts, financing, and other options such as leasing.

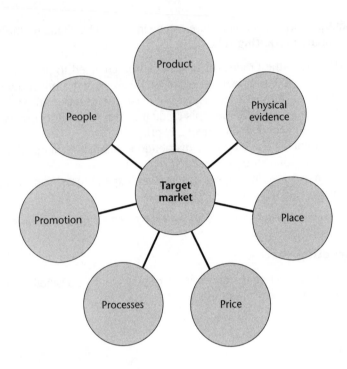

Figure 3 The 7 Ps of the marketing mix

- *Place* – Place (or placement) decisions are those associated with channels of distribution that serve as the means for getting the product to the target customers. The distribution system performs transactional, logistical, and facilitating functions. Distribution decisions include market coverage, channel-member selection, logistics, and levels of service.
- *Promotion* – Promotion decisions are those related to communicating and selling to potential consumers. Since these costs can be large in proportion to the product price, a breakeven analysis should be performed when making promotion decisions. It is useful to know the value of a customer in order to determine whether additional customers are worth the cost of acquiring them. Promotion decisions involve advertising, public relations, media types, sales promotions, exhibitions, word of mouth and direct marketing.

- *Physical evidence* – This is a relatively new element of the marketing mix, which focuses on the environment in which service is offered.
- *Processes* – This refers to the way in which services are actually delivered.
- *People* – This highlights the fact that the quality of many products and services relies on the quality of those who deliver them.

Arguably, there are more than seven elements within the marketing mix, which has developed considerably from the original 4 Ps. Other Ps could include periodicity, profitability and effectiveness, positioning, planning and performance of the organization.

Table 5 summarizes the marketing-mix decisions, including a list of some of the aspects of the original 4 Ps.

Table 5 Marketing mix variables

Product	Price	Place	Promotion
Functionality	List price	Channel members	Advertising
Appearance	Discounts	Channel motivation	Personal selling
Quality	Allowances	Market coverage	Public relations
Packaging	Financing	Locations	Sales promotion
Brand	Leasing options	Logistics	Exhibition
Warranty		Service levels	Word of mouth
Service/support			Direct marketing
Tangible			

Mass customization

Mass customization is an increasing trend and of considerable importance to manufacturers. Mass customization involves the production of mass-produced, standard products, with slight variations or customizations for particular market or customer segments. As the manufacturing process has developed technologically, and become more flexible, it is possible to produce these personalized products without having a detrimental effect on profit margins. Indeed, these customized products can often warrant a premium price, thus providing a margin in excess of what had previously been enjoyed by the manufacturer. Manufacturers have therefore realized that mass customization is a means by which they can improve their profitability without the attendant loss of production or productivity. A prime example of mass customization is the computer manufacturer and distributor Dell.

M

Gilmore, James H. and Pine, B. Joseph II (eds), *Markets of One: Creating Customer-unique Value through Mass Customization* (A Harvard Business Review Book). Boston, MA: Harvard Business School Press, 2000.

Materials management

Materials management involves the planning, organization and control of all aspects of a business's physical inventory, including shipping, distribution, warehousing and dealing with work in progress. For international businesses the essential problem is to minimize the total of all of the costs involved and to maximize savings where those savings can be identified. For international businesses this requires an integrated materials-management or **logistics** organization which takes full responsibility for supply, production and distribution. Clearly any reduction in cost can contribute to profit.

Arnold, J. R. and Chapman, Stephen, *Introduction to Materials Management*. Englewood Cliffs, NJ: Prentice-Hall, 2003.

McDonaldization

McDonaldization originally referred to the technological advances in the preserving and storing of foodstuffs and the growing ownership of automobiles during the 1950s, coupled with the development of US suburbs, which transformed the way in which Americans shopped and ate. The larger supermarkets in the US succeeded in overwhelming many smaller and longer-established businesses; a trend which has been replicated in many other countries. The emphasis of service had moved from quality to price and efficiency. The key characteristics of McDonaldization are:

- *Efficiency* – in as much as consumers can obtain what they need very quickly, with very little effort on the part of the business. The employees can perform their tasks more easily and, above all, quicker, thus serving customers more efficiently. Coupled with this increase in efficiency, the quality aspects are reduced, particularly given the fact that technologies which do not require the input of humans perform many of the tasks.
- *Control* – McDonaldization radically changed both the way in which employees were treated and expected to behave and the way in which customers were expected to interact with the business. For very much the first time, customers queued up at a cash register to collect their food, and cleared tables after they had finished eating.
- *Predictability* – was important as consumers knew exactly what they were purchasing, because to all intents and purposes, the product

was identical no matter which store or outlet the customers visited. This meant that McDonaldized businesses could more easily sell their business as a franchise operation.

McDonaldization has spread across the globe, not simply in the retailing of hamburgers and related products. The concept now revolves around the idea that the consumer can purchase standardized items at relatively low prices and that the quality of those products does not differ significantly in the various outlets scattered around the world. Given that there is a far greater availability of products and services on the global market, McDonaldization is said to have played an integral part in making these goods available to larger proportions of the population. Consumers, by purchasing standardized products, are able to obtain what they perceive they need without very much delay. Convenience and uniform quality have competed well against other economic alternatives, notably higher-priced customized products and services. In settling for standardized products, individuals in different countries around the world can now afford products and services which hitherto were beyond their means.

McDonaldization has been seen to be an ideal solution in providing faster, more efficient products and services to a working population which has considerably less free time than in the past. McDonaldized products provide a familiar, stable and safe alternative to taking risks in purchasing unknown products. It has also been a feature of McDonaldization that consumers can compare competing products easily.

Ritzer, George, The McDonaldization of Society. Thousand Oaks, CA: Pine Forge Press, 1996.

Mercantilism

Mercantilism makes the assumption that money will inevitably become scarce, which in turn would impede higher levels of output and have an impact upon employment. Mercantilists believe that low interest rates, which allow cheaper money to be available to businesses, is the ideal solution. Originally this was an economic viewpoint, dating back to the seventeenth century, and was very much a forerunner to the classical economics of the twentieth century. The classical economists, on the other hand, believed that in making money cheap, inflation would be created. Mercantilists were against **free trade** and they believed that protectionist policies, which would minimize imports and maximize exports, would create a trade surplus, thereby dealing with the problem of scarce money.

M

This viewpoint has largely been disproved as mercantilists believed that ultimately a nation's wealth was dependent upon its ownership or stock of precious metals. Later economic theorists undermined this view by stating that rather than precious metals being the most important consideration, it was a country's stocks of productive resources that were crucial. Each country's use of its land, labour and capital and how efficiently these were used would determine a nation's comparative wealth. With the increase in free trade, efficiency has also increased, which has allowed various countries to specialize in the production of products and services in which they have a **comparative advantage**. In other words, they use their land, labour and capital most efficiently in a particular way.

Vaggi, Gianni and Groenewegen, Peter, *A Concise History of Economic Thought: From Mercantilism to Monetarism.* New York: Palgrave Macmillan, 2002.

MERCOSUR

MERCOSUR, or the Southern **Common Market**, consists of Argentina, Brazil, Paraguay and Uruguay and came into force during the period 1994 to 1995. It was modelled on the European Community's **Treaty of Rome**, establishing common external **tariffs** and eliminating **trade barriers** in services.

Around 95% of MERCOSUR trade is carried out on a non-tariff basis. The MERCOSUR area covers some 12 million square kilometres (four times the size of Europe) and has a market of some 200 million people and a joint **gross domestic product** of $1 trillion. Technically, this places MERCOSUR amongst the four largest economies of the world, after **NAFTA**, the **European Union** and Japan.

www.mercosur.org.uy

Minimum efficient scale

The minimum efficient scale is taken to be the level of output at which a manufacturer's economies, achieved by an optimum level of produc-tion, have been eliminated by a scaling down of the output. The minimum efficient scale is the lowest output level which is economically viable,for the business to sustain, albeit for a short period of time.

Ministry of International Trade and Industry (MITI)

Japan's Ministry of International Trade and Industry (MITI) was created in 1949. It brought together the trade agency and the Ministry of Commerce and Industry in a nationwide effort to control postwar inflation and provide leadership towards productivity and higher levels of employment. MITI had the primary responsibility of formulating and implementing international trade policy. This was achieved through a consensus of opinion, including inputs from the Japanese ministries of Foreign Affairs and Finance. MITI, in coordination with the Economic Planning Agency, the Bank of Japan and the ministries concerned with agriculture, construction, forestry and fisheries, health and welfare, post and telecommunications, and transportation, framed Japan's trade policies.

By the 1980s MITI had far less control over the formulation of international trade policy than it had in the past, due to the growing strength and importance of other Japanese government ministries. MITI was also responsible for exports and imports, as well as for domestic businesses which were not covered by other ministries (primarily investment in plant and equipment, energy and power, pollution control, foreign economic assistance and consumer complaints). MITI's work with Japanese industry succeeded in strengthening domestic manufacturing, providing it with a platform through import control to become competitive on the world market. MITI was also integral in liberalizing Japan's import policies and the opening of the Japanese market, while continuing to promote the domestic industry.

In recent years MITI has been primarily involved in the encouragement of imports of foreign products into Japan and the supervision of export financing programmes, including Japan's export–import bank.

www.miti.gov.my

Mixed economy

In a mixed economy, economic decisions concerning the selling and purchasing of products, services and labour are made partly by businesses and partly by the government. A mixed economy has both private sector businesses and businesses which are owned by the government. Both take part in economic activity. Different countries have a radically different mix of public and privately owned businesses. In the UK, for example, during the 1980s and 1990s, many publicly owned businesses were sold through a policy of privatization, thus reducing the mix between public and private enterprise.

Mixed economies tend to have the following characteristics:

- They have features of both market and command economies.
- Both the government and private individuals own the businesses.
- Either employees have freedom to negotiate their wage deals with

M

their employers or, in other cases, the government regulates these wage deals.

- The government has the option to regulate prices if it deems it necessary.
- The government has the option to decide what products are produced and how they are produced.

Harvey, J., *The Organisation in its Environment: Business in the Mixed Economy.* Basingstoke: Palgrave Macmillan, 1980.

Monetarism

Monetarism is a strand of economic theory which suggests that control of the money supply in a given economy leaves the rest of the economy capable of balancing or taking care of itself. Monetarism is founded on the basis that inflation occurs when a government prints too much money. Milton Friedman argued his quantity theory of money, which suggested that governments need to keep a steady money supply, only expanding the money supply each year to allow for natural growth of the economy. This policy would allow market forces to control problems arising out of inflation, recession or unemployment.

Monetarism was eagerly grasped during the 1980s, primarily in the US and the UK. **Central banks** set targets for money supply growth and closely controlled the rates of interest. Since the 1980s the linkage between money supply and inflation has proved to be somewhat erroneous. At the time, the money supply was seen as a useful policy target, provided that the relationship between money and **gross domestic product**, and therefore inflation, remained predictable and stable. It was further believed that the money supply would necessarily affect both output and prices in as much as the money supply would determine how fast cash circulated around an economy. What monetarists had not considered was the speed at which money revolves around an economy (this is known as the velocity of circulation) and monetarists failed consistently to predict sudden changes. Gradually monetarists began to realize that the link between money supply and inflation was far more complex than they had believed. As a result, monetary targets set by central banks largely passed out of favour.

The natural alternative and successor to monetarist policy is the setting of inflation targets and manipulating the economy in order to achieve these targets.

See also **monetary policy.**

Vaggi, Gianni and Groenewegen, Peter, *A Concise History of Economic Thought: From Mercantilism to Monetarism.* New York: Palgrave Macmillan, 2002.

Monetary policy

The primary objective of monetary policy is to control inflation. A country will set a target for inflation and attempt to ensure that it does not deviate to any degree from this target. Since the UK left the **Exchange Rate Mechanism (ERM)** in September 1992, UK monetary policy has involved manipulating interest rates to control the level of inflation.

As the term 'monetary policy' suggests, it is a means by which the government controls the money supply. Adopting a monetarist policy relies on the belief that in controlling the money supply the price levels are also controlled. There are close links between interest rates, the money supply and the exchange rate. At times when the UK was tied to a fixed exchange rate system, both the rate of interest and the money supply had to be adjusted in order to maintain a **fixed exchange rate**. During the period between 1990 and 1992, when the UK was part of the ERM, the government effectively lost control of interest rates and the supply of money.

Monetarists realize that it is notoriously difficult to control interest rates, money supply and exchange rates simultaneously. In May 1997 the new Labour Chancellor, Gordon Brown, made the Bank of England independent, setting up the Monetary Policy Committee (MPC), and effectively taking the government and the Chancellor out of the decision-making loop with regard to interest rates.

In the US, monetary policy consists of efforts which are made by the US Federal Reserve (the **central bank** of the US) to influence the conditions of both money and credit in the US economy. It too has objectives in terms of stable prices, the maintenance of high employment and the promotion of maximum sustainable growth within the economy. The Federal Reserve formulates monetary policy by setting targets for Federal funds rates, which are the interest rates which banks charge one another for short-term loans. The Federal funds rate is what the banks pay when they borrow, and therefore affects the rates they charge when they lend. These rates, in turn, have an impact upon short-term interest rates in the economy and, ultimately, economic activity and the rate of inflation. In order to achieve this, the Federal Reserve uses open market operations, the purchase and sale of previously issued US Government securities, as a means by which they can influence how much banks can lend. This effectively raises or lowers the Federal funds rate. When the Federal Reserve buys securities, funds flood into the banking system; this gives them more money to lend and places a downward pressure on the Federal funds rate. When the Federal Reserve sells securities, the opposite occurs.

Walsh, Carl, *Monetary Theory and Policy*. Cambridge, MA: MIT Press, 2003.

Monopoly

A monopoly is the ability of a single business to control the prices within a particular product market, or geographical area. This term can also be used to describe the ability of a business to exclude competitors from doing business within a given product market or geographic market.

Monopolies tend to exist in situations where there is no close substitute for a monopolist's product. Although there are few examples of truly monopolistic markets, as there are often substitutes for even unique products, not all substitutes are perfect substitutes. A prime example would be an electricity supplier, who may have a monopoly of supply in a given area. Theoretically the electricity supplier could be replaced by a gas supplier, but gas is not always an ideal substitute.

Monopolies also occur when entry into the industry is very difficult. This means that a monopolist does not have to worry too much about competition. Therefore a monopoly organization has discretion over how much it chooses to produce and what price it deems reasonable to charge its customers. In the UK, for example, a business which has over 25 per cent of a defined market is considered to have a monopoly power and will therefore be investigated by the Monopolies and Mergers Commission. In 2003 a case which was referred to the Monopolies and Mergers Commission involved just such a monopoly situation. When the supermarket chain Safeway became available for **acquisition**, a number of potential suitors were interested in purchasing the business. The Monopolies and Mergers Commission considered the relative **market share** of the main supermarket chains and after due consideration decided that the four largest supermarket chains in the UK should not be eligible, and they were thus barred from purchasing Safeway. It was considered in this case, as in most monopoly cases, that to allow a large share of a specific market to be controlled by a single business would not be in the public interest.

Monopolies can occur naturally, usually through innovation, which requires businesses to take out international **patents** and **copyrights** to protect their products. This has become an extremely complex issue in the global market since individual patents and copyrights must be obtained in markets in which the business wishes to operate. In other cases monopolies are deliberately created by governments, such as the UK's National Lottery organizer, Camelot. Other nations have also decided to create their own monopolies in order to ensure that they have a national leader in a particular market. This is achieved by placing high **tariffs** on foreign imports, effectively preventing foreign competitors from entering the market.

Moore's law

Moore's law was suggested by a semi-conductor engineer, Gordon Moore, in 1964. He suggested that as the power of microprocessor technology doubles, the costs of production will halve every 18 months. He was speaking from a position of knowledge as he co-founded Intel some four years later. The logic behind his theory was that the amount of information that could be stored on a given amount of silicone had doubled every year since that technology had been invented. His theory held good until the late 1970s when the doubling period of microprocessor technology began to slow. With recent technological developments and the creation of better chips, the costs of production continue to fall broadly in line with his original theories.

Most favoured nation treatment

Under Article I of the **General Agreement on Tariffs and Trade (GATT)**, a country can extend the lowest possible **tariff** rates to another (most favoured) country, compared with all other tariffs it applies to other nations. When a particular country agrees to cut tariffs on a specified product imported from one country, the tariff reduction automatically applies to imports of the same product from any other country which is eligible for most favoured nation treatment.

Essentially this is a principle of non-discriminatory treatment of imports and did, indeed, appear on a number of bilateral agreements prior to GATT. There is no compelling obligation for any country to extend a most favoured nation treatment to another country unless they are both party to GATT. The most favoured nation treatment is one of the most important aspects in building the international trading system. The **World Trade Organization** does require member countries to give the same most favoured nation treatment that is given to the products of any one member, to the like products of all other members.

www.wto.org

M

Multi-domestic strategy

A multi-domestic strategy tends to lead a business with international operations to allow the operations in one country to be relatively independent of those in other countries. In essence, multi-domestic strategy emphasizes the unique conditions which apply to each country in which the multinational organization operates. This may involve separate design, production and sales operations.

In using multi-domestic strategy the business focuses upon local responsiveness to specific strategies wholly designed to suit that nation's market.

Multilateral Agreement on Investment (MAI)

The Multilateral Agreement on Investment (MAI) was negotiated by the **Organization for Economic Cooperation and Development (OECD)**. It is designed to make it easier for investors to move their assets across international borders. The negotiations got under way in 1995 and were finally passed in 1998.

Countries which ultimately sign the MAI will be required to fulfil the following obligations:

- Open all their economic sectors to foreign ownership.
- Treat foreign investors no less favourably than domestic businesses.
- Remove performance requirements which require investors to behave in particular ways in exchange for access.
- Remove restrictions on the movement of capital.
- Compensate investors if their assets are expropriated through seizure or regulation.
- Allow investors to sue a government for damages if that country's laws are in violation of the MAI rules.
- Ensure that all localities within their country comply with MAI.

Many of the 180 countries represented by the **World Trade Organization** objected to the MAI, which caused the negotiations to be transferred to the Organization for Economic Cooperation and Development. In contrast, the OECD represents 29 of the richest countries in the world, which are host to 95% of the total 500 trans-national corporations in the world. It is therefore unsurprising that many of the **lesser developed countries** were somewhat sceptical as to the true purpose behind the MAI.

www.oecd.org

Multilateral netting

Multilateral netting is a treasury management technique which is used by many larger international businesses in order to manage their payment processes, which often involve transactions in a multitude of different currencies. If multilateral netting is used, then businesses can expect to make huge savings in foreign exchange trading and improve the settlement of bills between different parts of the organization. In Figure 4, a complex organization has a situation where each overseas subsidiary settles its own obligations directly and individually with another part of the organization. Each time a payment transaction is made, the business incurs transaction costs. There is no overall base currency and payment is based on the current rate of exchange.

In Figure 5, the organization has reconfigured its payment systems and has established a netting centre, through which all transactions are routed. Each overseas subsidiary pays or receives a single local-

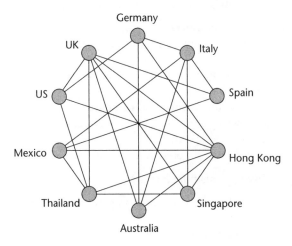

Figure 4   Multilateral trading patterns

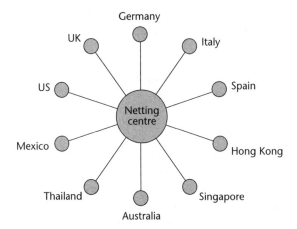

Figure 5   Multilateral netting centre

currency balance to or from the netting centre. The netting centre can then credit or debit one of the other subsidiaries automatically.

Multinational enterprise (MNE)

A multinational enterprise is a business which owns separate operations in at least two countries. Businesses become multinational enterprises and develop their foreign markets for a number of different reasons. These can be typified as being either proactive or reactive in nature. The key proactive (or pull) factors include the desire:

- to increase global **market share**;
- to satisfy demand for a unique product or service in a foreign market;
- to generate greater profits by reducing costs or acquiring new resources;
- to achieve greater **economies of scale**;
- to spread risks by diversifying their sources of sales and inputs;
- to satisfy managerial targets;
- to take advantage of potential tax benefits.

The key reactive (or push) factors are:

- to offer an alternative to the competitive pressures present in a domestic market;
- to seek an alternative to declining domestic sales;
- as a response to increasing costs of production in the domestic market;
- to seek alternative markets in a saturated domestic market;
- to provide a market for unused managerial or production capacity;
- to seek a market to sell excess stock due to over production in a domestic market;
- to prolong the life cycle of products which are reaching the end of their life cycle in the domestic market;
- to copy, for strategic reasons, their key competitors.

Multipoint competition

Multipoint competition arises when two or more international businesses compete with one another in different national markets or industries. They make these moves in order to keep their opponents in check, attempting to match one another's moves, so that globally a competitor does not acquire a distinct advantage in any given market. This is an increasing trend of international rivalry between **multinational enter-**

prises. The competition across borders gives international businesses the option to respond to an attack by a rival not only in the challenged market, but in any other market in which the two businesses compete.

Multipoint pricing

Multipoint pricing refers to situations where an international business's pricing strategy in one particular overseas market has a direct impact on a rival's pricing policies in another market. Should one international business choose to adopt an aggressive pricing policy in one market, then a rival may respond by adopting an aggressive pricing policy in another market that is vital to the first business.

Mutual recognition agreement

Mutual recognition agreements, or MRAs, are usually negotiated on a sector-by-sector basis. Under MRAs, testing and certification processes in sectors such as telecommunications, pharmaceuticals, chemicals and processed foods take place in the exporting country. Under MRA a European country would obtain a product certificate which would be applicable in the United States, thus enabling it to sell its products freely throughout the United States. The MRA requires a notified body to undertake some of the testing responsibilities, perhaps having recourse to a third country's testing laboratory. MRA exists between the **European Community** and the United States and between Japan and the **European Union**.

www.europa.eu.int/comm/enterprise/international/indexb1.htm

www.mofa.go.jp/region/europe/eu/agreement.html

M

NAFTA

See **North American Free Trade Agreement (NAFTA)**.

National member body

Participation in the work of organizations such as the **International Organization for Standardization (ISO)** is undertaken by a single body which represents a particular country within the ISO, its various sub-committees and working groups. These national member bodies can take part in the activities of organizations such as the ISO by becoming either participating or observer members.

www.iso.org

National trade databank

The national trade databank (NTDB) is a US system which holds information regarding international, economic and export promotion data. Some 19 US agencies provide data, which is updated on a monthly basis. Organizations contributing to the NTDB include the Departments of Agriculture, Commerce, Energy and Labour, the Central Intelligence Agency (CIA), the **EXIMBANK**, the **Federal Reserve System**, the US **International Trade Commission**, the Overseas Private Investment Corporation, the Small Business Administration, the **United States Trade Representative** and the University of Massachusetts (who provide data on state origins of exports).

www.stat-usa.gov

Nationalization

Nationalization occurs when a country's government chooses to take ownership of what had been a private sector business. Nationalization was a major component of many **mixed economies** in the post-Second World War period, until the 1980s. Nationalization was used as a means by which governments could attempt to remedy market failure. By being taken into government hands, industries enjoyed a form of legal protection, often becoming a **monopoly** through lack of competition in the marketplace. From the 1980s governments sought to reverse nationalization, which they saw to be a failure in as much as the nationalized businesses' performance had been poor compared with that of businesses in the private sector. As a result, a policy of **privatization** saw the vast majority of nationalized businesses returned to private hands. Arguably the former nationalized industries are now more economically efficient, but this has led to enormous numbers of closures and loss of jobs.

Chick, Martin, *Industrial Policy in Britain, 1945–1951: Economic Planning, Nationalization and the Labour Governments*. Cambridge: Cambridge University Press, 2002.

Natural resource based products (NRBP)

When the **General Agreement on Tariffs and Trade (GATT)** negotiating group was created as a result of the calls from resource-rich **lesser developed countries**, the primary aim was the removal of **trade barriers** in natural resource-based products. Considerable work was carried out during the early 1980s, focusing primarily on three traditional product areas: non-ferrous metals and minerals, fish and fish products, and wood and wood products.

Net foreign investment

Net foreign investment can be typified as being the total of a country's exports in products and services, the receipts from **factoring** and the capital grants received from the government, less the sum of imported goods, products and services, payments of factor income and transfer payments to foreign individuals or businesses. More simply, net foreign investment can be viewed as being the total of the **acquisition** of foreign assets by a country's residents, less the acquisition of that country's assets by foreign residents.

N

Net present value (NPV)

Net present value is used to help make the decision as to whether or not to make an investment. The 'net' aspect of the term refers to both the costs and the benefits of the investment. In order to calculate the net present value, a business will sum all of the benefits expected from the investment, both currently and in the future. It will then sum all of the expected costs on the same basis. In order to work out the future benefits and costs, a business will adjust its future cash flow using any appropriate discount rates. It will then subtract these costs from the benefits. If the result is a negative net present value then, in terms of expected returns, the investment would not be a good one and cannot be easily justified by the business. If the net present value proves to be positive then the business will compare the net present values of alternative investment opportunities before finally deciding whether or not to make the investment.

New trade theory

During the 1970s many economists wrestled with the problem of the differences between their predictions of **free trade** and actual world trade flows. New trade theory arose from this problem of prediction. Trade seemed to be growing faster between the industrialized countries which had similar economies. These economies had similar **factor endowments** and, flying in the face of free trade theory, none of the countries seemed to have a **comparative advantage**. Indeed the trade between the countries seemed to suggest that they were selling one another similar goods.

The explanation seemed to revolve around the fact that many markets had monopolistic competition and when a market such as this expands, it does so by more businesses and larger businesses offering greater product variety. Free trade expands the overall market size, thus allowing businesses to achieve greater **economies of scale**, which directly benefits their workforce, consumers and shareholders.

Grimwade, Nigel, *International Trade: New Patterns of Trade, Production and Investment*. London: Routledge, 2000.

N

Newly independent state

A newly independent state is one of the 12 republics of the former Soviet Union, namely Armenia, Azerbaijan, Belarus, Georgia, Kazakhstan, Kyrgyzstan, Moldova, Russia, Tajikistan, Turkmenistan, Ukraine and Uzbekistan.

Newly industrialized economy

A 'newly industrialized economy' is, in effect, a developing economy which has reached a fairly advanced stage of economic growth. These countries experience a rapid growth of **gross domestic product**, a rapid increase in industrial production and large rises in exports. Although the term was first applied to Hong Kong, Singapore, South Korea and Taiwan, it is now used as a general term to describe any such countries experiencing this form of development of their economy.

Newly industrialized economies are also known as 'newly industrialized countries' (NIC).

Nonconvertible currency

A nonconvertible currency is a currency which both residents and non-residents of a country are prohibited from converting into another currency. This state of affairs can lead to significant problems in international trade in as much as it may be desirable to sell products and services to a country which has a nonconvertible currency; the difficulty arises when payments received for those products and services in the form of a nonconvertible currency are to be moved out of that country. In effect, not only has the currency no value as it cannot be converted, but it also leaves an international business with a potential hole in its balance sheet.

There are, of course, alternatives when dealing with countries with nonconvertible currencies. A British clothing manufacturer, for example, may consider four different alternatives in getting around the problem of dealing with a country with a nonconvertible currency. Its options may include one of the following:

- The British clothing manufacturer may choose to use **barter**, in effect offering to trade its manufactured clothing for locally manufactured textiles, which it could either use itself or sell in another market to recoup the cash.
- The clothing manufacturer may choose to strike a compensation deal, where the local business in the overseas market covers the costs of any business travel and expenses undertaken by the British clothing manufacturer's employees, the balance being paid in the barter system as outlined above.
- The third alternative is to choose a buy-back system. The British clothing manufacturer may choose to fund a small production facility which makes the same items of clothing of similar quality to the ones produced at home. The British manufacturer would then be paid back over a period of time in finished goods.
- The fourth alternative is to use the **offsets** method, which means that the British manufacturer receives full payment in the nonconvertible currency. It can then use those funds to purchase products or services in the country and obtain goods which it can export and then, perhaps, resell.

N

Non-tariff barrier

Non-tariff barriers include **quotas** or charges other than traditional customs duties or domestic support programmes, stringent labelling and health standards or other business practices which limit the access of imported goods. Non-tariff barriers prohibit or restrict imports or require special procedures which make importing goods more difficult and, perhaps, more costly. Non-tariff barriers can occur as a result of either government intervention or private sector action.

United Nations, *Quantification of Non-Tariff Measures*. New York: United Nations, 2002.

Non-tariff measure

The most commonly used non-tariff measures (NTMs) include import **quotas**, quantitative restrictions, non-automatic import licensing and customs surcharges or other fees. They may also include customs procedures, export subsidies, unreasonable standards procedures, government-initiated procurement restrictions, or restrictions on investment. During the Tokyo Round of the **General Agreement on Tariffs and Trade (GATT)**, seven codes were negotiated: these included customs valuations, import licensing, subsidies and **countervailing duties**, **anti-dumping** duties, standards, government procurement and the trade in civil aircraft.

Despite the agreements during the Tokyo Round, non-tariff measures have still increased since that time.

North American Free Trade Agreement (NAFTA)

In 1993 the US, Canada and Mexico concluded their negotiations regarding the lowering of **trade barriers** between their three economies. The negotiations were hotly criticized, particularly in the US and Canada as many believed that the creation of a new regional trade area would mean that there would be job losses in their two countries as businesses would now have the opportunity to establish production facilities in Mexico. In-depth studies discovered that the economic gains would far outweigh the costs and consequently NAFTA came into force in January 1994. At the time, NAFTA's consumer population amounted to some 360 million (just 20 million less than the whole of the European economic area). It also had a combined output of $6 trillion; a full fifth larger than the **European Community**. Over a ten-year period progressive legislation has eliminated the majority of tariffs between the US and Mexico. Smaller tariffs in trade-sensitive areas were to be phased out within a

15-year period. Meanwhile, tariffs between Mexico and Canada were also to be phased out over a 10-year period. The tariff reductions between the US and Canada would fall in line with the already negotiated Canadian Free Trade Agreement.

In essence, NAFTA seeks to eliminate barriers to trade (import licensing and customs fees) and also seeks to establish the principle of national treatment (products from other NAFTA countries to receive treatment equal to that of domestic products). NAFTA also seeks to provide guarantees for investors and the right to sell services across the borders, and it established five basic principles in order to protect foreign investors and their investment in the free trade area:

- non-discriminatory treatment;
- no performance requirements;
- free fund transfers related to investment;
- expropriation would only occur under international law;
- the right to seek international arbitration in cases of violation.

www.sice.oas.org/trade/nafta/naftatce.asp

www.ustr.gov/regions/whemisphere/nafta.shtml

N

Ocean bill of lading

An ocean bill of lading is a receipt for the cargo and a contract for transportation between a shipper and an ocean carrier. Ocean bills of lading can also be bought, sold or traded as an instrument of ownership while the goods are in transit. In order for it to fulfil this function, the ocean bill of lading needs to be negotiable.

There are several associated terms, which include the following:

- *Clean bill of lading* – which is issued when a shipment is received in good condition. If there is damage or if there are shortages then a clean bill of lading will not be issued.
- *Onboard bill of lading* – which certifies that the cargo has been placed aboard a named vessel. This is signed by the master of the vessel or their representative.
- *Inland bill of lading* – this is used primarily to document the transportation of goods between a port and the point of origin or destination.

Off balance sheet financing

This is a form of borrowing in which the obligation is not recorded on the borrower's financial statements. Off balance sheet financing can employ several different techniques, which include development arrangements, leasing, product financing arrangements or recourse sales of receivables (recourse sales are the rights of a holder of a negotiable instrument to recover from a secondary liable party). Off balance sheet financing does raise concerns regarding the lenders' overall risk, but it improves their debt to equity ratio, which enhances their borrowing capacity. As a result, loans are often easy to arrange and are given lower interest rates because of the improved debt structure on the balance sheet. Off balance sheet financing is a technique often used by multinational businesses in order to secure additional loans on the worldwide loan market.

Ketz, J. Edward, *Hidden Financial Risk: Understanding Off Balance Sheet Accounting*. New York: John Wiley, 2003.

Office of International Cooperation and Development (OICD)

The OICD is part of the US Department of Agriculture. It is responsible for cooperative international research, liaison with international agricultural organizations and the exchanging of scientific and technical information. The OICD's other primary objective is to assist in training and the provision of technical assistance to around 80 **lesser developed countries**.

www.usda.gov

Official development assistance (ODA)

Official development assistance (ODA) is loans or grants which are made on the basis of concessionary financial terms by either the Development Assistance Committee (DAC) of the **Organization for Economic Cooperation and Development (OECD)**, or members of the **Organization of Petroleum Exporting Countries (OPEC)**. The loans are made to promote both economic development and welfare.

Offsets

Offsets involve establishing overseas production, which results in the creation or expansion of an international business's industrial capacity or output. Offsets include co-production, licensed production, subcontractor production, general overseas investment and the transfer of technology. In this respect co-production permits an overseas producer to acquire the technical information to manufacture, or part manufacture, the international business's products.

Licensed production in this respect involves the transfer of technical information, whilst subcontractor production involves a direct commercial arrangement between the international business and an overseas producer. Overseas investment, in the offset sense, involves a capital contribution by an international business to assist the establishment, or expansion, of a subsidiary or a **joint venture** in an overseas country.

Technology transfer in this sense is an agreement to conduct research and development in an overseas country, perhaps to provide technical assistance or to perform other activities. Many countries require offsets in order to ease (or offset) the enormous burden that is often associated with the importation of technologically superior or advanced products.

At the same time offsets also help to increase domestic employment and help the country build up specific industrial sectors. In many cases

O

overseas governments impose offset requirements on foreign exporters in order to reduce the adverse impact of a major purchase, or series of purchases. Offsets can be either direct or indirect: in the case of a direct offset, an international business will sell a product which uses components that are made in the purchasing country; in cases of indirect offsets the exporter would undertake to buy products which are peripheral to the manufacture of its main product.

See also **counter-trade**.

Hammond, Grant Tedrick, *Counter-Trade Offsets and Barter in International Political Economy*. Basingstoke: Palgrave Macmillan, 1990.

Offshore

'Offshore' is a term used to describe an area in which an individual's or international business's **home country** rules do not apply. 'Offshore' can also mean a **tax haven**, which may, or may not, be literally offshore. Offshore locations can also be merely legally offshore, such as the City of London, in which certain financial transactions can be deemed for regulatory purposes to have actually taken place offshore.

Scheidr, Jerome, *The Complete Guide to Offshore Money Havens*. Prima Lifestyles, 2001.

Offshore banking unit

An offshore banking unit is an entity which acts as an intermediary in financial transactions between non-resident borrowers and lenders. Offshore banking units are normally foreign banks which conduct business in the domestic money market. They can deal in foreign exchange settlements and in **Eurocurrencies**, for example. Offshore banking units cannot accept domestic deposits and their activities are unrestricted by domestic authorities. Offshore banking units tend to be located in major financial centres, which are often known as offshore banking centres. Normally these financial centres have fairly liberal tax and capital market requirements.

Typical offshore banking activities include:

- borrowing or lending;
- providing guarantees;
- trading;
- contracting;
- investment;
- advisory work;
- **hedging**.

Scheidr, Jerome, *The Complete Guide to Offshore Money Havens*. Prima Lifestyles, 2001.

Ohmae, Kenichi

In his book published in 1995, *The End of the Nation State: The Rise of Regional Economies*, Ohmae put forward three key theories:

- World markets, particularly services, will continue to become highly globalized.
- The modern nation state has developed too many rigid rules and practices to be able to cope with the perpetual change in the international economic environment.
- New region states, consisting of between 5 million and 20 million people, which quite possibly could cross national boundaries, represent a new natural unit for economic growth. They would enjoy **economies of scale** in terms of services, but would not be self-sufficient in any other products.

Ohmae suggested that these regional clusters were the future of international trade, and successful clusters would spread their economic benefits to neighbouring regions. Whilst the first two ideas are fairly common, the third is somewhat novel. In principle, these region states are not unlike some of the smaller European countries.

Ohmae suggested that areas such as Hong Kong are ideal examples of this form of region state. Its **gross national product (GNP)** per capita stands at around $12,000. When it was brought into China as part of the Shenzhen Province, it boosted the province's GNP per capita to $5,695 compared with an average of $317 for the rest of China.

Ohmae, Kenichi, *The End of the Nation State: The Rise of Regional Economies*. New York: Free Press, 1995.

Oligopoly

An oligopoly occurs when a relatively small number of businesses dominate a market. To all intents and purposes they act together and behave as if they were a **monopoly**. This collusion is sometimes formalized, albeit illegally, in the form of a **cartel**. The businesses tend to compete with one another on the basis of non-price competition. In other words, one of the businesses periodically takes the lead in terms of adding additional value to its products and services, making the products or services slightly more attractive to consumers.

O

OPEC

See **Organization of Petroleum Exporting Countries (OPEC)**.

Optimal currency area

An optimal currency area is a geographical region which would benefit from having a single currency. Optimal currency areas could, in theory, cover several countries, as the benefits of having one currency mean lower foreign exchange rates and currency hedging costs, and a far more transparent pricing. A single currency would mean a single **monetary policy**, which would mean that no part of the currency area would be allowed to change its exchange rate with another part of the area.

One of the major problems with optimal currency areas is that changes in economic conditions may affect one part of the area more than others, but provided employees in affected parts of the area are able to move to other countries, and both wages and prices are flexible, then the affected area should not have an adverse impact upon the rest of the region. In these optimal currency areas there should be no barrier to labour mobility. There should also be wage flexibility and a system of transferring resources to regions which are less replete or are suffering problems.

In practice, few areas of the world which have single currencies are indeed optimal currency areas. In time, however, even areas with immense difficulties, such as the **European Union**, will gradually become optimal currency areas.

Options

Options are a prerogative, purchased by an individual or a business, which gives them the right to buy or sell specified securities or commodities from another person if they choose, at an agreed upon price, at any time within an agreed period.

Ordinary course of business

'Ordinary course of business' refers to business transactions which have been carried out in accordance with the common usages and customs of international trade. These are generally standard contractual terms, which can then be applied in the case of disputes.

Organization for Economic Cooperation and Development (OECD)

The Organization for Economic Cooperation and Development was formed in 1961 in order to stimulate the economic progress of western industrialized nations and to further expand world trade. It has variously been described as a 'think tank', a 'rich man's club' or a 'monitoring agency'. The OECD has some 30 members which produce two-thirds of the world's products and services. Originally the membership was exclusively European and North American, but it now includes Japan, Australia, New Zealand, Finland, Mexico, the Czech Republic, Hungary, Poland and the Slovak Republic. Non-members can subscribe to OECD agreements and treaties and now the OECD works with 70 non-member states, including Russia, Brazil and China.

The OECD operates as a forum in order to develop economic and social policies. This is achieved by the sharing of common problems and the coordination of both domestic and international policies. The agreements are legally binding to combat policies which would otherwise inhibit the free flow of both capital and services. The OECD also issues guidelines for **multinational enterprises**.

There is a constant exchange of information and analysis between the OECD governments and this contributes to the organization of the world's most reliable sources of economic and social data. The OECD grew out of the Organization for European Economic Cooperation (OEEC), which was formed in the aftermath of the Second World War in order to administer US and Canadian aid under the terms of the Marshall Plan. The OECD took over responsibilities from the OEEC in 1961. The OECD has more recently been involved in sustainable development, economic commerce and biotechnology. The OECD works out of a Paris headquarters which employs 2,300 staff. They are supported by 700 economists, lawyers and scientists. The OECD is funded by its member countries; the national contributions are based on each member's economy. Some 25% of the budget is provided by the United States; Japan is the second largest contributor. The OECD has a budget of around $200 million per year.

Unlike the **International Monetary Fund** and the **World Bank**, the OECD does not act as a lender. It primarily works through the collection and analysis of data and the collective discussion of policy issues. The OECD played a critical role in the conclusion of the **Uruguay Round**.

www.oecd.org

O

Organization of African Unity (OAU)

The OAU was founded in 1963 and originally had 32 member countries. Its primary aim was to coordinate political, economic, cultural, scientific and defence policies. Above all, it sought to end colonialism in Africa. In 1999 the heads of state and government of the Organization of African Unity established the African Union, calling on all member states to adopt coordinated positions on matters of common concern.

The objectives of the African Union include:

- The achievement of greater unity and solidarity.
- Defence of the sovereignty and territorial integrity of its members.
- To speed up political and socio-economic integration.
- To promote common African positions on issues of interest.
- To encourage international cooperation.
- To promote sustainable development.
- To coordinate and harmonize policies between the various economic communities.
- To advance the development of science and technology.

These are amongst the many objectives of the African Union, although the above relate specifically to international business.

The Organization of African Unity itself was officially disbanded in July 2002.

www.africa-union.org

Organization of American States (OAS)

The Organization of American States, or the Pan-American Union, is a regional organization which came into existence in 1948 and began operations in 1951. The OAS currently has 35 member states and is the main political forum for multilateral negotiations in the region. Each of its member states has one vote. The regular decision making is undertaken by a permanent council based at the OAS headquarters in Washington, DC. Each country appoints an Ambassador to sit on the permanent council.

Initially the OAS had 21 nations as its membership; since then the organization has expanded to include several nations in the Caribbean, as well as Canada. Officially, Cuba is still a member of the OAS, but its government has been excluded since 1962. The original membership, who signed the 1948 OAS Charter, were Argentina, Bolivia, Brazil, Chile, Colombia, Costa Rica, Cuba, the Dominican Republic, Ecuador, El Salvador, Guatemala, Haiti, Honduras, Mexico, Nicaragua, Panama, Paraguay, Peru, the United States, Uruguay and Venezuela. Barbados, and Trinidad and Tobago joined in 1967, Jamaica in 1969, Grenada in 1975, Suriname in 1977, Dominica and St Lucia in 1979, Antigua and Barbuda, St Vincent and the Grenadines in 1981, the Bahamas in 1982, St Kitts and Nevis in 1984, Canada in 1990 and Belize and Guyana in 1991.

The OAS has four specialized areas: trade, sustainable development, education and the promotion of democracy.

www.oas.org

Organization of Petroleum Exporting Countries (OPEC)

OPEC was formed in 1960 in order to coordinate petroleum production and pricing policies. It is effectively a **cartel**, which arguably has caused enormous havoc to industrialized countries, primarily during the 1970s and 1980s, which resulted in high inflation and slow economic growth.

OPEC describes itself as being an international organization of developing countries which are reliant on their oil revenues as their primary source of income. Officially at least, membership is open to any country which is a net exporter of oil, but it must share ideals with the other members of the organization. The current membership consists of Algeria, Indonesia, Iran, Iraq, Kuwait, Libya, Nigeria, Qatar, Saudi Arabia, the United Arab Emirates and Venezuela. The 11 members supply approximately 40% of the world's oil output and control over 75% of the world's crude oil reserves.

Since OPEC's influence on world trade in the 1970s and 1980s, many international businesses have switched their production methods to require less oil and indeed less energy. Equally, non-OPEC producers, such as the United Kingdom and the United States, offer a viable alternative to OPEC-controlled oil. Some members of OPEC have also chosen not to restrict their oil production, which has meant lower oil prices.

www.opec.org

Organizational architecture

Organizational architecture is taken to mean the totality of an international business's organization, including its formal structure, **organizational culture**, processes, incentives and human resources. It is believed that in order for an international business to be profitable, three conditions related to its organizational architecture need to be in place, these are:

O

- The various elements of the business's organizational architecture must be consistent from an internal standpoint.
- The organizational architecture must match the strategy of the business.
- Both the organizational architecture and strategy must be consistent with the prevailing competitive conditions in the markets in which the organization operates.

Organizational culture

There are a number of ways in which an organization's culture can be classified. The main classifications were suggested by a number of researchers, including Harrison, Handy, Deal and Kennedy, and Quinn and McGrath. As years have passed, so these classifications have become more developed, making it possible only to generally approach them in broad terms.

In 1972, J. Harrison suggested four main categories of organizational culture – power, role, task and person. Charles Handy reworked Harrison's theory and identified them as described in Table 6.

Table 6 Categories of organizational culture

Culture	Description
Power	This type of culture is based on trust and good personal communication. There is little need for rigid bureaucratic procedures since power and authority are based on only a few individuals. The power culture is dynamic in that change can take place quickly but is dependent on a small number of key, powerful individuals. This culture tends to be tough on employees because the key focus is the success of the organization, often resulting in high labour turnover.
Role	This type of culture tends to be bureaucratic in nature, thus requiring logical, coordinated and rational processes with heavy emphasis on rules and procedures. Control lies with a small number of employees who have high degrees of authority. They tend to be stable organizations, operating in a predictable environment with products and services that have a long lifespan. Not considered to be innovative organizations, they can adapt to gradual, minor change, but not to radical ones.
Task	This type of organizational culture relies on employee expertise. The matrix structure tends to prevail in these organizations, with teams of individuals specializing. They need and tend to be flexible organizations with individual employees working with autonomy, allowing fast reaction to changes in the external environment and having set procedures in place to address this aspect.
Person	This type of culture relies on collective decision making, often associated with partnerships. Compromise is important and individuals will tend to work within their own specialist area, coordinating all aspects and working with autonomy without the need to report to other employees.

During the 1980s Terence Deal and Allen Kennedy developed their own set of theories about organizational culture and the way in which it affected how management made decisions and formed strategies. Their conclusions are shown in Table 7.

Table 7 Organizational culture according to Deal and Kennedy

Culture	Description
Macho	These types of organization have to make decisions quickly and adopt a tough attitude towards their employees and fellow managers. There is a high degree of internal competition and the operations tend to be high risk. The majority of these organizations do not form strategies or plan for the long term but are considered short-termist, with a low level of cooperation within the organization itself. There is a high labour turnover, resulting in a weak organizational culture.
Work hard/ play hard	This type of culture tends to be associated with sales. The majority of individual employees are sales-orientated but the level of risk is low. It is the employees' ability to accumulate sales that is important and the culture tends to encourage team building and social activities for employees. The organization encourages competition and offers rewards for success, but does not necessarily rate quality as highly as volume.
Company	These types of organization are often in high-risk areas and operate on the basis that decisions take a long time to come to fruition. Decision making takes place at the top of this hierarchical organization and the overall approach can often be old-fashioned. Each new invention or technical breakthrough will pose a threat to the business.
Process	This type of culture operates in a low-risk, slow feedback environment where employees are encouraged to focus on how they do things rather than what they do. It tends to be systems- and procedures-based, requiring employees to work in an orderly and detailed fashion, attending meetings and work groups. There will be rigid levels of management in the hierarchical structure, but because the organization operates in a predictable environment, reactions from management are often slow.

R. E. Quinn and M. E. McGrath also identified four different organizational cultures, as shown in Table 8.

Table 8 Organizational culture as seen by Quinn and McGrath

Culture	Description
Rational	The rational culture is firmly based on the needs of a market. The organization places emphasis on productivity and efficiency and encourages management to be goal-orientated and decisive. All activities are focused on tangible performance and employees are rewarded on achievement.
Adhocracy	This type of culture is an adaptive, creative and autonomous one where authority is largely based on the abilities and charismatic nature of leaders. These organizations tend to be risk-orientated and emphasis is placed on employees' adherence to the values of the organization itself.
Consensual	These types of organization are often concerned with equality, integrity and fairness and much of the authority is based on informal acceptance of power. Decisions are made by collective agreements or consensus and dominant leaders are not often present. Morale is important, as is cooperation and support between employees in order to reach organizational objectives. Employee loyalty is high.
Hierarchical	This type of culture relies on stability and control through the setting of rigid regulations and procedures. Decisions are made logically on facts alone with the management tending to be cautious and conservative. The employees are strictly controlled, with the management expecting obedience.

It should be remembered that no one organization fits neatly into any one of the categories mentioned and the majority are too complex to be categorized generally. The classifications should be regarded only as a reference point for comparison of extremes.

Handy, C. B., *Understanding Organizations*. Harmondsworth: Penguin, 1985.
Quinn, R. E. and McGrath, M. R., *The Transformation of Organizational Cultures: A Competing Values Perspective in Organizational Culture*, edited by C. C. Lundberg and J. Martin. Thousand Oaks, CA: Sage Publications, 1985.
Scholz, C., *Organizational Culture and Leadership*. New York: Jossey-Bass, 1985.

Organizational structure

Organizational structure is a crucial consideration for all international businesses. Efficient organizational structure requires three main criteria. These are:

- The way in which the organization is divided into sub-units. This is known as horizontal differentiation.
- The location of the decision-making responsibilities within the structure. This is known as vertical differentiation.
- How the business has established integrating mechanisms.

Arguably, there is a fourth consideration, which is known as 'control systems'. This is taken to mean how the performance of sub-units within the organization is assessed and how well the managers of those sub-units control the activities within their area of responsibility.

It is essential for organizations which are pursuing a variety of different strategies as part of their international business activities to choose and then adopt appropriate **organizational architecture** which is responsive enough to implement the identified strategies. The organizational structure or architecture of a multinational business organization will very much depend on whether it is a multi-domestic business, global or trans-national in its nature. As multinationals spread their interests across the globe they inherently become more complex in their nature. In addition to this, they also become less able to change. None the less, the move towards increased **globalization** of industry has meant that businesses trading internationally must be able to adapt or amend their organizational structure to incorporate new strategies and operations in new markets.

Outflows of FDI

The outflows of FDI are simply the sum of all **foreign direct investment** out of a given country. In other words, the total of the outflows of FDI is equal to that nation's investments over a given period of time in overseas nations.

Output controls

The term 'output controls' has a specific reference to international businesses in as much as it suggests the inherent difficulties in setting goals for subsidiaries and then expressing those goals in terms of objective criteria. The more complex an international business becomes, perhaps with a series of subsidiaries in different nations, the more difficult it becomes for the parent company to judge the performance of those subsidiaries. There is no simple solution, yet output controls seek to provide an objective means by which the goals can be expressed. The objectivity needs to be applied equally to all subsidiary organizations; only then can it be used as a true performance measurement and a means by which the subsidiaries' ability to meet those goals can be judged.

Overseas Economic Cooperation Fund

The Overseas Economic Cooperation Fund (OECF) was created in 1961 and was a Japanese government institution providing development finance, based in Tokyo. It was designed to provide developing countries with grants and low-interest loans. There was a considerable reorganization in 1975 as it became difficult to distinguish between the Export–Import Bank of Japan and the OECF.

Currently the operation, specifically the Official Development Assistance, is provided by what is now known as the Japan Bank for International Cooperation (JBIC). Its purpose is to contribute to the development of Japanese and international trade and economies by providing loans and other financial support. It is also concerned with the promotion of Japanese exports and Japanese economic activity abroad. The JBIC is concerned with political, economic and social stability in developing areas of the world. Its 2002 Overseas Economic Cooperation operations amounted to some 6,285 billion yen. In the same period it had outstanding loans and other financing of 11,178 billion yen.

O

Pacific Rim

'The Pacific Rim' refers to economies which border the Pacific Ocean. Generally it is regarded as referring to East Asia, the United States and Canada. The term is somewhat flexible as it may also include Mexico, many of the Central American states and South American states which have a coastline on the Pacific Ocean. In its broadest sense it includes Canada, Japan, the People's Republic of China, Taiwan, the United States, Australia, Brunei, Cambodia, Indonesia, Laos, North and South Korea, Malaysia, New Zealand, the Pacific Islands, the Philippines, Russia and the Commonwealth of Independent States.

Paris Club

The Paris Club is an informal group of official creditors who seek to coordinate sustainable solutions for payment problems experienced by debtor nations. The Paris Club has 19 permanent members, which are Austria, Australia, Belgium, Canada, Denmark, Finland, France, Germany, Ireland, Italy, Japan, the Netherlands, Norway, the Russian Federation, Spain, Sweden, Switzerland, the United Kingdom and the United States. The Paris Club's first meeting with a debtor country was in 1956 when a meeting was arranged with Argentina.

The Paris Club meets debtors that need debt relief, and requires the debtor nations to implement reforms to help restore their financial and economic position. The countries tend to have current programmes in existence with the **International Monetary Fund**. Since 1956 the Paris Club has reached 369 agreements with some 78 debtor countries. Since 1983 the total amount of debt covered by these agreements has reached $410 billion. The Paris Club is essentially informal, allowing the creditors to take a more flexible approach to each debtor country. However, there are rules and regulations which are required in order to secure agreements.

The latest three agreements concern the following countries:

- Nicaragua (December 2002) owed $1,638 million to the Paris Club; $406 million was cancelled and $174 million was rescheduled.

- Mali (January 2003) owed $276 million to the Paris Club; $145 million was cancelled and $10 million was rescheduled.
- Benin (April 2003) owed $219 million to the Paris Club; $65 million of which was cancelled.

The Paris Club also dealt with debt rescheduling for Gambia in January 2003 and Ecuador in June 2003.

See also **London Club**.

www.clubdeparis.org

Paris Convention

The Paris Convention was first signed in 1883 and was revised in Brussels in 1900, Washington in 1911, The Hague in 1925, London in 1934, Lisbon in 1958, Stockholm in 1967, and the last amendment took place in 1979. The convention is an international agreement which seeks to promote trade amongst member countries and is also devised to protect industrial property. At present the convention has 151 members.

The Paris Convention covers the protection of industrial property, including:

- **patents**;
- utility models;
- industrial designs;
- trademarks, service marks and trade names;
- the source of appellations of origin;
- the repression of unfair competition.

The term 'industrial property' can apply to all forms of industry and commerce, including agriculture, the extractive industries, and all manufactured and natural products. Patents include various kinds of industrial patents which are recognized by the laws of member countries.

The principal features of the Paris Convention are:

- National treatment – which seeks to provide equal treatment to applications from member countries, and for members not to differentiate between the nationals of their own country and other nationals.
- Right of priority – industrial property rights are granted for a fixed period of time. Applications need to be filed on the same day in member countries in order to have rights starting from the same day.

- Independence of patents.
- Parallel importation.
- Protection against false indications and unfair competition.

There are a number of international conventions and treaties which are only available to members of the Paris Convention. These include:

- the Patent Cooperation Treaty (CPT);
- the Budapest Treaty (which covers the deposit of micro-organisms);
- the Union for Protection of New Varieties of Plants;
- the Madrid Agreement (which seeks to stop false or deceptive indications of the source of goods);
- the Madrid Protocol (concerning registration marks);
- the Hague Agreement (the deposit of international designs).

Patent

The concept behind a patent is that an individual or a business that has made a considerable investment, in terms of both time and money, in creating a new innovation should have a degree of protection for a period of time so that they can be fully rewarded for their invention. Patents aim to achieve this by granting an inventor a temporary monopoly for their innovation, and seek to prevent others from imitating the new invention, as they have not borne any of the costs or risks involved.

Despite the fact that in 1899 the then Commissioner of the American Office of Patents recommended that the office be abolished because he believed that everything that could be invented had already been invented, there are more patents being granted now than at any other point in the past. One of the major criticisms of patents is that they stifle competition and in many cases it is argued that the inventor is unable to fully exploit the potential of the new invention. There is also a degree of debate as to how long patents should be granted for.

See also **Patent Cooperation Treaty (PCT)**.

www.patent.gov.uk

www.uspto.gov

Patent Cooperation Treaty (PCT)

The **Patent** Cooperation Treaty was originally concluded in 1970 and subsequently amended in 1979 and 1984. The treaty is only open to nations which have signed the **Paris Convention** of 1883.

Under the terms of the treaty it is possible for an individual or a busi-

ness to seek patent protection for an innovation simultaneously in a
number of countries, by completing an International Patent Application.
The application is filed with the National Patent Office of the nation in
which the applicant is a national or a resident. It can also be filed at the
International Bureau of the World International Patent Office based in
Geneva. The application is then subjected to what is known as an international search. This means that published documents which might
affect the patent ability of the invention are investigated. On the basis of
the findings, either the patent is granted or the applicant is requested to
withdraw the application.

www.wipo.org/pct/en

Pegged exchange rate

A pegged exchange rate occurs when a nation's government or **central
bank** officially announces the **Gold par value** of its currency and then
seeks to maintain its market rate within a narrow band above or below
that official exchange rate. The pegging is achieved by the country's
central bank buying and selling its own currency in order to influence its
price.

There are inherent dangers in doing this as it may well affect the
country's money supply and its monetary stability.

Petrodollar

The term 'Petrodollar' refers to the oil earnings of petroleum exporting
countries which are in excess of their domestic requirements, and which
are therefore deposited in the form of $s in overseas banks. Huge finan-
cial surpluses were created, primarily by **OPEC** countries as a result of
their near **monopoly** power. This caused, particularly in the 1970s, a
huge glut of capital, which became known as the Petrodollar market. For
many countries that required large oil imports, there was an increasing
problem of how these countries were to deal with their **balance of
payments**. In some respects the oil trade was a one-way traffic in terms
of international trade. As a result, much of the reserves of Petrodollars
was lent to oil-importing countries in an attempt to balance very
lopsided international accounts. This was a particular problem for many
developing countries that had no access to oil reserves of their own. To
some extent the availability of the Petrodollars aided these countries
over a difficult period. None the less, it only served to push the **lesser
developed countries** into deeper debt. These issues are only now
being addressed. Rather than providing aid programmes, there are

increasing moves to help lesser developed countries deal with their debt servicing.

Spiro, David E., *The Hidden Hand of American Hegemony: Petrodollar Recycling and International Markets*. Ithaca, NY: Cornell University Press, 1999.

Pioneering costs

The term 'pioneering costs' is associated with the costs and risks facing an international business entering a new overseas market for the first time. In many respects they are trail-blazing organizations that do not have the benefits of knowing how to deal with that overseas country, either from experience or by learning lessons from other international businesses that have come before. Pioneering costs include the time and effort required to learn how the market operates and how that country's government, rules and regulations can have an impact upon the business's ability to be successful. Pioneering costs are borne alone by the first entrant into the market. Later entrants can benefit from lessons and mistakes learned by the pioneer. However, assuming the pioneer has been successful, later arrivals may find it as difficult, if not more so, to establish themselves in the new marketplace.

Policy framework paper (PFP)

The term 'policy framework paper' refers to a debtor country's economic plan, when it is used as part of a structural adjustment programme. A PFP is most closely associated with the **International Monetary Fund** and the **World Bank**. Both the IMF and the World Bank, in cooperation with the debtor country, prepare a first draft of the PFP and then engage in consultation and negotiation before the IMF itself drafts the final PFP and submits it for approval by its own board. Assuming the PFP is approved, it is used by the Structural Adjustments facilities of the two financial institutions to form the basis of negotiations regarding financing and future policy.

Political economy

'Political economy' refers to the study of how political factors can influence the functioning of an economic system. In essence, a political economy involves the study of social relations and mechanisms which regulate production, distribution and consumption of products and services in a country. Using this approach, it is assumed that all economic phenomena are a product of the country's social relations and structures. Analysts who use this approach believe that economic phenomena and variables cannot be explained without reference to politics. They argue that both economic phenomena and variables are influenced by a country's institutions, conflicts, alliances, culture, interests and power structures.

The political economy approach states that the relative power of financial groups within the country, and the degree of regulations and supervisory institutions, have a direct impact upon how the economic system of the country operates.

Gilpin, Robert, *Global Political Economy: Understanding the International Economic Order*. Princeton, NJ: Princeton University Press, 2001.

Political risk

Political risks are issues which international businesses would need to consider before deciding whether or not to involve themselves in trade or **foreign direct investment** in a country which either has a history of instability or the potential to be unstable, or has a government which may well involve itself to the detriment of the international business in some way. These risks would include war, civil unrest, expropriation, defaults or losses and the possibility that the local currency is not convertible to an international currency.

Politics and international trade

For various domestic and political reasons, different countries may adopt radically different trade policies. While, on the face of it, it may appear that **free trade** is in the interests of a country, and of international businesses and consumers, many countries seek, for political reasons, to protect their domestic markets from imports or **foreign direct investment**. Each protectionist policy has implications. For example, the imposition of **tariffs** will raise the costs of imported goods. Whilst the government receives extra finance from the revenues, and domestic producers are protected from foreign competitors, the nation's consumers lose because imports are more expensive.

A political alternative may be to lower the costs for domestic producers so that they can more easily compete against foreign imports and, perhaps, secure export markets. Again this may be a political decision, but the cash to pay for subsidies must be found, which inevitably places an additional burden on the taxpayers.

Countries also take the political decision that there should be a local content requirement, which requires a specific proportion of particular products to be produced within the domestic market. Once again the

P

producers of the component parts will benefit, but this raises the prices of imported components, which again affects consumers.

Government intervention in international trade is either political or economic. In the case of political interference, governments are, in effect, protecting the interests of certain groups within their nation, whilst other groups in the country suffer as a result. Political intervention inevitably affects consumers and many governments tread the risky path of threatening to intervene in international trade primarily as a means by which they can open up overseas markets. In many cases this policy fails and results in higher **trade barriers**. In many cases all these policies succeed in doing is protecting inefficient domestic industry.

Any political interference in international business can bring about retaliation from other countries that feel that their own domestic industries are being unfairly penalized by any form of protectionist policy adopted by another nation. A prime example of this was the **Smoot–Hawley Tariff**, which was introduced by the United States in 1930. In effect it erected huge tariff barriers to imports. As a result, other countries brought in their own tariffs, which arguably forced the world further into depression in the 1930s.

The **General Agreement on Tariffs and Trade (GATT)** was introduced in the aftermath of the Second World War and managed to lower trade barriers, particularly on manufactured goods and commodities. For some time this did stimulate economic growth. When the **World Trade Organization** extended the original GATT rules to services and sought protection for **intellectual property**, ordered a reduction in agricultural subsidies and introduced mechanisms to monitor and enforce free trade, businesses began to look for other alternatives to get around the possibility of trade barriers being erected. This move on behalf of international businesses brought about the setting up of production facilities in optimal locations around the world. Establishing production facilities in a country was seen as an ideal solution to political intervention by governments. Therefore, the impact of political intervention has become less drastic for international business as it is increasingly difficult to legislate against multinationals that provide a significant source of income and employment in a domestic market.

Gilpin, Robert, *Global Political Economy: Understanding the International Economic Order*. Princeton, NJ: Princeton University Press, 2001.

Polycentric staffing

Polycentric staffing is a human-resource management policy which appoints **host country** nationals to manage overseas subsidiaries in multinational businesses. It uses **home country** nationals for the primary positions in the corporate headquarters. Host country nationals are recruited to manage the subsidiaries in their own countries and in doing so the international business can reduce the possibility of it becoming culturally myopic. There are several primary advantages in adopting a polycentric human resource policy:

- By employing host country nationals initial language difficulties are avoided.
- There is an avoidance of the problems **expatriate managers** and their families have in adjusting to new roles abroad.
- Expensive training programmes associated with the reorientation of expatriate managers are also eliminated.
- Using host country nationals allows the multinational businesses to adopt a lower profile, particularly if politically sensitive situations occur.
- Host country nationals are less expensive, even if the best applicants are taken on.
- Polycentric policy provides a degree of continuity in the management of overseas subsidiaries.

Polycentric staffing policy is ideal for international businesses that have a **multi-domestic strategy**.

Porter, Michael

Michael E. Porter is currently a professor at the Harvard Business School. He is considered to be the leading authority on competitive strategy and competitiveness. He graduated with an MBA from Harvard in 1971 and a PhD in 1973. He has written some 16 books and 75 articles, including *Competitive Strategy: Techniques for Analyzing Industries and Competitors* (1980), *Competitive Advantage: Creating and Sustaining Superior Performance* (1985), *The Competitive Advantage of Nations* (1998) and *On Competition* (1998).

Over the years he has received a number of awards, including the Adam Smith Award from the National Association of Business Economists. Porter serves as an advisor to several different countries and has led major economic studies into countries as diverse as New Zealand and Peru.

Michael Porter's classic Five Forces model appeared in his 1980s book *Competitive Strategy: Techniques for Analyzing Industries and Competitors*. It has become the standard analysing tool for many businesses (see Table 9).

Table 9 Porter's Five Forces – simple model

Force	Description
Industry competitors	Rivalry amongst existing businesses
Potential entrants	Threats of new entrants into market
Buyers	Bargaining power of buyers in the market
Substitutes	Threat of substitute products/services
Suppliers	Bargaining power of suppliers to businesses in the market

The Five Forces shape every market and industry and help a business to analyse the intensity of competition, as well as the profitability and attractiveness of the market and industry. The Five Forces can be best explained as in Table 10.

Porter, Michael E., *Competitive Strategy: Techniques for Analyzing Industries and Competitors*. New York: Free Press, 1980.

Porter, Michael E., *Competitive Advantage: Creating and Sustaining Superior Performance*. New York: Free Press, 1985.

Porter, Michael E., *The Competitive Advantage of Nations*. New York: Free Press, 1998.

Porter, Michael E., *On Competition*. Boston, MA: Harvard Business School Press, 1998.

Porter's diamond

Michael Porter's theory on the **competitive advantage** of nations was published in 1990. He suggested that there are four attributes of a nation which shape the environment in which businesses compete and that these attributes either promote or impede the creation of competitive advantage. He arranged his four attributes in the form of a diamond, arguing that the diamond is a mutually reinforcing system. In other words, the effect of one attribute affects the state of the others. His four attributes are:

- **Factor endowments**, which are a nation's position in factors of production, such as skilled labour or infrastructure.
- Demand conditions – the nature of the **home country**'s demand for products and services.

P

Table 10 The Five Forces

Five Forces	Description	Implications
Threat of new entrants	The easier it is for new businesses to enter the industry, the more intense the competition. There may be factors which may limit the number of new entrants, which are known as **barriers to entry**.	Customers may already be loyal to major brands. Incentives may be offered to customers in order to retain them. Fixed costs will be high and there may be a scarcity of resources. Businesses and customers may find it expensive to switch suppliers and take the attendant risks.
Power of suppliers	This measures how much pressure suppliers can place on businesses within the industry. The larger the supplier and the more dominant, the further it can squeeze a business's margins and profits.	In some markets there are few suppliers of particular products as there are no available substitutes. Switching to other suppliers may prove difficult, costly and risky. If the product is extremely important to the buyers they will continue to purchase it. In many cases the supplying industry has a higher profitability than the buying industry.
Power of buyers	This is a measure of how powerful customers are and what pressures they can apply to a business. The larger and more reliant customers are, the more likely they are to be able to affect the margins and volumes of business.	There may be a small number of buyers who purchase large volumes of products and services. Buyers may be tempted to switch to an alternative supplier. If a product is not at the core of their business or requirements, buyers may choose not to purchase for a period of time. The more competitive the market, the more price sensitive the customers may be.

$\Rightarrow$

Table 10 The Five Forces (*continued*)

Five Forces	Description	Implications
Threat of substitute products	This is a measure as to how likely it is that buyers will switch to a competing product or service. Assuming the cost of switching is low, then this will be a serious threat.	Businesses should be aware that similar products, if not exact substitutes, may tempt the buyer to switch, temporarily at least, to another supplier. If, for example, supermarket chains are offered considerably cheaper alternatives to plastic shopping bags, they may be tempted to move over to cardboard boxes or paper sacks.
Competitive rivalry	This measures the degree of competition between existing businesses in an industry. It is usually the case that the higher the competition, the lower the return on investment. Margins are pared down to the lowest levels.	Assuming there is no dominant business, then many of the competitors will be of a similar size. There will also be little differentiation between competitors' products and services. The more stagnant the industry, in terms of market growth, the higher the possibility that competitors will focus on taking customers away from other businesses, rather than attempting to develop the market themselves.

P

- Relating and supporting industries – the presence or absence of supplier industries and related industries and whether they are internationally competitive.
- Business strategy, structure and rivalry – concerning how businesses are created, organized and managed, as well as the nature of domestic rivalry.

Porter went on to suggest that there may be two other variables which could influence the diamond, these were:

- Chance – including innovations or major events which could reshape the structure of the industry and provide opportunities for one nation's businesses to overtake another's.
- Government – through its adoption of policies such as regulation, **anti-trust laws** or investments, the government can have an impact for good or ill on the nation's advantages.

Positive sum game

The term 'positive sum game' suggests that in terms of international trade all countries involved benefit, even though some may benefit more than others. Indeed international trade only occurs because both parties benefit from the exchange. International trade is considered to enhance world prosperity, therefore economic integration, or **globalization**, is a positive sum game and not, as some suggest, a process of exclusion and marginalization. Adopting the 'positive sum game' viewpoint, the inference is that all countries, both the developed and the **lesser developed countries**, achieve material gains from international trade, regardless of whether the trade is imbalanced. By removing any restrictions to international trade, resources can be to a greater or lesser extent more fairly distributed throughout the world. Any increase in the transfer of technology, skills or competition increases productivity, which in every nation should bring about economic growth and a rise in real incomes. This is a positive sum game for all countries.

Power distance

Power distance is a theory regarding how a nation, or indeed the world, deals with the fact that individuals are unequal in terms of either their intellectual or their physical capabilities. There are many power distance cultures which allow inequalities to grow over a period of time. These inequalities are exemplified in huge disparities in power and in wealth.

Hofstede, Geert, *Culture's Consequence: Comparing Values, Behaviour, Institutions and Organizations across Nations.* Thousand Oaks, CA: Sage Publications, 2003.

Predatory pricing

Predatory pricing is a pricing strategy adopted by some businesses in order to inflict financial damage on competitors by forcing them to cut their profit margins and matching the unfeasibly low prices the business is offering. This is an extremely aggressive and often short-term policy, used to drive competitors out of a market. Invariably it is adopted by businesses that already have a substantial **market share** and enjoy considerable **economies of scale**, allowing them to temporarily offer products and services at prices well below the market norm. In recent years predatory pricing has become a feature in a number of areas, particularly with regard to supermarkets, where basic stock items, such as bread, baked beans and tinned tomatoes, have been offered at virtually cost price. Extreme cases of predatory pricing do in fact aim to drive competitors out of business. If this purpose is revealed and proved, the strategy is deemed illegal.

Preferential Trade Area for Eastern and Southern African States (PTA)

The PTA was first established in 1981 in order to support economic development and cooperation between its members. The membership includes Burundi, Comoros, Djibouti, Ethiopia, Kenya, Lesotho, Malawi, Mauritius, Rwanda, Somalia, Swaziland, Tanzania, Uganda, Zambia and Zimbabwe.

The treaty established a Common Market for Eastern and Southern Africa in 1994. This organization replaced the Preferential Trade Area for Eastern and Southern African States, which had been operational since 1981. The new Common Market for Eastern and Southern Africa (COMESA) now has some 20 members. COMESA seeks self-sustained development through cooperation, primarily in trade promotion, financial and monetary cooperation, the development of agriculture, investment, and an improvement in communications and transportation. The ultimate objective is to bring about a regional common market and an economic community. The aims and objectives of COMESA are to remove some of the inherent institutional and structural weaknesses of the member states by pooling their resources. The organization's main means of achieving this are:

- Through promoting a more balanced development in production, they hope to achieve sustained growth and development.
- By promoting joint development in economic activities and the adoption of joint economic policies and programmes, they hope to bring about closer relations between the member states and raise the standard of living.
- By providing an enabling environment for overseas investment, they hope to promote research, science and technology.
- By ensuring peace, security and stability within the region, they hope to enhance economic development.

- By strengthening the relationships between COMESA and the rest of the world, they hope to adopt common international positions.
- By achieving the above, they hope to bring about an African economic community.

The member states have agreed to allow **free trade**, the adoption of a **customs union**, the free movement of investment and capital, the eventual establishment of a payments union and common visa arrangements.

www.africatrade.com

Preliminary determination

'Preliminary determination' refers to the announcement by the **International Trade Administration (ITA)** of results of an investigation on **dumping**. The preliminary determination is completed within 160 days in most cases, or in more complex issues within 210 days.

The ITA makes a preliminary determination as to whether there are reasonable grounds to believe or suspect that specific merchandise has been sold, or was likely to be sold, at less than a fair trade price.

The term 'preliminary determination' also refers to decisions made by the **International Trade Commission** in cases where there is reasonable indication that a US industry has been injured or threatened by imports which are the subject of a petition. The ITC makes its preliminary determination within 45 days.

President's Export Council (PEC)

The President's Export Council (PEC) was established by Executive Order in the United States in 1973. It was originally composed of business executives but it was reconstituted in 1979 to include leaders of labour and agricultural communities, the Congress, and members of the Executive Branch. There are some 28 private sector members, 5 US Senators, 5 members of the House of Representatives, the Secretaries of Agriculture, Commerce, Labor, State and Treasury, the Chairman of the **Export–Import Bank of the US** and the US trade representative.

PEC directly advises the President on government policies and potential programmes which may impact upon US trade performance. They are also concerned with the promotion of exports and provide a platform for the discussion and resolution of trade-related problems.

www.ita.doc.gov/td/pec

Price discrimination

Price discrimination occurs when an international business charges its customers in different nations, different prices for the same product. Realistically, in more integrated areas of the world, such as areas of economic or monetary union, it is increasingly difficult for international businesses to adopt this policy. Theoretically, of course, businesses would like to charge each customer a different price for the same product, based on the price that each customer is willing to pay. In reality, however, sellers do not often know what purchasers are willing to pay.

Price discrimination is not necessarily related to additional costs incurred by an international business in getting products to a particular market. Indeed it is generally accepted that an international business will charge an additional sum to cover transportation and distribution costs. Price discrimination, therefore, refers wholly to the actual price of the products or services once any additional costs have been stripped out. Clearly in different markets in the world there are what could be considered to be acceptable and unacceptable prices. International businesses seek to find an equilibrium price in each market in which they operate. In framing a different pricing structure for each market an international business can enjoy a greater surplus or profit in certain markets. However, this policy only works for as long as the markets remain separate. Once any form of economic or currency union has been adopted, price differences are far more transparent as they do not require any currency-exchange calculation to be undertaken in order to compare the prices directly.

In most cases price discrimination is not a long-lasting policy and ultimately prices are framed as a direct reflection of prices achieved in other overseas markets.

Price elasticity

Price elasticity, or price elasticity of demand, measures the responsiveness of quantity demanded to a change in price. The most commonly used formula compares the proportion in change in quantity divided by the proportion in change in price. The effects are summarized in Table 11.

Tellis, Gerard J., *The Price Elasticity of Selective Demand: A Meta-analysis of Sales Response Models.* Cambridge, MA: Marketing Science Institute, 1988.

P

Table 11 Price elasticity

Elasticity	Demand is price elastic: $\eta_p > 1.0$	Demand is price inelastic: $\eta_p < 1.0$
Price reduction	Expenditure increases	Expenditure decreases
Price increase	Expenditure decreases	Expenditure increases

Privatization

Privatization involves the sale of government-owned businesses to private investors. In the UK, privatization was a key policy of the Conservative government during the 1980s, during which time many public utilities were sold into private hands. By the 1990s privatization had become a key element of many government policies around the world. The primary argument for the privatization of nationalized businesses was that it improved the performance of those industries.

Privatization can also be typified as being the transformation of what had been a state-owned **monopoly** into a competitive market by liberalizing and deregulating the industry itself. It has been argued that whilst privatization has seen some improvement in performance, the main purposes of privatization were to break the power of the trade unions within those nationalized industries and to provide considerable sums of money which could then be reinvested in other forms of public spending, as opposed to increasing taxation levels.

Clifton, Judith, Comin, Francisco and Diaz Fuentes, Daniel, *Privatization in the European Union: Public Enterprises and Integration*. New York: Kluwer Academic Publishers, 2003.

Product life cycle theory

The academic Raymond Vernon, who was a member of the Marshall Plan team and one of the key individuals involved in the development of the **International Monetary Fund** and the **General Agreement on Tariffs and Trade (GATT)**, proposed the product life cycle theory in response to the failure of the **Heckscher–Ohlin Theory** and its inability to explain patterns of international trade.

Vernon suggested that most new products are produced and exported from the country in which they were developed. As the new product becomes more accepted internationally, production begins in other countries. As a result of this the product ends up being exported back into the country where it was originally developed. Vernon argued that many of the mass-market products being produced in the world today were originally developed and sold in the US market, notably cars, televisions, photocopiers, computers and semi-conductor chips.

Vernon believed that the size of the US domestic market gave these US businesses a strong incentive to develop new consumer products. Essentially most of these products were produced using cost-saving processes on account of the fact that US labour was comparatively expensive. These pioneering businesses not only developed new products, but also developed low-cost production facilities. Demand grew for these products within the US and ultimately the US began exporting them. Over time, demand began to grow for these products in countries such as the UK, France, Japan and Germany. In the end it became advantageous for overseas producers to make the products themselves.

At first this meant that there was a reduced demand for US-made products and that the products became standardized. In the case of standardized products the main competitive weapon is price and therefore producers in overseas countries which have lower labour costs than the US are in a position to begin exporting not only to other overseas nations, but also to the US. In essence, the innovating country that first produced the product can no longer compete on a cost basis. Developing countries, such as Thailand or South Korea, have a huge production advantage over more advanced countries. This leads to a movement in the global production of these products, first to other advanced nations and then to developing countries. Over a period of time in the case of the US, the country moves from being a primary exporter of products to an importer of products.

Vernon, Raymond, *Beyond Globalism: Remaking American Foreign Economic Policy*. New York: Free Press, 1989.

Protocol

A protocol is a government-to-government agreement which usually frames the reciprocal trade agreements between two countries. The protocols may precisely set out the terms governing the reciprocal trade with respect to turnover of specific products or commodities. These bilateral government protocols effectively lay down the ways in which the governments are expected to treat one another's suppliers.

Protocol of provisional application (PPA)

The protocol of provisional application was the legal device used to enable the contracting parties to accept the benefits and obligations of the **General Agreement on Tariffs and Trade (GATT)**. This was despite the fact that some of the countries' domestic legislation at that time actually discriminated against imports and was inconsistent with some of the GATT provisions. The arrangement was meant to be a temporary solution for those countries which signed the PPA in 1947. As it transpired, countries which joined GATT after 1947 have continued to sign under the terms of the protocol of provisional application. Originally the PPA was to be developed until such a time as the Havana Charter could be ratified. The PPA itself stated that the governments would apply Parts 1 and 3 of GATT and that Part 2, with regard to **non-tariff barriers**, would apply only if it was not inconsistent with existing legislation.

The PPA was signed by 23 countries in 1947; these were Australia, Belgium, Brazil, Burma, Canada, Ceylon (now Sri Lanka), Chile, China, Cuba, the Czechoslovak Republic (now the Czech Republic and Slovakia), France, India, Lebanon, Luxembourg, the Netherlands, New Zealand, Norway, Pakistan, Southern Rhodesia (now Zimbabwe), Syria, South Africa, the United Kingdom and the United States.

The protocol of provisional application came into force on 1 January 1948.

www.wto.org

Purchase power parity

Purchase power parity is essentially a theory which contends that exchange rates between different currencies are in equilibrium when the purchasing power is the same in both countries. It is a means by which it is possible to compare the average costs of products and services between countries. The theory does require assumptions in as much as importers and exporters are motivated by cross-country price differences and changes in the **spot exchange rate**.

PPP theory is an integral part of the theory of the **law of one price**. Should a vehicle in the UK cost £10,000, then an identical model in the US should cost $20,000, on the assumption of the law of one price and given that the exchange rate is £0.50 to the $. If the exchange rate was higher and perhaps rose to £0.60 to the $, then it would be prudent for a US resident to purchase the vehicle in the UK because $16,666 would obtain £10,000. This would save the US resident $3,334 compared with the purchase price of the vehicle in the US.

Those who follow the theory of purchase power parity argue that the exchange rate must adjust itself to ensure that the law of one price continues to hold internationally for identical products and services. In the example above, this would mean that the price of the vehicle in the US should be brought down in order to re-establish purchase power parity.

P

Quantitative restrictions

Quantitative restrictions are explicit limits which are usually expressed by volume, giving the amount of a specified product or commodity which may be imported into a particular country. The term may also be used to describe the total amount of those goods which may be imported from any given supplying country.

When compared with **tariffs**, quantitative restrictions are more predictable. They are, in effect, **quotas**, which can also be used to favour particular sources of supply. In the majority of cases the **General Agreement on Tariffs and Trade (GATT)** prohibits the use of quantitative restrictions, except those which are specifically cited under Articles XX and XXI. These two articles deal with public health, national gold stocks, items of archaeological or historical interest and goods which are in the interests of national security.

Quotas

Quotas are deemed to be an absolute limit on the number of units of a particular product, or products, which can be imported over a specified period of time. The quotas can also apply to exports.

A variation of this is the tariff rate quota, which allows a specific quantity of a particular merchandise to be either imported or exported at a reduced rate over a given period of time.

In the US, quotas are usually established by Presidential proclamations or Executive Orders. In essence, quotas are a form of protectionism, which either imposes a limit on the imports of particular products from another country or limits the amount of exports from a country bound for another named country.

Quotas limit the supply, and therefore the price of quota-restricted imported goods is higher. In theory this process should make it easier for domestic producers to compete.

Rate of exchange

The rate of exchange is the basis upon which the currency of one country can be exchanged for the currency of another. Rates of exchange are usually established on the basis of demand, supply and stability of the currencies in question.

See also **exchange rate.**

Reciprocity

Reciprocity is concerned with the reduction of a country's trade restraints or import duties in return for comparable changes related to trade from another country. Usually reciprocity involves a reduction of customs duties on imports in return for **tariff** concessions.

Reciprocity is an integral part of the **General Agreement on Tariffs and Trade (GATT)** negotiations, which call for an equality of concessions between participants who are engaged in reciprocity negotiations. As far as GATT is concerned, reciprocity only applies to trade negotiations between developed countries. This is on account of the fact that the relationships between developed and developing countries rarely allow for truly equivalent trade concessions to be agreed, largely because the countries have widely different economic capabilities and potential.

The negotiations in regard to reciprocity between developed and **lesser developed countries** are described as relative reciprocity, in as much as the developed country does not seek full reciprocity from the developing country during the trade negotiation.

Regional economic integration

Regional economic integration can range from a **free trade area**, a **customs union**, a **common market** and an **economic union** or a full political union. Free trade areas involve the removal of all **trade barriers** of all member countries, but each country is left to determine its own external trade policies with other nations.

In customs unions, the internal barriers to trade are also removed, but in this case a common external trade policy is developed. A common market bears a striking resemblance to a customs union but it also allows **factors of production** to move between countries.

Economic unions involve the establishment of a common currency and usually a harmonization in tax rates. Political unions are a culmination of all of the above, moving the countries closer to full economic integration.

Countries are tempted towards economic integration in order to gain the full benefits from the free movement of trade and investment. However, integration is not without grave difficulties, principally as can be seen in the case of the **European Union**, where national sovereignty is a major stumbling block. In Europe the **Single European Act** sought to create a single market by pulling down all of the administrative barriers to the free flow of trade and investment. The **Maastricht Treaty** took the European Union further towards economic union. Arguably attempts are already being made at full political union in Europe, notably by the **European Commission** becoming involved in competition policy, and its attempts to restrict the number of **acquisitions** and mergers, which it believes will have an impact upon competition within the European Union.

The European Union is the closest example in the world, of economic and political union. Other attempts at various stages are being made in other parts of the world, such as the **Andean Pact** and **MERCOSUR** in Latin America, the **North American Free Trade Agreement**, and **ASEAN** in South-East Asia.

Schirm, Stefan, *Globalization and the New Regionalism: Global Markets, Domestic Politics and Regional Cooperation*. Cambridge: Polity Press, 2002.

Rescheduling

Rescheduling involves amendments being made to the payment schedules for debts following an agreement between the borrower and the lender. Rescheduling usually takes place when the borrower is finding it increasingly difficult to make regular payments under an original schedule. Rescheduling can involve extending the period over which the payments are collected, the postponement of the date for the repayment of the loan, a reduction of interest payments (but increasing the amount that has to be repaid at the end of the period) or simply a reduction of the interest rates. Rescheduling can mean that the lender has to accept some degree of financial loss.

Reserve tranche

A reserve tranche is an amount of cash which may be made available to a member country of the **International Monetary Fund** in addition to the extent of the quotas of IMF holdings of its currency (held in the General Resources Account). The member country may obtain up to the full amount of its reserve tranche at any time, but this is subject to the requirement of **balance of payments** needs.

www.imf.org

Retaliation

Under the terms of the **General Agreement on Tariffs and Trade (GATT)**, countries are permitted to impose limited restraints on imports from another country which has raised its **trade barriers** against them. Retaliation therefore is action taken by a particular country whose exports have been adversely affected by some form of trade restriction, perhaps the raising of tariffs, by another country. Theoretically at least, under the terms of GATT the retaliatory measures should be broadly in proportion to the value of trade which was affected by the other country's import protection policy.

Reverse preferences

Prior to the signing of the **Lomé Convention** reverse preferences were tariff advantages which were offered by developing countries to particular imports from specified developed countries which had, in turn, granted the developing country trade preferences.

Right sizing

Right sizing is a considerable feature in expanding international businesses who seek to ensure that the totality of their **organizational structure** reflects the requirements and needs of the business processes in which they are involved. Right sizing involves an investigation into the number of employees, their positions and job roles and how both the formal and informal patterns of interaction all contribute towards accomplishing the international business's objectives. Right sizing seeks to eliminate duplicated work and unnecessary tasks and it also aims to improve and prioritize the passage of the most important functions of the business. In effect, right sizing attempts to reshape the

R

whole organizational structure of an international business. Right sizing can be synonymous with down-sizing in as much as it seeks to eliminate functions which are unnecessary, and to reduce expenditure and redesign systems and policies. Right sizing can also involve the process of up-sizing, which effectively increases the number of employees by identifying areas of the business's operations which are undermanned and require an injection of new employees in order to ensure that they function to optimal levels.

Massoudi, Robert and Astrid, Julienne, *Right-Sizing for Corporate Survival*. Englewood Cliffs, NJ: Prentice-Hall, 1994.

Rio Group

The Rio Group is an organization of Latin American countries which currently consists of Mexico, Costa Rica, Guatemala, Honduras, Nicaragua and El Salvador. It also includes the members of the Central American System of Integration (SICA), namely Panama, Colombia, Venezuela, Ecuador, Peru and Bolivia. The group also includes the members of the **Andean Pact**, which are Brazil, Argentina, Uruguay and Paraguay. The members of **MERCOSUR** are also represented, namely Chile, the Dominican Republic and a representative member of **CARICOM**.

The Rio Group has met annually since 1987 with the aim of strengthening both political and economic relations between the countries in Latin America and the Caribbean. They are primarily concerned, through this informal mechanism, with the growth and consolidation of the region. The Rio Group does not have a permanent headquarters and its secretariat is rotated on an annual basis within its membership. The Rio Group acts mostly within the confines of the **United Nations** and represents its member states in multilateral discussions.

www.europa.eu.int/comm/external_relations/la/rio/28_03_03.htm

Risk analysis

Risk analysis is the process of identifying potential loss exposures and measuring the degree of loss that could result from these exposures. Risk analysis also involves an estimation of the probability that losses may occur, and evaluation of the potential actions which could be undertaken in order to meet risk management objectives.

See also **risk management**.

Risk management

Risk management is a procedure usually undertaken by a bank in order to manage its exposure to various forms of risk. Risk management involves internal risk reduction and the framing of contractual safeguards in respect of each individual loan contract. Risk management also seeks to secure **insurance** coverage to cover various forms of potential risk.

See also risk analysis.

Bessis, Joel, *Risk Management in Banking*. Chichester: John Wiley, 2002.

Rollback

'Rollback' is a term related to the **Uruguay Round** of the **General Agreement on Tariffs and Trade (GATT)** in which the participating countries undertook to dismantle any trade restrictions or distortions which would be inconsistent with GATT. Rollback issues meant that specific trade restrictions would be brought into conformity with GATT within an agreed period of time and no later than the formal completion of the GATT negotiations. In effect, rollback was a commitment by countries not to impose any further trade restriction measures, or at least not to impose any which were in excess of those that already existed.

Rounds

The term 'rounds' refers to the periodic cycles of trade negotiations under the **General Agreement on Tariffs and Trade (GATT)**. They culminated in a series of agreements in which the participating countries agreed to reduce both tariff and non-tariff **trade barriers**. These were:

- The first round – Geneva 1947, which brought about the creation of GATT.
- The second round – in Annecy, France, in 1949, which brought about tariff reductions.
- The third round – in Torquay, England, in 1951, which dealt with accession and further tariff reductions.
- The fourth round – in Geneva in 1956, which again dealt with accession and tariff reductions.
- The fifth round – also in Geneva between 1960 and 1962, which was known as the Dillon Round, which revised GATT and allowed more countries to join.

R

- The sixth round – also held in Geneva, between 1964 and 1967, was known as the Kennedy Round.
- The seventh round – again in Geneva, between 1973 and 1979, also known as the Tokyo Round.
- The eighth round – in Geneva between 1986 and 1993, which is otherwise known as the **Uruguay Round**.

Rugman, Alan M.

Alan M. Rugman has published widely in the areas of economics and the managerial strategic considerations of multinational enterprises, as well as on trade and investment policy. He is considered to be one of the leading writers on international trade and international business issues, together with his insightful analysis of markets and economies.

Amongst his most recent books are *Environmental Regulations and Corporate Strategy* (1999), *International Business: A Strategic Management Approach* (2000), *The End of Globalization* (2000) and *The World Trade Organization in the New Global Economy* (2002).

Rugman, Alan M. and Hodgetts, Richard M., *International Business: A Strategic Management Approach*. Englewood Cliffs, NJ: Prentice-Hall, 2002.

R

Safeguards

Under the terms of the **General Agreement on Tariffs and Trade (GATT)**, there are two forms of permitted multilateral safeguards, these are:

- The right of a country to impose temporary import controls or other trade restrictions in order to prevent the commercial injury of its domestic industries.
- The right of exporters not to be denied access to markets in an arbitrary manner.

Scope determination

Scope determination aims to address the product coverage of **anti-dumping** and **countervailing duty** orders. In the US, for example, the US Department of Commerce will determine, as a result of an application or on its own initiative, whether particular products are included in an anti-dumping or countervailing duty order.

Section 201

Section 201 is known as the escape clause of the US Trade Act 1974. It allows temporary import relief, which cannot exceed 8 years, to a US industry which has been injured or threatened with injury due to increased imports. The import relief, which is granted at the President's discretion, takes the form of either **quantitative restrictions** or increased **tariffs**. A US business, in order to be eligible for relief under Section 201, must have the backing of the **International Trade Commission (ITC)** which has determined the following:

- The industry has been seriously injured or has been threatened with injury.
- The imports which caused this injury were substantive in their impact.

Should the ITC agree that there has been serious injury and a substantial cause, the US President may increase tariffs or impose quantitative restrictions.

Should the President not grant relief, he must explain his decision to the US Congress.

Section 232

Section 232 refers to the US Trade Expansion Act 1962 and its subsequent amendments. The US Commerce Department must make a ruling as to whether a specific product which has been imported into the US in a particular quantity, or under particular circumstances, may seriously threaten national security. The US Commerce Department must make recommendations within 270 days, and, within 90 days of the Commerce Department's report being delivered to the President, he must make a decision as to whether to adjust imports. The President is also required to inform Congress of his decision within 30 days.

Section 301

Under Section 301, US businesses can complain about a foreign country's trade policies which they believe to be harmful to US trade opportunities. Section 301 involves the investigation of the allegations and the immediate commencement of negotiations to remove those **trade barriers**. Section 301 requires that the dispute resolution process of the **General Agreement on Tariffs and Trade (GATT)** be commenced and, if the negotiations fail, they allow the US to retaliate within 180 days of discovering that the trade agreement violation has taken place. The Section 301 investigations are carried out by the US Trade Representative (USTR).

See also **Special 301**.

Section 337

This refers to Section 337 of the US Tariff Act 1930. Under the terms of this section investigations are carried out with regard to unfair practices in import trade. The **International Trade Commission** uses existing US law on unfair competition to judge as to the fairness of the importation of goods into the US. Section 337 expressly prohibits both unfair competition and unfair importing practices. Should a violation be identified, it must be proved that one of the following has occurred:

- that the importation has destroyed or substantially injured US industry;
- that it has prevented the establishment of a US industry;
- that it has otherwise monopolized or restrained US trade.

Section 337 also refers to the infringement of US-held trademarks, copyrights and patents.

Severely indebted countries

The **World Bank** defines severely indebted countries as nations whose present value of debt services is equal to 80% of their **gross national product** and where the present value of their debt services is 220% of the value of their exports.

See also **Toronto terms.**

Shipper's export declaration (SED)

Shipper's export declarations are used primarily to control exports and to act as a primary source of statistical information in the compilation of export figures. SEDs are prepared by the exporter and the exporter's agent and delivered to the exporting carrier. The exporting carrier then presents a number of copies of the shipper's export declaration to the customs service at the port of export.

Shipping terms

Shipping terms are essentially price quotations which include the cost of merchandise plus the cost of any other services which a beneficiary of a **letter of credit** is required to pay for shipping the merchandise. Typically, the following forms of shipping terms include a number of different pre-paid services:

- CFR (cost and freight) – which includes the cost of the merchandise, transportation to the dock, loading onto the vessel, forwarders' fees for preparing the documents, and ocean freight.
- CIF (cost, insurance and freight) – which includes the cost of the merchandise, transportation to the dock, loading onto the vessel, forwarder's fees for the shipping documents, ocean freight and an insurance premium.
- CIP (cost and insurance) – which includes the cost of the merchandise, marine insurance and transportation charges, with the exception of the ocean freight to the named destination.

S

- DDP (ex-dock duty paid) – which includes the cost of the merchandise, transportation to the dock, loading onto the vessel, forwarder's fees for preparing the documents, ocean freight, insurance premium, unloading of the merchandise at the dock, import duties and delivery to a named destination.
- EXW (ex-factory) – which only includes the cost of the merchandise.
- FAS (free alongside) – which includes the cost of the merchandise, transportation to the dock, but not the forwarder's fees for the shipping documentation.
- FOB (free, or freight, onboard) – which includes the cost of the merchandise, transportation to the dock, loading onto the vessel and freight forwarder's fees for preparing the shipping documents.

Single European Act

The Single European Act came into force in 1987 and was essentially a revision of the **Treaty of Rome**. The Single European Act revised the European Economic Community Treaty and provided both the legal and procedural framework for the achievement of a single European market by 1992. The Single European Act also introduced majority decisions for the votes which faced the Council of Ministers, strengthened the role of the European Parliament and required a unanimous decision on fiscal policy.

Single Internal Market Information Service (SIMIS)

The Single Internal Market Information Service is operated by the US Commerce Department's **International Trade Administration**. It provides information, assistance and advice to US businesses on how to carry out trade and other business in the internal market of the **European Community**.

www.doc.gov

Smoot–Hawley Tariff

The Smoot–Hawley Tariff, which was enacted in 1930 by the US Congress, was a major policy blunder which hastened and deepened the 1930s depression. The Smoot–Hawley Tariff only succeeded in creating similar tariff barriers around the world, which meant that US products found few markets in other countries. As soon as US domestic demand had been satisfied, US businesses were faced with the prospect of overproduction, which led to industrial cut-backs. As increasing numbers of employees were laid off, the demand for US domestic products fell and a vicious circle was created, leading to ever deeper cut-backs in industry and an ever-increasing decline in demand for products and services.

Thousands of US banks failed during the period. The Smoot-Hawley Tariff threw 13 million US workers into unemployment.

See also **tariff**.

Soft currency

A soft currency is a national currency which is notoriously difficult to exchange. Usually soft currencies belong to countries that have enormous deficits in their **balance of payments** and have only minimal exchange reserves.

Soft loan

'Soft loan' is normally associated with loans made by international banks, or agencies, to help encourage economic activity in developing countries. They may also be granted to support other non-commercial activities. A soft loan is typified by the interest rate being pegged at lower than the normal market interest rate, thus making the loan more attractive and affordable to the developing country.

Special and differential treatment

The principle of special and differential treatment came about during the Tokyo Round of the **General Agreement on Tariffs and Trade (GATT)** negotiations. It sought to confer benefits to the exports of developing countries provided they were consistent with their development, financial and trading needs. In effect, special or differential treatment involves the reduction, or perhaps the elimination, of tariffs on developing countries' exports under the terms of the **generalized system of preferences (GSP)**.

The special and differential treatment allows for the expansion of either product or country coverage of the GSP and an accelerated implementation of tariff cuts which had been agreed during the Tokyo Round and were subsequently stated in the Tokyo declaration. It allows for a substantial reduction or elimination of tariffs, and contains special provisions covering **non-tariff measures**. Above all, it agreed in principle that developed countries would not necessarily expect full **reciprocity** for any trade concessions they might grant developing countries.

S

Special drawing rights

Special drawing rights were created by the **International Monetary Fund** in 1970 and are, in effect, international reserve assets which are allocated to each of the member nations. Provided these countries adhere to the conditions set by the IMF, special drawing rights can be used to help deal with deficits in their **balance of payments**. They can help settle debts that they have with another nation, or with the IMF itself. The value of special drawing rights is calculated as a weighted average of several internationally traded currencies.

Special 301

Special 301, which is a variation of **Section 301**, was created by the US Omnibus Trade and Competitiveness Act 1988. Under the terms of Special 301 the US Trade Representative (USTR) is instructed to make annual reviews of **intellectual property rights** protection amongst US trading partners. The USTR considers whether a country can be considered as having excessive **trade barriers** with the US as a result of its inadequate protection of intellectual property. Should a country be named as being a potential problem, it is either designated as a priority foreign country, or placed on the priority watch list or simply on the watch list, according to its level of intellectual property protection.

Specific tariff

A specific tariff is a fixed charge which is levied for each unit of a particular product which is imported.

> See also **tariff**.

Spot exchange rate

The spot exchange rate is the current market rate for the purchase or sale of foreign exchange whose settlement will be made within one or two business days.

Standard industrial classification (SIC)

Standard industrial classifications are attempts to categorize each form of business activity using a 4-digit code for each group. The exact nature of the SIC in any given country will necessarily have an entirely different mix. In terms of marketing, the SIC or, as it is known in North America, the NAICS (North American Industry Classification System), allows a

business to specifically target businesses within specified classif
An alternative is the Business Activity Classification (BAC)
comprises seven categorized areas, with a number of subdivisic...

SIC codes were developed to facilitate the collection and presentation, and ultimately the analysis, of uniform and comparable statistical data covering all economic activities.

Stationery Office Books, *Indexes to the Standard Industrial Classification of Economic Activities*. London: HMSO, 2002.

Stationery Office Books, *UK Standard Industrial Classification of Economic Activities*. London: HMSO, 2002.

Standard International Trade Classification (SITC)

The SITC is the standard classification for reporting international trade statistics. The SITC consists of detailed categories for the classification of various commodities and has a hierarchy of five levels. It was developed by the United Nations and is broadly compatible with other international classifications of industries and products.

Standardization

The term 'standardization' refers to an organization's efforts to ensure that all its workers are performing their tasks or activities in a consistent manner. An organization striving for standardization would do so to assist in ensuring consistent levels of safety, productivity, and quality. The term 'standardization' may also refer to an organization's desire to standardize the parts and components which it uses.

In international business, standardization very much relies upon the specific arrangements required by overseas nations in their moves towards standardized procedures and classifications.

See also **Levitt, Theodore.**

Standards code

The term 'standards code' can be applied to a wide variety of different international business-related areas of operation. Clearly there are standards codes which are applicable to issues such as financial reporting, marketing, health and safety, employment rights, equality of opportunity and a host of other areas which may have a direct impact upon the way in which a business organization configures its activities. Many international businesses attempt to ensure that they have a series of standards codes which are applied to all areas of their operations, regardless of the

S

fact that they may include foreign subsidiaries. Until such a time as more nations adopt similar standardized approaches to business practice, the standards codes can at best be only considered as guidelines of best practice.

Standby arrangements

A standby arrangement is essentially an extended arrangement which assures a member of the **International Monetary Fund** that it will be allowed to make purchases up to a specified amount from the fund over a given period, provided the member has met specified criteria and other terms enshrined within the agreement. Standby arrangements can cover three years, during which the member state can make purchases from the general resources of the IMF. The standby arrangement will specify which funds will be available, how much will be available and whether there are any conditions attached to the access of those funds. The terms of any standby arrangement are agreed after consultation between the member state and the fund itself. A standby agreement is not an international agreement as the arrangement is not legally binding upon the member state.

www.imf.org

Standstill

'Standstill' refers to the **Uruguay Round** negotiations of the **General Agreement on Tariffs and Trade (GATT)**. During this time the countries involved undertook the following:

- Not to impose any restrictive trade or trade distorting measures which were inconsistent with GATT.
- Not to impose any restrictive trade or trade distorting measures beyond those consistent with GATT.
- Not to impose trade measures in order to improve their negotiating position.

See also **rollback**.

Statistical Office of the European Community (Eurostat)

The Statistical Office of the European Community, or Eurostat, exists to provide **European Union**-wide statistics on a variety of different subjects, including economics, finance, foreign trade, industry, energy, agriculture, forestry, services and transportation. It began life as a statistical service in 1952 and in 2002 adopted a Pan-European statistical system.

www.europa.eu.int/comm/eurostat

Strategic alliances

Strategic alliances are either short-term or long-term alliances between two businesses with the purpose of sharing resources. Strategic alliances may include **joint ventures**, but in general they are a business relationship in which the two businesses pool their strengths, share risks and try to integrate their business functions for mutual benefits. Unlike any other form of close cooperation, both business entities remain independent throughout the arrangement. Strategic alliances are an important way of being able to break into new markets, acquire new technical skills and improve on the business's competitive position. Businesses may create a strategic alliance in one of the following ways:

- through internal growth;
- through merger and **acquisition**;
- through spin-offs;
- through short-, medium- or long-term contractual agreements with another business.

The alliance strategy is particularly attractive to international businesses that wish to operate in foreign markets which are relatively politically stable, or in developing countries which have free market systems (and are not usually suffering from high inflation or high private-sector debt). Strategic alliances can be used to offset many of the risks associated with **pioneering costs** as the risks are spread.

There are in effect six different ways in which a strategic alliance could assist international businesses in entering a foreign market. These include:

- Exporting – which has all the advantages of avoiding the setup costs of manufacturing in an overseas market, but may have the disadvantage of higher transport costs and potential **trade barriers**. A strategic alliance could be used to form an association with a marketing subsidiary in the **host country**.
- **Turnkey** projects – this allows an international business to become involved in an overseas market where there may be prohibitions related to **foreign direct investment**. In essence, the international business exports only its process abilities and understanding, but this may inadvertently create a competitor in the longer run.

S

- **Licensing** – this involves framing a strategic alliance on the basis that a host country's industry undertakes to manufacture products in accordance with the trademarks and **patents** of the international business. The international business may risk losing control over its licences and will be passing on its technological know-how to a potential long-term competitor.
- **Franchising** – this involves a strategic alliance with a host country business which will bear the risks and the costs of opening up a new market. There are often problems in dealing with quality control issues with distant franchisees.
- **Joint ventures** – this involves establishing a strategic alliance based on the sharing of costs and risks and the gaining of local knowledge and perhaps political influence. Again the international business may lose a degree of control and protection of its technologies.
- Wholly-owned subsidiary – whilst the international business will have to bear all of the costs and risks in opening up the overseas market, a wholly owned subsidiary offers tighter control of technology and other aspects of the business operation.

In order to make strategic alliances work, both businesses need to have sophisticated formal and informal communication networks and take steps to build trust between one another. Both parties need to take proactive steps in order to learn as much as they can from the operations of their partners.

Doz, Yves and Hamel, Gary, *Alliance Advantage: The Art of Creating Value through Partnering*. Boston, MA: Harvard Business School Press, 1998.

Structural adjustment facility (SAF)

A structural adjustment facility is an **International Monetary Fund** programme which aims to implement structural adjustment programmes. SAFs provide assistance with **balance of payments** to low-income developing countries on favourable terms. The primary objective of an SAF is to help the member country to restore its balance of payments position and move towards more sustainable growth.

See also **structural adjustment programmes (SAP)**.

www.imf.org

Structural adjustment programmes (SAP)

The structural adjustment programmes (SAP) are the conditions imposed by the **International Monetary Fund** and the **World Bank** on conditional loans. The aim of the programmes is to encourage the borrowing country to make changes to its economy to improve its financial performance. SAPs can include currency devaluation, interest rate rises, the lowering of **quotas** and **tariffs**, **privatization** of public companies and the general promotion of exports. The primary aim of SAPs is to help borrowing countries reduce their budget deficits and enable them to meet debt repayment obligations.

SAPs are strongly criticized in as much as they often lower the per capita income of the country's population, reduce the value of real wages, increase unemployment and reduce nutritional standards.

www.imf.org

Structural Impediments Initiative (SII)

The Structural Impediments Initiative is a series of negotiations which began in 1989 between the US and Japan in order to bring their trade with one another into a better balance. The SII sought to identify and solve structural problems which would restrict the achievement of this balance. The US was concerned regarding its allegations that Japan had not effectively enforced national competition law (namely the Anti-Monopoly Act), and perceived that there were adverse consequences with regard to access to the Japanese market by foreign exporters.

Subrogation

Subrogation is an operation in which an insurance company, on the payment of a particular claim, assumes the assureds' rights to recovery from any third party. In effect, subrogation is the substitution of one creditor for another creditor.

Subsidy

Although the **General Agreement on Tariffs and Trade (GATT)** does not define the term 'subsidy', it is generally regarded as either a bounty or a grant which is paid to support the production, manufacture or export of a product or a commodity. Export subsidies clearly apply to products and commodities which will be exported, whilst domestic subsidies apply to forms of production or manufacture which are not necessarily related to exporting. Subsidies can take various forms; occasionally they may be direct payments to specific businesses. More usually, however, subsidies take an indirect form, such as tax breaks, preferential terms for loans, and support for research and development. In essence, subsidies help to keep prices lower than they would be normally in a free market. Subsidies can also ensure that specific businesses can still remain operational. In other cases subsidies ensure that research, development and innovation can take place in conditions where otherwise they could not have been undertaken. In many respects subsidies are a form of protectionism which keeps domestic goods artificially competitive against imports from overseas countries.

Summit conference

The term 'summit conference' is probably derived from the Geneva Big Four Conference of 1955. It now refers to an international meeting of nations where the heads of government assume the role of chief negotiators. These meetings aim to achieve substantive results and outcomes and are differentiated from other meetings of heads of government, which can be purely ceremonial.

Supplier credit

Supplier credit is normally delivered through commercial banks and involves the supplier organizing deferred payment terms on behalf of an overseas buyer. The arrangement allows the supplier or exporter to give the customer, under the terms of the sales contract, the opportunity to make deferred payments. In order to facilitate this the buyer issues the supplier promissory notes or accepts **bills of exchange**, as under normal circumstances a supplier could not afford to produce and deliver goods without receiving financial compensation for them. The supplier then presents the promissory notes or bills of exchange to a bank, which buys them at a discounted rate. In effect this means that the commercial bank, via the supplier, has provided credit to the buyer.

S

Supply access

'Supply access' refers to agreements or assurances that are made with overseas countries to ensure that an importing country will continue to have fair and reasonable access, at reasonable prices, to supplies of essential imports, notably raw materials. Supply access assurances usually include explicit agreements which constrain the use of export embargoes as a means of foreign policy by the exporting country.

Sustainable competitive advantage

A sustainable competitive advantage can be typified as being a competitive advantage which either an international business has, or a specific country has, which cannot easily be imitated and will be difficult to erode over a period of time. In order to have a sustainable competitive advantage a business or a nation needs to have a unique **core competence** which is difficult to copy, unique in itself, sustainable, superior to the competition and, above all, applicable in a number of different situations. Typical forms of sustainable competitive advantage include:

- a vastly superior product in terms of quality;
- well established and extensive distribution channels;
- a positive reputation and a strong brand equity;
- low-cost production techniques and processes;
- the ownership of **patents** or **copyrights**;
- a **monopoly** in the form of government protection;
- a superior management team and/or employees.

See also **Porter, Michael.**

Swaps

Swaps involve the exchange of one asset or payment for another. Currency swaps, for example, involve converting a lender's currency into the debtor's currency and the receiving of interest payments in the debtor's currency. Swaps are made to protect a principle from future changes in foreign exchange rates. Debts swaps, for example, involve the replacing of foreign liabilities of a debtor country with ownership. Debt-for-equity swaps replace foreign liabilities with a stake in the debtor country's national enterprises. Debt-for-export swaps similarly replace foreign liabilities with the right to receive proceeds from the overseas sales of the debtor country's products and commodities. Debt-for-debt swaps replace existing foreign liabilities with new commitments from the debtor country. Single-currency interest rate swaps involve exchanging future cash flow in the same currency whilst offering a means of modifying the impacts of future changes in interest rates. Cross-currency interest rate swaps involve the exchanging of future cash flows between one currency and another (traded on either a fixed or a floating rate basis) whilst offering the means for limiting the risk of converting financial interest between currencies.

Swaps can also involve an arrangement between different sellers of similar commodities. This allows them to swap and deliver to each other's customers in order to cut down on transportation costs.

Switch trading

Switch trading involves the conversion of bilateral clearing balances into convertible currencies through the sale of the clearing balance to switch traders at a discounted price. The switch traders reduce or eliminate the imbalance through any import or export transactions with which they are involved. Switch trading is also used to describe various non-clearing transactions which involve multiple sales of different goods through various brokers. Through this series of trades at discounted prices an exporter can effectively convert a **soft currency** payment, or a **counter-traded** product, into **hard currency**.

Systematic risk

Systematic risk recognizes that the value of overseas investments may decline over a period of time as a result of economic change. International businesses use the potential threats which may arise from systematic risk as a key determining factor in choosing how they allocate their assets and diversify in different markets. By becoming involved in different overseas markets they can, to some extent, insulate themselves from events which would have a detrimental impact on a specific market. By spreading their risk they avoid the dangers of systematic risk affecting their whole operations. In making investments in different overseas countries, international businesses can afford the detrimental impacts of under-performance in certain markets at different times, provided that this under-performance is not widespread across all of the markets in which they operate.

The term 'systematic risk' is also known as 'market risk'.

S

Tariff

A tariff is, in its simplest form, a tax on products, raw materials or commodities which have been produced abroad, and is imposed upon them by the government of the country into which they are being exported. Governments will set the level of tax in accordance with their own **tariff schedule** and it may indeed be applied to goods entering or leaving the country. Tariffs are levied primarily in order to protect domestic industries from imported goods, as tariffs inherently make the imports more expensive. Tariffs are also used as a primary source of revenue for the government.

Increasingly, many countries have reduced their tariffs, though without having wholly dispensed with them, as part of the continuing process of freeing up world trade.

See also **Smoot–Hawley Tariff.**

Tariff anomaly

A tariff anomaly may exist when the tariffs on raw materials or semi-manufactured products are actually higher than the tariff on the finished product.

Tariff escalation

Tariff escalation is a shorthand means of explaining the comparative tariffs on raw materials, semi-processed products and completely finished manufactured goods. In the majority of circumstances the tariffs on raw materials are extremely low, or there may not be any tariffs levied at all. The tariffs on semi-processed goods or components may be deemed moderate compared with the tariffs on raw materials. Manufactured goods tend to attract relatively high tariffs in comparison with the other two.

The primary reason for tariff escalation is a country's determination to protect its own industry, which may be reliant upon raw materials or semi-processed products and components. Ultimately the domestic industry will be able to turn these raw materials and semi-processed goods into manufactured goods, possibly for re-export. As a result, the work carried out on these two sets of items will contribute positively to the country's **balance of payments**. Manufactured goods, on the other hand, can only ever contribute a negative total to the balance of payments and are therefore, comparatively speaking, penalized by the importing nation, partly to recoup some of the costs to the economy through taxation, but also to protect their existing domestic business, which may manufacture similar products.

Tariff quota

A country may use a tariff quota in an attempt to restrict the amount of a specific imported product or commodity coming into the country. A quota will be set, based on the country's needs for a particular commodity. This will usually be a lower tariff rate than is normally expected. This is to encourage the importation of these goods up to that quota level and ensure that overseas businesses remain financially committed to providing that amount of goods. Once the tariff quota has been reached, however, the country then imposes a far higher tariff rate on the imported goods, thus making it less attractive for overseas businesses to continue to import above the tariff quota level.

Tariff schedule

A tariff schedule is a comprehensive list of products, goods and commodities which a country is prepared to allow to be imported. The tariff schedule not only details all of these different products, goods and commodities, but it also details the relevant import duties which are applicable to each of them.

Jackson, John H., *The World Trading System: Law and Policy of Economic Relations.* Cambridge, MA: MIT Press, 1997.

Tax arbitrage

Tax **arbitrage** involves the creating of transactions or financial instruments which allow two businesses to exploit the loopholes or differences in their tax exposures at home. The purpose of tax arbitrage is to ensure that both parties pay a lower amount of relevant tax than would otherwise have been due had the tax arbitrage not taken place.

Tax haven

A tax haven is often known as an offshore financial centre. It is a term which is usually applied to low-tax economies which aim to attract foreign investment. The United Nations, for example, defines an **offshore** institution as 'any bank anywhere in the world that accepts deposits and manages funds on behalf of persons legally domiciled elsewhere'. The US has a far more practical definition, as framed by its Financial Stability Forum, describing offshore financial centres as 'jurisdictions that attract a high level of non-resident activity'.

There are undoubtedly a large number of tax havens around the world. The United Nations recognizes between 60 and 90 nations and territories. The US Department of State recognizes 52, including the US itself. The **Organization for Economic Cooperation and Development** identifies 41 low-tax jurisdictions. Countries such as the Cayman Islands, Bermuda and the Bahamas have no income tax, whilst others, such as Guernsey, Lichtenstein and Hong Kong, have low flat-rate taxation systems.

Many commercial banks, however, and government **central banks** consider tax havens to be nothing more than undesirable tax competition that has entirely different rules on disclosure, or the protection of minority shareholder rights, and many other missing features in regulatory competition rules.

Tax treaty

A tax treaty defines and specifies precisely how particular income is to be taxed in the event that two countries have jurisdiction over the income in question. A new tax treaty between the UK and the US was ratified in March 2003. It was originally signed in July 2001 and was amended by a **protocol** in July 2002. The treaty in this case affects income tax and capital gains tax, corporation tax, Federal income taxes and the withholding of tax in both countries. These elements were all phased in between April 2003 and January 2004.

Technology transfer

Technology transfer involves the transference of knowledge which has been created and developed in one country to another country, where its use has definite practical applications. Technology transfer can occur in many different ways, including the following:

- Free technology transfer – which includes conferences, the emigration of technical experts, technical assistance programmes and technical journals.

- Industrial espionage – literally the theft of technological know-how by subversive means.
- Sales – notably of **patents**, industrial processes and blueprints.

The most common form of technology transfer is through the activities of multinational organizations. Each time a multinational organization chooses to establish new operations in an overseas environment, inherently it transfers technology. Technology need not be the stereotypical view of a technological innovation, as the term 'technology transfer' also refers to the way in which an organization runs or operates particular processes, and it may, of course, include the knowledge which has been accumulated by managers and employees. In establishing a relationship with an overseas business, whether this is as a subsidiary or by **acquisition**, technology transfer is immediate and ongoing as its transference has mutually beneficial connotations for both the multinational and the overseas business.

Temporal method

The temporal method is a currency translation methodology in which the choice of exchange rate depends on the underlying method of valuation. Normally assets and liabilities are valued at the market cost, or historical cost rate, and then translated at the historical or current rate. In other words, balance sheet items are translated using the exchange rate which corresponds to their valuation base in a local currency. The temporal method applies what is known as a single entity theory to currency translation. The assumption is that the consolidation group represents a single economic unit. The consolidation units post data and prepare balances in the currency of the upper unit, regardless of the country in which they operate. Currency translation should not affect the valuation base on the balance sheet, nor the temporal consideration of either expenses or revenue. It simply entails changing the unit of measure and not the base evaluation.

Terms of trade

'Terms of trade' refers to the economic factors which affect a country's foreign trade in products and services. Typically its terms of trade may be dependent upon foreign sourcing or competitiveness in production.

Third country initiative (TCI)

Third country initiative (TCI) was originally created to establish an export control system with regard to strategic commodities. The third country initiative was proposed and run by the Coordinating Committee for Multilateral Export Controls (COCOM), but COCOM itself was dissolved in 1994, leaving no multilateral means of controlling exports of militarily useful products and technology. The TCI, however, included:

- import certifications and delivery verifications;
- controls over re-exports of controlled goods;
- cooperation in pre-licensing and post-shipment checks;
- cooperation in enforcement issues.

The TCI itself sought to assist countries in establishing export controls despite the fact that they were not members of COCOM.

Through bill of lading

A through bill of lading is a single **bill of lading** which covers both the domestic and international carriage of an export shipment. Although an **air way bill** is essentially a through bill of lading, ocean shipments usually require two documents: an **inland bill of lading** (which covers the domestic carriage) and an **ocean bill of lading** (for the international carriage). Through bills of lading are not sufficient for ocean shipments.

Tiger economy

'Tiger economies' describes countries including Indonesia, Malaysia, Singapore, South Korea and Taiwan, who are seen as the model of successful development. Tiger economies have many of the following key features:

- Under heavy state direction of both resources and planning, production is largely carried out under private ownership.
- Certain sectors are protected from international trade.
- The key thrust is behind export-led growth and the promotion of major export sectors (this was a strategy adopted by Japan in the 1950s).
- Higher levels of saving in cultures where savings and investment are a long-held tradition.
- Strong links between the banking system and industry, where long-term investment finance and deregulation are the key aspects.

T

- **Pegged exchange rates** fixed to the $US.
- Business restructuring, notably in the strategic industries, to obtain **economies of scale** so that they can compete internationally.
- High levels of social and political cultural conformity.
- Fairly autocratic, single-party political systems.
- An anti-trade-union stance by government, coupled with a pro-business approach.
- Large levels of **foreign direct investment** from the US and Japan.

Toronto terms

In 1988 at the Toronto Summit, the major creditors of the **Paris Club** were asked to offer more favourable **rescheduling** terms to heavily indebted or poor countries. The Toronto Summit ended in agreement on three key areas, which became known as the Toronto terms. The three options were:

- To write off one-third of the whole debt owed by a specific country under the proviso that the balance is to be repaid over 14 years (with an 8-year grace period) at standard market rates.
- To reschedule all outstanding debt over the same 14-year payment period, with the 8 years' grace, with the market rates of interest being either reduced by 50% or set at 3.5%, whichever is less.
- To reschedule all of the outstanding debts to make them due over 25 years, with a 14-year grace period, at market interest rates.

Trade Act 1974

The Trade Act 1974 is a piece of US legislation which grants the US President the authority to enter into international agreements with the aim of reducing import barriers. The main purposes of the Act, which became law in 1975, were four-fold:

- To stimulate US economic growth and to maintain and enlarge overseas markets (primarily for agriculture, commerce, industry and mining).
- To strengthen economic relations with other countries through non-discriminatory and open trade practices.
- To protect US industry and employees against unfair import competition.
- To provide adjustment assistance for areas of US business, or indeed geographic areas, which had been affected by increased imports.

The Act further allowed the President to extend **tariff** preferences to particular imports from specific developing countries. In effect it would allow the President to set similar conditions under the **most favoured nation treatment**.

Trade Agreements Act 1979

The Trade Agreements Act 1979 followed up the **Trade Act 1974** by authorizing the US to implement trade agreements to deal with the **non-tariff barriers** which had been negotiated during the Tokyo Round. In effect the Act incorporated the Tokyo Round agreements in respect of customs valuations, **dumping**, government procurement, import licensing, products standards and various other products and duties. In addition the act extended the US President's authority which he had gained under the Trade Act 1974 to reduce or eliminate non-tariff barriers to trade.

Trade area

Over the past 50 years around 150 regional trade agreements have been notified to the **General Agreement on Tariffs and Trade (GATT)** or the **World Trade Organization**. Although some of these were revisions to previous arrangements, around half of these agreements have come into force since 1990. The best known trade areas are the **European Union**, the **North American Free Trade Agreement** and **MERCOSUR**.

Trade areas have been established largely as a result of the fact that most countries have reduced their tariff barriers, which has now made transportation costs one of the most important aspects in terms of price. Trade areas effectively deal with overseas countries' **comparative advantages**. If, for example, Taiwan had a comparative advantage in the production of computers, but the UK could purchase German computers tariff-free, then Taiwan's main benefit of trade would be lost. Many critics of trade areas believe that regional trade actually impedes global trade on the basis that members of trade areas are more likely to trade amongst themselves than with the rest of the world.

Trade barrier

A trade barrier can be any impediment to the free flow of products, services and capital into a country. Typically, trade barriers are exemplified by one or more or the following:

- import barriers, including tariffs and import charges, **quantitative restrictions**, import licensing, customs barriers;
- the imposition of standards, testing, labelling and certification;
- strict controls over government procurement;
- the granting of export subsidies;
- lack of protection for **intellectual property rights**, including **technology transfer**;
- barriers to services;
- investment barriers;
- barriers which encompass a selection of measures that affect a particular sector.

Trade concordance

Trade concordance involves matching harmonized system codes to other statistical definitions, including **standard industrial classification (SIC)**. In effect it means having a set of definitions which can cross-classify products. Trade concordances are essential for countries to be able to relate trade and production data.

Trade credit

Trade credit is provided by exporting businesses, multinationals, government or governments, to either other businesses or organizations, usually in the form of a delay in the payment for products or services received.

When trade credit is offered it is common practice to obtain trade credit insurance, which minimizes the risk of possible default and insolvency. Trade credit insurance can provide cover against the risk of a bad debt and is an essential tool in the export business. Trade credit insurance effectively replaces working capital when bad debts or late payments have an impact on the cash flow of a business.

A number of insurance companies underwrite trade credit insurance and international businesses could choose to seek to cover what is known as whole turnover, which covers the whole of the policy-holders' business and allows them to grant credit up to a stated limited. Alternatively businesses may choose to take out a specific account policy, which can be either fixed or adjustable to cover a number of named buyers. The premiums are usually based on the amounts of debts outstanding. In determining the correct trade credit insurance policy for the business, and for insurers to set the premium rate, the following criteria are usually examined:

- the annual turnover of the exporting business;
- the previous experience of bad debts;
- the efficiency of the business's credit control systems;
- the length of credit granted by the business;
- the historical and current status of the buyers;
- the trade sector in which the exporting business operates;
- the size of individual accounts and the proportion they actually represent in relation to the exporting business's total turnover.

Trade credit insurance does not necessarily cover the exporting business for all of its loss, but normally covers between 75% and 95% of any given loss.

Briggs, Peter, *Principles of International Trade and Payments*. Oxford: Blackwell, 1994.

Trade mission

A trade mission is an international trade and investment promotion activity. It is designed to increase international business opportunities and sales for participating businesses. Usually the trade mission consists of a number of businesses who are ready to export from one country or region to a target market. Trade missions are well organized and often offer customized, pre-screened meetings, educational seminars and networking opportunities. Trade missions have the following key advantages:

- They are cost-effective in as much as they can assist a business, at a relatively low cost, to enter or expand into an overseas market. They therefore offer a high return on investment.
- They are invariably led or guided by export specialists, as part of either the exporting country's government or the importing country's government.
- They should provide targeted contacts which match the exporting company's needs.
- Through increased market intelligence provided by the organizers of the trade mission, medium- and long-term sales should be easier to achieve.
- They should develop stronger, longer lasting business relationships with importing businesses and expand the exporting business's cultural awareness.

There are a number of different types of trade mission, which include:

- multi-industry trade missions;
- industry-specific trade missions;

- trade missions designed for the gathering of market intelligence;
- trade missions to foster partnering opportunities, such as **joint ventures** or **strategic alliances**;
- trade show trade missions.

Trade Promotion Coordinating Committee (TPCC)

The TPCC is a US initiative which aims to coordinate the trade promotion efforts of all Federal agencies. The committee members consist of some 19 Federal agencies, including representatives from the US Departments of Commerce, Agriculture, Defense, Energy, the Interior, Labor, State, Transportation and Treasury. The committee also consists of a representative from the Agency for International Development, the Council of Economic Advisors, the Environmental Protection Agency, **EXIMBANK**, the Office of Management and Budget, the Overseas Private Investment Corporation, the Small Business Administration, the Trade and Development Agency, the Information Agency and the **United States Trade Representative**. The TPCC was established in 1993 and has a primary purpose of ensuring that US products and services have the best possible opportunities in foreign markets.

www.ita.doc.gov/td/advocacy

Tranche

In international trade the term 'tranche' has three relevant meanings. The first refers to funding commitments made by organizations such as the **World Bank**, which are, in effect, loans or credit facilities which are structured into parts and form the basis of cash advances to countries requiring additional funding.

The second key definition is with reference to the **International Monetary Fund**, where a tranche represents the first 25 per cent of a member country's contribution to the fund, which is normally made in the form of gold bullion.

The third key definition of 'tranche' is with reference to debt securities, issued as part of a bond or an instrument. The securities themselves are issued in tranches, each maturing at a different date. The maturities are set in order to help meet the investor's objectives.

Transaction exposure

Transaction exposure is a form of currency risk that can occur when an international business deals with either another business or a subsidiary in an overseas market. Transaction exposure refers to gains and losses which may be incurred when transactions are paid in a foreign currency. The funds received from the transaction may have to be converted to the home currency, but are obviously subject to fluctuations in the foreign exchange market. Transaction exposure can occur when a company buys or sells on credit in a foreign currency, or when a business borrows or lends in a foreign currency.

Transit zone

A transit zone is essentially a **free trade zone**. It is usually an area close to a port of entry which effectively serves as a storage and distribution centre, often for the convenience of a neighbouring country which is landlocked or lacks adequate port facilities. Products, merchandise or commodities which enter the transit zone are considered to be 'in transit' either to or from that neighbouring country, and are therefore not subject to customs duties or import controls which would normally be relevant in the host country where the transit zone is located. A transit zone itself is a somewhat more limited facility than a free port or a free trade zone, as all operations are geared towards storage and distribution rather than sales, manufacturing or marketing.

Translation exposure

'Translation exposure' is another term for **transaction exposure**. It concerns the effect of currency conversion on individual transactions and how fluctuations in the foreign exchange rates affect the value of, and ultimately the income derived from, that transaction.

Trans-national corporation

The United Nations defines a trans-national corporation as a business which possesses means of controlling production and services outside the country in which they were established. Trans-national corporations are, in effect, the most influential of all international businesses. Increasingly they control trade investment, technology finance and communications. Trans-national corporations use their country of origin as a base and usually establish their headquarters there. All profits tend to return to their **home country**. Some 90% of all trans-national corporations are based in industrialized countries, whilst the remaining 10% are mainly in South-East Asia.

It has been estimated that there are around 40,000 trans-national corporations in existence. The 10 largest trans-national corporations have a higher total income than the world's 100 poorest countries. It has been estimated that trans-national corporations sell in excess of $7 trillion worth of products and services per year through their foreign **affiliates**. This is a figure which rivals the world's total exports in any given year. It has also been estimated that trans-national corporations (actually the top 500 trans-national corporations) control upwards of two-thirds of all world trade. They are responsible for 80% of all foreign investment, and in excess of 30% of all international trade occurs within the trans-national corporations themselves. Trans-national corporations collectively have some 250,000 affiliated companies worldwide and employ more than 70 million people. In effect they employ between 5% and 10% of the global workforce.

During the 1970s and 1980s the United Nations were concerned with assessing the impact of trans-national corporations and how this was affecting the world economy.

The term 'trans-national corporation' is now virtually synonymous with the term 'multinational corporation'.

Transparency

Transparency is a measure of how clear, open, verifiable or measurable various laws, agreements, **protocols**, regulations and practices are between countries which have an impact upon international trade. Ideally any such trade agreements should be clear and unambiguous for both parties and should not contain clauses which are impenetrable, either in their intent or in their practice, so that they are not disadvantageous to the signatories.

Treaty of Rome

The Treaty of Rome was signed in 1957 by France, Germany (West), Italy, Belgium, the Netherlands and Luxembourg. Effectively this established the European Economic Community. The Treaty of Rome was the second of three founding treaties; the others being the Treaty of Paris in 1951 and the Euratom Treaty, which was also signed in 1957. The Treaty of Rome was succeeded by three amending treaties: the **Single European Act** (1986), the **Maastricht Treaty** (1992) and the Treaty of Amsterdam (1997). Each of these treaties further expanded the scope of the Treaty of Rome.

The Treaty of Rome came into force, and with it the founding charter of the European Economic Community, on 1 January 1958. The Treaty of

Rome contributes some three-quarters of the consolidated Treaty on the **European Union**. Articles cover citizenship, the free movement of goods, the establishment of the **Common Agricultural Policy**, the free movement of individuals and capital, asylum and immigration, competition, legal and tax harmonization, the **Exchange Rate Mechanism**, a common commercial policy, health and safety, environmental policy, overseas aid, relations with former colonies of the member states, and the budget.

www.europa.eu.int/abc/obj/treaties/en/entoc05.htm

Trigger price mechanism (TPM)

In its more general sense, 'trigger price mechanism' refers to a price point at which a certain action is taken. However, trigger price mechanism is more closely associated with the US **anti-dumping** mechanism, which was designed to protect US industries from under-priced imports. It was specifically created to monitor imported steel and a minimum price using this system is estimated when the steel is landed at a US port. Imported steel which enters the US below a specified price triggers automatic anti-dumping investigations, which are carried out by the US Department of Commerce and the **International Trade Commission**. The TPM was used between 1978 and March 1980. It was reinstated in October 1980 and suspended once again in January 1982. It was used once more between April 1982 and June 1988.

Under the terms of TPM, if imports are considered to have been brought in under-priced then duty is levied on the steel equal to the difference between the trigger price and the actual price.

Trinidad terms

The Trinidad terms were proposed in 1990 by the then British Prime Minister, John Major. He suggested that the industrialized nations cancel some 50% of the debts currently owed by the lowest-income countries in the world, whilst providing a relief fund of some £18 billion. Eventually around 67% of the debt was finally written off following a **G-7** summit in 1994, but this was only applied to a relatively small number of the poorest countries' debts. The Trinidad terms were proposed in response to the **Toronto terms** as the latter were considered inadequate to meet the needs of the **lesser developed countries**. The debt relief proposed was to cancel some two-thirds of all debt owed by eligible countries, whilst **rescheduling** the remaining debt over a 25-year period. The Trinidad terms were never fully adopted by G-7.

T

Turnkey

A turnkey project is a means by which an international business can expand, consolidate or rationalize its operations. Turnkey projects aim to achieve a specific task and achieve it quickly within a set budget. Turnkey projects tend to be new means of carrying out a business process, or, perhaps, a new way of carrying out operations. Increasingly, international businesses will seek to create innovative turnkey projects with the intention of gaining a competitive advantage over their competitors, by creating an exemplar facility, or series of systems, either in the home market or in overseas markets.

Turnkey projects are typified by the speed at which they are developed and implemented. In many respects turnkey projects begin at concept stage and develop or evolve during the construction and implementation phase.

Typically, turnkey projects will include new management services, engineering projects, site installation and reconfiguration. Turnkey projects seek to consolidate an international business's control or position in a specific market. They seek to identify more efficient means of operating, thus reducing costs, while simultaneously being more effective in that marketplace.

T

Umbrella agreement

An umbrella agreement is usually a bilateral trade agreement which stipulates the conditions related to trade, and which is reviewed on an annual basis. An umbrella agreement incorporates other agreements which form a part of a greater whole. The term is often used to describe a series of negotiations and agreements which collectively form the basis of an interlocking set of negotiated arrangements between countries.

'Umbrella agreements' can also refer to trade agreements which are made between international businesses and an overseas government and foreign businesses or overseas subsidiaries.

Unfair trade practice

The term 'unfair trade practice' refers to an act or a policy which may be adopted by an overseas government and that may deny benefits, perhaps under an existing trade agreement, to other overseas businesses. It is considered to be a practice which is unreasonable, discriminatory, restrictive or unjustifiable.

As far as the US is concerned, an unfair trade practice is one which is inconsistent with a **Section 301** determination by the **United States Trade Representative**.

In actual fact, an unfair trade practice may be considered by one country to be unreasonable, whilst another country may consider it to be purely a form of protection. In terms of the US, if their own domestic trade laws were applied on an international basis, a vast majority of US businesses would be guilty of **dumping** products across the world. In the US the Supreme Court has set their standards so high that very few US businesses could be successfully prosecuted.

Unfair trade practices revolve around the protection of a country's industry from what is known as predation. In effect this means that many developed countries undermine fair trade by selling their products and services at below cost in overseas markets. Whilst in the short term profits are dented, in the longer term domestic industries are unable to compete. Ultimately they are either driven to bankruptcy or acquired by international businesses at lower than market rates. Once overseas businesses have gained a foothold in an overseas market and have dealt with the domestic competition, they are then free to increase their prices; this process is known as predation.

There are undoubtedly double standards in any definition of unfair trade practices. Increasingly, trade negotiations attempt to determine what is fair and what is unfair. Given the fact that many trade negotiations are rather imbalanced, the liberalization of overseas markets only makes them more susceptible, and therefore, overseas countries are accused of creating unfair trade practices as a means of resisting sharp business practice, such as predation.

United Nations (UN)

The term 'United Nations' was first used by the US President Franklin D. Roosevelt in 1942 when 26 nations pledged their countries' determination to continue the fight against Germany, Italy and Japan. The forerunner of the United Nations was the League of Nations, which had been established in 1919 under the terms of the Treaty of Versailles.

In 1945 the representatives of some 50 countries met in San Francisco in order to draw up the United Nations' charter. The charter was finally signed in June 1945 (it was later signed by Poland, making the original total of member states 51). The United Nations itself came into existence in October 1945, after the charter had been ratified by the UK, the US, the Soviet Union, China and France.

The primary functions of the UN were to:

- help to maintain international peace and security;
- continue to develop friendly relations between states;
- achieve cooperation in respect of economic, social, cultural and humanitarian problems;
- act as a centre for harmonization for countries to achieve these common ends.

The current UN membership is some 191 countries, the latest of which were East Timor and Switzerland, who joined in September 2002. States which join the UN agree to accept the obligations of the UN Charter. The UN itself has six main sub-organizations, which are:

- The General Assembly – which has a single, equal representative from each of the member states. They discuss various issues and require a two-thirds majority to pass the UN budget. It meets annually between September and December.

- Security Council – which is responsible for helping to maintain peace and security. There are 15 council members, with China, France, the Russian Federation, the UK and the US as permanent members and the other 10 members being elected by the General Assembly to serve a two-year term.
- Economic and Social Council – which has 54 members and is a forum for discussing international economic and social issues.
- Trusteeship Council – which was established to provide international supervision for 11 trust territories. By 1994 all of the trust territories had obtained self-government or independence.
- **International Court of Justice** – which consists of 15 judges elected by the General Assembly. It is also known as the World Court and is the main judicial organ of the UN.
- Secretariat – which consists of some 7,500 people drawn from 170 different countries. They carry out much of the administrative work, as directed by the other parts of the UN.

In terms of international business, the UN is concerned with international law, principally through the **United Nations Commission on International Trade Law**, which seeks to form the basis upon which trade law is harmonized throughout the world.

www.un.org

United Nations Commission on International Trade Law

The UN Commission on International Trade Law, or UNCITRAL, aims to achieve progressive harmonization, as well as unification, of international trade law. According to the UN General Assembly Resolution 2205 (XXI), it seeks to achieve this by:

1 Coordinating the work of organizations active in this field and encouraging cooperation among them.
2 Promoting wider participation in existing international conventions and wider acceptance of existing model and uniform laws.
3 Preparing or promoting the adoption of new international conventions, model laws and uniform laws and promoting the codification and wider acceptance of international trade terms, provisions, customs and practices, in collaboration, where appropriate, with the organizations operating in this field.
4 Promoting ways and means of ensuring a uniform interpretation and application of international conventions and uniform laws in the field of the Law of International Trade.

U

5 Collecting and disseminating information on national legislation and modern legal developments, including case law, in the field of the Law of International Trade.

6 Establishing and maintaining a close collaboration with the **United Nations Conference on Trade and Development**.

7 Maintaining liaison with other United Nations' organs and specialized agencies concerned with international trade.

8 Taking any other action it may deem useful to fulfil its functions.

In essence, UNCITRAL, having been established in 1966, aims to harmonize and unify international trade. It focuses on the sale of goods, payments, commercial **arbitrage** and legislation relating to shipping.

www.uncitral.org

United Nations Commission on International Trade Law (UNCITRAL arbitration rules)

The UNCITRAL arbitration rules are generally used where parties are reluctant to refer their disputes to a permanent institution. Arbitration carried out under the UNCITRAL rules are binding on both parties. The UN has also created the UNCITRAL Model Law on International Commercial Arbitration, which is a comprehensive text on how international arbitration should be treated. Ultimately the goal of the model law is to both harmonize and modernize national legislation. The model law has been adopted by a number of different countries, including Australia, Canada and Nigeria.

www.uncitral.org

United Nations Conference on Environment and Development

The UN Conference on Environment and Development met in Rio de Janeiro in June 1992. It reaffirmed the Declaration of the United Nations Conference on the Human Environment, which had been adopted in Stockholm in 1972. The primary goal of the conference was to establish equitable global partnerships in key sectors throughout the world. It sought to achieve this by working towards the foundation of international agreements which would not only protect the environment, but also ensure a sustainable development.

The conference agreed some 27 principles covering four major areas, which were:

• poverty and the environment;

- growth and consumption patterns and demographic pressures;
- economic problems;
- sustainable development.

www.unep.org

United Nations Conference on Trade and Development

The UN Conference on Trade and Development, or UNCTAD, was established in 1964 as a permanent part of the UN General Assembly. The primary purpose of the UNCTAD is to promote international trade, primarily between developing countries and countries with different social and economic systems. Based in Geneva, UNCTAD examines economic development and international trade, seeking to harmonize development, trade and regional economic policy.

www.unctad.org

United Nations Development Program

The UN Development Program, or the UNDP, was established in 1965 and based in New York. In essence it is a multilateral grant-providing agency and has six key areas of interest:

- democratic governance;
- poverty reduction;
- crisis prevention and recovery;
- energy and the environment;
- information and communications technology;
- HIV/AIDS.

The UNDP operates in some 166 countries. At the heart of its current policies and actions are the millennium development goals, which have set targets for reducing poverty, hunger, disease, illiteracy, environmental degradation and discrimination against women, by 2015.

www.undp.org

United Nations Environment Program (UNEP)

The UNEP was established in 1972 and seeks to provide a worldwide environmental monitoring system. Its mission is to 'provide leadership and encourage partnerships in caring for the environment by inspiring, informing, and enabling nations and peoples to improve their quality of life without compromising that of future generations'.

In terms of international business the UNEP is primarily engaged in the following:

- The Division of Technology, Industry and Economics, which focuses on solutions to industrial and urban environmental problems.
- Industry Outreach, which seeks to promote responsible entrepreneurship, focusing primarily on environmental reporting, voluntary initiatives and **technology transfer**.
- The Production and Consumption Unit, which seeks to develop cleaner and safer production and consumption patterns.
- Environmental Management Tools, which provide an introduction to a number of different management tools to ensure businesses' care for the environment.

The UNEP is also concerned with financial initiatives, tourism, mineral resources, oil and gas, agri-food production and consumption, economics and trade, environmental law, the Convention on International Trade and Endangered Species, and world conservation monitoring.

www.unep.org

United Nations Industrial Development Organization (UNIDO)

The UNIDO was established in 1966 and became a specialist agency of the UN in 1984. The UNIDO is responsible for the promotion of industrialization throughout the developing world. It is based in Vienna and is represented in some 35 developing countries. Its core functions and services are:

- To act as a forum which generates and disseminates knowledge related to industry.
- To provide technical assistance with implementing industrial development.
- To strengthen industrial capacities.
- To achieve cleaner and more sustainable industrial development.

www.unido.org

United Nations Regional Commissions

The United Nations Regional Commissions promote economic development primarily as a regional commission for the UN Education, Scientific and Cultural Organization. There are five regional commissions, which are:

- Economic Commission for Africa – which was established in 1958 and has implemented a number of economic and social policies, expanded regional trade and begun to integrate Africa into the world economy.
- Economic and Social Commission for Asia and the Pacific – this was originally the Economic Commission for Asia and the Far East, which was established in 1947. It became ESCAP in 1974. It has 52 members and 9 associate members and is the largest of the five regional commissions. It is concerned with socio-economic development, the sharing of regional experiences, training and information, and the building of inter-country networks.
- Economic Commission for Europe – which was created in 1947 and encompasses some 55 states. It is involved in transport, the environment, industry, trade and energy.
- Economic Commission for Latin America and the Caribbean – this was originally the Economic Commission for Latin America, which was established in 1948 and became ECLAC in 1984. It is concerned with the coordination of economic development in Latin America and the development of international trade.
- Economic and Social Commission for Western Asia – which was set up in 1973 and is concerned with the improvement of economic and social conditions in the area, notably in the form of trade, the environment, energy and water.

www.un.org/partners/civil_society/reg-comm.htm

United States Trade Representative (USTR)

The United States Trade Representative was created under the terms of the Trade Expansion Act (1962) and was brought into being by President Kennedy's Executive Order 11075 in January 1963. The USTR was originally known as the Office of the Special Trade Representative. Under the terms of the **Trade Act 1974** the office became a cabinet-level agency, giving it powers and responsibilities to coordinate trade policy. The agency officially became the USTR in 1980 and is now considered to be the United States' chief trade negotiator and the primary representative of the nation in major international organizations.

The USTR is primarily responsible for the development and coordination of US international trade. It is also concerned with direct investment policies, and negotiations with overseas countries. Its major areas of responsibility include:

U

- All of the US dealings with the **World Trade Organization**.
- Negotiations regarding trade, commodities and direct investment, particularly in relation to matters managed by the **Organization for Economic Cooperation and Development** and the **United Nations Conference on Trade and Development**.
- Moving towards the expansion of market access for US products and services.
- Managing the industrial and services trade policies.
- Implementing international commodity agreements and policies.
- Dealing with bilateral and multilateral trade and investment.
- Dealing with **intellectual property rights** protection concerns.
- Negotiating with other countries in respect of US import policies.

The USTR is primarily based in Washington, DC, and Geneva in Switzerland.

www.ustr.gov

Uruguay Round

The Uruguay Round was the 8th **round** of multilateral negotiations related to the **General Agreement on Tariffs and Trade (GATT)**. The negotiations first began in Geneva in November 1982, and after four years negotiations began in Punta del Este, Uruguay. The negotiations ranged across all forms of trading policies, notably the trade in services, and **intellectual property rights**. The primary aim was to reform trade in some sensitive sectors, such as agriculture and textiles. The negotiations began once again in Montreal, Canada, in December 1988, to clarify the agenda for the next two years, but the talks ended in deadlock. Work continued through a meeting in Brussels in December in 1990 and again in Geneva in December 1991.

The Uruguay Round still looked as if it was doomed to failure, but in November 1992 both the **European Union** and the US settled the majority of their differences with regard to agriculture and in July 1993 the European Union, the US, Japan and Canada could report considerable progress on **tariffs**. In December 1993 most issues had finally been resolved and negotiations for market access could be concluded. The deal was eventually signed in Marrakesh on 15 April 1994 by the majority of the 123 participating countries.

www.wto.org/english/thewto_e/whatis_e/tif_e/fact5_e.htm

Value added

The term 'value added' can be taken to mean the value of a business's output less the value of all of the inputs. In other words value added can be a measure of the profit which a business has created by carrying out particular processes, or becoming involved at some point in the distribution chain. Clearly, the more value a business can add to its products or services, the more successful or profitable it becomes.

The term 'value added' can also be applied to a form of indirect taxation. A **Value Added Tax** is levied on the value which is created at each stage of a production process. It is also charged in many cases to the end-user or consumer of the products and services.

A further definition of 'value added' can be applied to the changes in the economic value of a business. The base economic valuation of a business is the combined value of its assets, shares, debts and other liabilities. The 'value added' component comes in when a comparison is made between what a business was worth economically in these terms before and after a specified period of time, perhaps a period of new management, or a period which had seen the business introduce new products or services.

Value Added Tax (VAT)

Value Added Tax is a consumption tax which is assessed on the **value added** to products and services. It is in effect a consumption tax charged as a percentage of the final price of a product or service. It is also charged at each stage of the production and distribution chain. In other words, it is collected fractionally. This means that there is a system of deductions made, with taxable individuals or businesses allowed to deduct from their liability the amount of tax they have paid to other individuals or businesses for purchases for their own activities.

VAT was brought in under the first VAT Directive (11 April 1967), requiring that **European Union** member states replace any of their indirect taxes by a common system of value added tax. The national laws of each of the member states in respect of VAT were specified by the

Directive 77/388/EEC. Non-EU businesses which export to the European Union are taxed at import stage, whilst export goods are zero-rated and not subject to VAT.

Directive 2001/4/EC requires all member states to set a minimum standard VAT rate of 15%, to be effective until at least December 2005.

www.europa.eu.int/eur-lex/en/lif/reg/en_register_093010.html

Vehicle currency

Since the introduction of the **Bretton Woods** system, which required the majority of countries to buy and sell US dollars in order to meet their **International Monetary Fund** exchange rate obligations, the US dollar has assumed the role of a vehicle currency. In international business it is common for pairs of currencies to trade each of the two currencies against a common third currency, known as a vehicle currency. This is as opposed to trading the two currencies directly with one another. In adopting a vehicle currency the transaction is made simpler and usually cheaper. The dollar remains one of the most common vehicle currencies as it is considered to be relatively stable.

Vernon, Raymond

See **product life cycle theory**.

Visible trade

'Visible trade' describes the physical exports and imports between countries. Visible trade includes raw materials, vehicles, computers and any other tangible item. In some countries visible trade is known as merchandised trade. Collectively, visible trade and **invisibles** (or invisible trade, which refers to services or intangible imports and exports) are detailed on a country's **balance of payments**.

V

Voluntary export restriction

A voluntary export restriction is essentially an agreement or an understanding between trading partners in which the exporting nation, as a means of reducing trade friction, agrees to limit its exports of particular products or services. Voluntary trade restrictions are also known as **voluntary restraint agreements**.

Voluntary restraint agreement

A voluntary restraint agreement is an arrangement in which an exporting country agrees to reduce or restrict particular exports without the importing country needing to impose import controls. Voluntary restraint agreements tend to occur when an importing country feels that increased imports may injure or even close its domestic industry. Voluntary restraint agreements are often an ideal alternative to the imposition of more direct import controls, which may well be at variance with the **General Agreement on Tariffs and Trade (GATT)**. Voluntary restraint agreements are also known as **voluntary export restrictions** or orderly market agreements.

V

West African Economic Community (CEOA)

The West African Economic Community was created in 1974 and is essentially a **free trade area** of former French African colonies. The CEOA is primarily concerned with the free movement of agricultural products, raw materials, industrial products and other approved products and services. It has a regional cooperation tax, which replaces import duties between members. Its community fund provides loans to its least developed nations, including Mali, Mauritania and Niger.

Western European Union (WEU)

The Western European Union was created in 1948 and amended by **protocol** in 1954. At its heart is the Brussels Treaty, which was signed by the UK, the Netherlands, Luxembourg, France and Belgium. In essence it was a response to the Soviet Union's control over many central European nations. The Brussels Treaty was instrumental in persuading the US and Canada to sign the North Atlantic Treaty in 1949. Denmark, Iceland, Italy, Norway and Portugal all ultimately signed the North Atlantic Treaty.

The WEU now has some 40 members and is based in Brussels. Its primary function is to promote mutual defence and progressive political unification based on three key areas: humanitarian aid, peace keeping and crisis management.

www.weu.int

World Bank

The World Bank began its operations in 1946 in close cooperation with the **International Monetary Fund**. It was formerly known as the International Bank for Reconstruction and Development. It was an institution created with the IMF at **Bretton Woods** in 1944. The World Bank has three main areas: the International Bank for Reconstruction and Development (IBRD), the International Development Agency (IDA) and the International Finance Corporation (IFC).

The World Bank is essentially one of the specialized agencies of the **United Nations**, which now has a total of 184 member countries. The World Bank has 109 country offices and some 10,000 development professionals, in virtually every country in the world. Currently the bank is involved in over 1,800 projects in almost all countries and sectors of the world. On average it lends $30 billion each year.

www.worldbank.org

World Bank's project cycle

With approximately three-quarters of all of the **World Bank**'s loans designated for specific development projects, each of these development projects must pass along a six-step project cycle. The cycle consists of:

- An identification phase, which determines whether the project is suitable for funding.
- The preparation phase, during which the borrower conducts a feasibility and design study, as well as an implementation strategy.
- The appraisal phase, during which the bank conducts its own assessment of the project.
- A negotiation and approval phase, where the bank and the borrower negotiate the loan agreement.
- The implementation phase of the project in accordance with the terms of the loan agreement.
- The evaluation phase, where the bank evaluates the borrower's reports and considers its own project study.

www.worldbank.org

World Federation of Development Financing Institutions (WFDFI)

The WFDFI was created in 1979 and aims to improve the technical operations and coordination amongst worldwide development banking. Its members include development financing institutions.

www.wfdfi.org.pe

World Intellectual Property Organization (WIPO)

WIPO was established in 1967 and officially came into being in 1970, becoming a specialist agency of the **United Nations** in 1974. In 1996 WIPO entered into a cooperation agreement with the **World Trade Organization**. Its primary function is to administer moves to promote creativity by protecting **intellectual property rights** in the context of the management of globalized trade. WIPO administers 11 treaties which set out internationally agreed rights and common standards. At the centre of WIPO's treaties are the Berne and Paris Conventions. Its two latest treaties, on **copyright** and on performances and phonograms, came into effect in 2002.

www.wipo.org

World Tourism Organization

The World Tourism Organization was created in 1974 and is closely associated with the **United Nations**. It aims to operate as a clearing house for the collection and analysis of tourism information and also offers national tourism organizations the opportunity to enter into international discussions and negotiations. It also aims to promote and develop tourism as a component part of sustained economic development.

The World Tourism Organization has seven strategic priorities, in order to attain sustainable travel and tourism development. It therefore recommends to nations the following:

- To have a clear vision of the future of travel and tourism.
- To measure and promote the economic importance of travel and tourism.
- To put forward a positive image of the travel and tourism industry as both career and job opportunities.
- To encourage free access, open markets and the removal of barriers to growth.
- To improve infrastructure in proportion to customer demand.
- To provide access to capital resources and technological advancement in the travel and tourism field.
- To promote responsible travel and tourism in terms of the preservation of natural, social and cultural environments.

www.world-tourism.org

World Trade Organization (WTO)

The World Trade Organization was created in January 1995 directly by the **Uruguay Round** negotiations (1986–94), as part of the **General Agreement on tariffs and Trade (GATT)**. As of April 2003 it had a membership of 146 countries and a 2003 budget of 154 million Swiss francs. Its primary functions are:

- to administer WTO trade agreements;
- to act as a forum for trade negotiations;
- to handle trade disputes between members;
- to monitor the national trade policies of its members;
- to provide technical assistance and training for developing member countries;
- to act in coordination with other international organizations.

By the time the WTO was set up, GATT was already 50 years old. Merchandise exports had been growing at a rate of 6 per cent on an annual basis. Indeed by 2000 the level of world trade was 22 times greater than the level that had been achieved in 1950. GATT and subsequently the WTO developed the world trading system through a number of trade negotiations, dealing first with **tariffs**, then with **anti-dumping** and **non-tariff measures**.

It was the Uruguay Round which led to the creation of the WTO, but it was not until February 1997 that agreements were reached with regard to telecommunications, leading to 69 governments agreeing to liberalize their measures. Also in 1997, 40 governments agreed tariff-free trade in information technology products, whilst 70 members concluded deals regarding financial services. In 2000, discussions began with regard to agriculture and services. This was formally launched at the WTO Conference in Doha, Qatar, in 2001. The Doha Development Agenda (DDA), which seeks to conclude negotiations by the beginning of 2005, incorporates non-agricultural tariffs, trade and the environment, anti-dumping, **subsidies**, investment, competition policy, **transparency** and **intellectual property rights**.

GATT still remains the WTO's principal set of rules in regard to international trade, consisting of 30 agreements and a series of commitments or schedules. The WTO and its membership has clear, non-discriminatory trading rules in which each member country is guaranteed that its exports will be treated in a fair and consistent manner in other nations' markets.

The WTO is active in trade dispute settlements and member countries bring it their disputes if they believe that their rights are being abused. In the past nine years, over 300 cases have been put forward to the WTO; virtually the same number that was dealt with by GATT during the whole of the period 1947–94.

With over 75 per cent of WTO members being identified as either least developed or developing nations, the WTO seeks to arrange agreements which contain special provisions. These nations generally have longer to implement agreements and commitments. The WTO assists them in handling disputes and the implementation of technical standards. The

W

WTO has over 100 technical cooperation missions in developing countries and regularly runs trade policy courses in Geneva. There are also regional seminars and other training programmes, to assist countries in the move from a **command economy** to a **market economy**. The WTO has also over 100 trade ministries and regional organizations in least developed and developing countries. These centres liaise with the countries' officials in order to feed back information regarding the WTO to these nations.

www.wto.org

World Traders' Data Reports (WTDR)

World Traders' Data Reports are provided on a fee basis by the International Trade Administration. The WTDRs provide background reports on specific overseas businesses, which have been prepared by commercial officers in the nation concerned. The WTDRs cover the following:

- type of organization;
- year established;
- relative size;
- number of employees;
- reputation;
- markets or territories in which the business is involved;
- language preferences;
- products offered;
- ownership;
- financial and trade references;
- reliability.

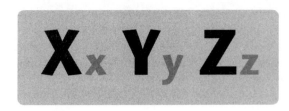

X-efficiency

'X-efficiency' refers to attempts by businesses to produce their output at the minimum possible cost. The term relates to varying the quantity of output so that the business can maximize its profits by ensuring that the market is not oversupplied with that produce, thereby driving the price of those products down. X-efficient manufacturers or producers seek to strike a balance between the most cost-effective level of output and the actual demand for the product itself. This is a form of economic efficiency which aims to minimize the costs related to production while maximizing the sell-on price of the product to either consumers or distributors.

X-efficient international businesses have considerable advantages in as much as they can optimize their output whilst driving down costs, and then choose to supply each of their overseas markets with as close as possible to an ideal supply, without flooding any individual market with their products. In doing this they have not only maximized their output and minimized their costs, but have also ensured that they have maximized the profits from the sales in different countries.

Zero sum game

Zero sum game is the antithesis of the **positive sum game**. Given that most economic transactions are, to some degree, positive sum games, there are examples of zero sum games which suggest that the business which has engaged in an international transaction gains to the same degree as its trading partner loses. In other words, a gain by one business is equal to the losses of another business.

Examples of popularly held beliefs about zero sum games are that increased imports into a country will necessarily mean that there may be fewer jobs in the importing market as a result of the increased competition. Equally, zero sum games can be applied to the internal dynamics of a business. Prime examples include higher automation and greater productivity leading to fewer jobs in the business. Equally, a business which is seeking to maximize its profits may often do this at the expense of the remuneration to its employees.

In actual fact, there are few true examples of zero sum games, as in the majority of cases most economic transactions are a positive sum game, but this is always just a measure of degree.

Z

Index

Note: page numbers in **bold type** refer to definitions. References are to the UK, except where otherwise indicated.